CINDERELLA CHURCH:
The Story Of Early Christianity

R. John Kinkel

iUniverse, Inc.
New York   Bloomington

Cinderella Church
The Story of Early Christianity

Copyright © 2008 by John Kinkel

All rights reserved. No part of this book may be used or reproduced by any means, graphic, electronic, or mechanical, including photocopying, recording, taping or by any information storage retrieval system without the written permission of the publisher except in the case of brief quotations embodied in critical articles and reviews.

The views expressed in this work are solely those of the author and do not necessarily reflect the views of the publisher, and the publisher hereby disclaims any responsibility for them.

iUniverse books may be ordered through booksellers or by contacting:

iUniverse
1663 Liberty Drive
Bloomington, IN 47403
www.iuniverse.com
1-800-Authors (1-800-288-4677)

Because of the dynamic nature of the Internet, any Web addresses or links contained in this book may have changed since publication and may no longer be valid. The views expressed in this work are solely those of the author and do not necessarily reflect the views of the publisher, and the publisher hereby disclaims any responsibility for them.

ISBN: 978-0-595-52348-1 (pbk)
ISBN: 978-0-595-62402-7 (ebk)

Printed in the United States of America

In memory of:

Michael Ciaramitaro
Vince Meli
Lara Rutan

Three young people from Michigan who died tragically;
I think they would have enjoyed this book.

ACKNOWLEDGMENTS

I wish to thank my students for their insightful questions and interest in the topic of early Christianity. The classroom experience has helped all of us. My readers, and still my friends, helped me improve the manuscript and deliver a quality product to the consumer. Norma Josef, Francis Strunk, Jonathan Kinkel, Danielle Kinkel, and many others are in my debt. As always, the mistakes are all mine. In addition to these personal notes, I wish to thank various authors and publishers fo permission to use their work in writing *Cinderella Church*. I aknowledge my gratitude to the editots of Christianity today, author Richard Carrier, Seven Locks Press, HarperCollins, and The Teaching Company for letting me utilize quotations from various works.

JK

Contents

Introduction	1
Chapter One: The New Wine	5
Chapter Two: The Pauline Churches	23
Chapter Three: The Post-Apostolic Church	43
Chapter Four: The Blood Of Martyrs	69
Chapter Five: Religions In Conflict	77
Chapter Six: The Bishop Of Rome	85
Chapter Seven: The Gnostic Christians	95
Chapter Eight: What Hath God Wrought?	103
Chapter Nine: A Church For Sinners	111
Chapter Ten: The Will Of Constantine	122
Chapter Eleven: Early Monastic Life	132
Chapter Twelve: Augustine Of Hippo	139
Chapter Thirteen: Conclusion	157
Appendix A: Was Jesus Married?	162
Appendix B: Popes, Condoms, And Aids	168
Notes	189
Index	201

PREFACE

I have spent most of my adult life teaching and mingling with college and university students in the Midwest. After reading student essays for some 30 years, it bothers me to see any of the following: I don't believe in God anymore; I don't go to church…..; I used to be a Catholic until…. In the old days (1950s) these people would be called backsliders, apostates, lapsed Christians, and now this label has emerged: FARC, i.e. fallen away Roman Catholic. Today, however, the culture police are saying, "Not so fast." There is clear evidence that some religious expressions turn people off. Services are uninspiring, preachers are boring, and "there are too many rules." The religious institutions are driving people away. Is it the people or the church? Are we facing a decadent society or a corrupt church?

A recent study by the Pew Research Center offers us data for reflection.[1] Nearly one-third (31%) of U.S. adults say they were raised Catholic, but only 24% say they are affiliated with the Catholic church any longer. That is a net loss of 7%--the largest decline of any religion studied in the survey. Where are these lapsed Catholics? Who is seeking them out? What is their problem?

To explore this topic and others I have re-coined an old phrase from philosophy: we have found religion standing on its head, and it must be turned right side up. People—especially the young—are leaving the churches in droves. This is true in the United States and Europe as well. How can this trend be reversed? I have decided that the God-fearing people I know could benefit from an old fashioned return to tradition. I am not suggesting the catechism or Sunday school but rather a return to one's roots to discover the ancient religious heritage of the founders, namely, what it meant for the early Christians to live their new faith. Such a study could lead to personal renewal as well as a change in church structures. The journey begins by trying to understand the term: Cinderella church.

R. John Kinkel
Rochester, Michigan

Introduction

"I have come to bring fire to the earth and how I wish it were blazing already" (Luke 12:49).

Today we find Roman Catholics polarized and segmented, but they are not alone. Protestant churches also struggle with issues such as gays in ministry, the papacy, and the ordination of women, etc. Many Roman Catholics are under the illusion that the Catholic one-size-fits-all mentality will work in our contemporary world. This dogmatic approach turns people off and many have left the church because of it. Yet in the Jewish faith, for example, we find these major divisions: orthodox, conservative, reform.[2] All are considered legitimate expressions of the Jewish faith. Protestant pluralism is obvious to anyone familiar with the phone book. From the liberal Episcopal church to the fundamentalist Southern Baptist tradition, we find many expressions of what it means to be a son or daughter of the Reformation. Many Catholics, however, continue on their merry way thinking that it is "my way or the highway" or "you can't be your own pope," as a conservative friend recently told me. Today the conservative Catholic branch feels it is their birthright to attack fellow members for their beliefs and convictions. They think they are correct; they have the whole truth. They are not alone: Orthodox Jews look down on Reform Jews and

Schaefer contends that this so-called purist form of the Jewish faith sees "Reform Jews as little better than nonbelievers."[3] Without question we find in many religions a group of people claiming that they are the "proto-orthodox" version of religious reality and that everyone should conform to their views.[4] In this respect the Roman Catholic church is no different. Some Catholics are refused communion by conservative clergy while others are excommunicated. Lay people do not trust their bishops and some say with good reason. Is there any way out of this quagmire?

After writing the book, **Chaos in the Catholic Church**, which outlines many of the problems the contemporary Catholic church faces, I was often asked: "What should the church actually look like? How should it operate? Where did we go wrong?" This new book, which reviews the history and structure of early Christianity, continues the theme of "chaos," but now we must look to the words of Genesis (1:1-2) for clarification. Here we find, according to the sacred writer, Yahweh bringing order out of the primordial chaos. The creation narrative shows God at work, transforming the primordial abyss into life, beauty, and splendor. To follow the theme of Genesis we must try to bring order out of the chaos we find in today's Christianity. For the believer, this means working hand-in-hand with God to transform the cosmos, the church, and the individual person.

We must go back to the beginning—the early days of Christianity—and to do this I have suggested to many of my friends that we ought to look to the birthplace of Christianity: how these people lived, worshipped, and dealt with problems/conflict. The first generation of Christians gave us their witness to the risen Christ: the Gospels and St. Paul's letters offer us a working constitution for all Christian believers who want to follow in the path of Christ (Messiah). The entire New Testament is a road map for rebuilding the Christian community today. The problem we face as a Church is that many Catholics and Christians are not very familiar with Church history and how the people of God prayed and practiced their faith after the death and resurrection of Christ. The editors of **Christianity Today** have urged their readers to rediscover the roots of their faith: "One of the most promising developments among evangelical Protestants is the recent 'discovery' of the rich biblical, spiritual, and theological treasures to be found within the early church."[5] The call for more education for all Catholics was sounded by Pope Benedict XVI in his first visit to the U.S. as pope. He stated that education is an integral part of the mission of the Church to proclaim the good news.[6] Admittedly, tomes by Raymond E. Brown, *An Introduction to the New Testament* (800pp) and Hans Küng, *Christianity: Esssence, History, and Future* (700pp) are not on the reading lists of fund-raising bishops, busy laity, and overworked priests. Hence I have prepared this book about the epic struggle of a small group of believers who held fast to their fundamental principles and succeeded against all odds in establishing a great world religion. By all accounts they should have failed; they should have gone unnoticed. But like the Cinderella story, the early church surprised everyone. Through their efforts the Gospel was preached throughout the known world. In these pages I try to examine the major themes and controversies that we know of during the first centuries of post-resurrection Christianity. I have tried to tell the story of the early church. It was then that the church was coming into being, and if we examine closely the key historical documents of these early days we can get to know how men and women worked together to fashion a dynamic religious movement. Hence, this book can be useful to Protestants and Catholics alike. The early Christians were given the rich deposit of faith known only to the first witnesses to the risen Christ. They heard the sermons of Jesus; His actions inspired them. They took seriously the command: be faithful to the Gospel. Or, as St. Paul put it: conduct yourselves "in a manner worthy of the Gospel of Christ" (Philippians 1:27). They were a fellowship of believers who were committed to the risen person of Jesus. They had met with him, talked with him and understood his way of life. They embraced his message and the truths he enunciated in the few years of his public life and ministry. Their testimony is crucial in resolving some of our contemporary problems and disputes. Their story can help us out of the conflicts we face today.

Christ's death was a great loss to them. Like Jesus, when he heard of John the Baptist's death, they wanted to go off to a quiet place and grieve. But that could not go on forever. As one studies the life of this fledgling band of religious men and women, we find patterns of behavior, ways of doing things and a clear focus on what they considered essential. Raymond E. Brown[7] has suggested in various ways that the social and behavioral sciences can help us understand the meaning of sacred scripture. There are 15 references in his book on the New Testament pointing to the social or sociological applications present in the New Testament. He appreciates the work of Gerd Theissen who has studied the church in Corinth sociologically and was responsible for coining the term "Jesus Movement." Brown notes elsewhere: "Literary criticism and sociology have enriched the study of the letter [to Philemon]...."[8] Anyone using the social historical approach in studying the early church will be heartened to know that a world renowned biblical scholar like the late Raymond E. Brown approved such a method and utilized it. The key to this method is twofold: 1) understanding the facts that constitute the real Christian experience; 2) examining the social structures that the early Christians created to aid them in the quest for salvation.

The people of God whom Christ inspired grew in numbers because many people were impressed with Jesus' life and the example of His community of believers. We need to know more about this movement. Were the apostles faithful to the founder? Did the second generation Christians follow the Apostles' lead? What changes and developments were implemented in the 2nd century and were they in line with Gospel values? Were women treated fairly? How was the role of Peter, the head of the Apostles, acknowledged and understood by the early church?

If this book has any substance at all, it will force Christians to ask two basic questions: first, how do I measure up to the first Christian believers? Do I really understand the message of the Good News? Second, we have to honestly examine the church and its officials to determine if this is the kind of organization that would warrant Jesus' approval. What are its flaws and how can they be corrected? The answers will not come easy. We hope to give a realistic response to these profound religious and sociological questions and more.

CHAPTER ONE:

The New Wine

"For I am about to create new heavens and new earth; the former things shall not be remembered or come to mind" (Isaiah 65:17).

"The one who sat on the throne said, 'Behold, I make all things new'" (Rev. 21:5).

Two questions are fundamental to the story of early Christianity: Who was Jesus? How did the Jesus movement develop and thrive in the first few decades after his death and resurrection?

1. Jesus as the Founder. As a child preparing for first holy communion in Wisconsin many years ago, I learned that Jesus was the Christ child who was born in a manger near Bethlehem. I thought of Him as the young boy who was lost in the temple for three days only to emerge unscathed and full of wisdom and promise. This Jesus would soon come to me in the host to help me be a good Catholic. All my grade school friends probably held similar beliefs, but today the discussion about Jesus has expanded a bit.

We must start with the fundamental truth that Jesus was a Jew who with his parents faithfully observed the law of Moses. He was a religious thinker who emerged out of Judaism and lived near the Sea of Galilee—a hotbed of Zealot fervor.[9] Modern biblical scholars are asking us to focus on this often neglected fact: Jesus and his family were thoroughly Jewish. The first Christians were all Jews and the entire New Testament was probably written by Jewish scholars who joined the first generation of the Jesus movement. We are now in the "third phase" of our modern quest to understand Jesus—the Jewish apocalyptic prophet who came to announce the coming of the kingdom.[10] The first modern quest to find the Jesus of history was directed by Albert Schweitzer who wrote the landmark book ***The Quest of the Historical Jesus*** (1906). As an ordained Lutheran minister with degrees in theology and medicine, he sought to separate the true sayings of Jesus in the Gospel from those he considered mere words attributed to him by the later followers of the Messiah. After considerable research and effort he conceded that this was an impossible task.

In his classic treatment of the historical Jesus, Rudolf Bultmann initiated the second quest for the historical Jesus and in 1926 published ***Jesus and the Word.*** Here he argues that we can know very little about the life and person of Jesus since the primitive record is fragmentary and often based on legend. Bultmann's followers refined his approach and method to preserve some authenticity for the New Testament writings. The third quest for the historical Jesus is perhaps best summed up in the work of John Meier, ***A Marginal Jew: Rethinking the Historical Jesus (1991),*** wherein he attempts to understand Jesus within the context of first century Palestinian Judaism.

There were a number of factions in the Jewish religious tradition that Jesus and his family must have been aware of. The Pharisees were one of the more prominent groups at the time and they were strict followers of the Jewish law. They frowned upon Hellenistic Jews who did not always follow the letter of the law. The Sadducees adhered to the Mosaic law but not the many commentaries and interpretations of it. They did not believe in the resurrection and the immortality of the soul. A third group that was well known to Jews was the separatist movement called the Essenes. They felt the priests in the Temple (Jerusalem) were corrupt and not practicing the true principles of Judaism. The Essenes, therefore, withdrew from Jerusalem and established a settlement near the Dead sea. This group produced the Dead sea scrolls that were found near Qumran in 1947. The Essenes were known for their many ritual washings, rejection of violence, belief in equality (no slaves), and celibacy for full members. Finally, there were the Zealots, founded by Judas of Galilee ca. 6 A.D., who opposed Roman occupation and taxes; they wanted to establish a free Jewish state. Aside from the role of priest, there were prophets, teachers, rabbis, and so forth. Jesus and John the Baptist knew of the many Pharisaic traditions but they were clearly prophets who sought religious and social reform.

Raised in the rural areas of Galilee, Jesus eventually embarked on his public life of preaching and teaching. His inspiring words and miraculous deeds attracted a large following. Several scholars argue that Jesus "did not come as a founder of a new religion, and yet a new religion, Christianity, was founded in his name or, more precisely, in his memory."[11] Many historians of religion today call him an apocalyptic prophet who tried to call his people back to their solid religious traditions. His message was eschatological in that he warned people that the end was near. The kingdom of God was at hand. According to his message, which is clearly recorded in the Gospels and other writings, God would soon come to overthrow the forces of evil and bring his kingdom here on earth.[12] Thus, his type of preaching did not necessarily mean that the end of the world was imminent but rather God's action in human history was about to take place. Most scholars agree that Jesus lived for about 30 years before he was executed by order of Pontius Pilate at the urging of some Jewish leaders. After selecting 12 apostles and teaching them and others for about 3 years he went up to Jerusalem to observe the Passover with his disciples. He was viewed as a leader and wonder worker, and at times He even spoke in the synagogues with great power and authority. Jesus was held in high esteem by many Jewish leaders, as is clear in this passage from Mark 5:22ff:

And behold, one of the rulers of the synagogue came, Jairus by name. And when he saw Him, he fell at His feet and begged Him earnestly saying, "My little daughter lies at the point of death. Come and lay Your hands on her, that she may be healed, and she will live…" Then He took the child by the hand, and said to her, "talitha cumi," which means, "Little girl, I say to you, arise!"

Jesus was not just some obscure rural preacher from a backwater town in the Roman empire. Rulers of the local synagogue came to him for help. Mark's account of the healing shows that Jesus spoke Aramaic (talitha cumi) and we should note that the first oral tradition of the Gospel was probably in that language; later a Greek oral tradition emerged. The four canonical Gospels, written in Greek, give us a brief sketch of Jesus' life but these documents are really "salvation history" and many critics remind us that such writings are not objective accounts of what most scholars consider historical reality. They are documents written by believers for believers. This is where we get most of our information about the life of Jesus. Josephus, a non-Christian historian who lived several decades after Christ, only mentions Jesus in passing, with little attention to his life or teachings. In the ***Testimonium Flaviannum***, he writes: "About this time came Jesus, a wise man, if indeed it is appropriate to call him a man. For he was a performer of paradoxical feats, a teacher of people who accept the unusual with pleasure and he won over many of the Jews and also many Greeks. He was the Christ."[13] Parts of this document are widely considered a product of Christian forgery. But there is no question that Josephus acknowledged Jesus' existence and his considerable impact on society. Another secular observer, Pliny the Younger, wrote a letter to Emperor Trajan in 112 A.D. asking what he should do with followers of Christ who meet together before dawn and "sing a hymn to Christ, as to a god...."[14] He was rather concerned about this new religious sect. Despite these two commentaries we have very little information about the life and teachings of Christ save the writings of his committed followers.

The four canonical Gospels and other books of the New Testament, therefore, are our major source of information regarding the life of Jesus; they provide us with the good news of salvation but have limitations in that they are written by committed followers whose intentions at times were to promote a certain point of view and not necessarily to present objective truth. But the spirit and message of these documents is clear: the first Christians believed God sent Jesus, his son, to save all humanity from sin and eternal death.

One of the most moving and insightful stories found in all of the Gospels describes an event in Jesus' life which had profound implications to his followers. One day Jesus traveled to the town of Nain (Lk 7:11ff) which was south of the Sea of Galilee.

7:11 Soon afterward Jesus went to a town named Nain, accompanied by his disciples and a large crowd.

7:12 Just as he arrived at the gate of the town, a funeral procession was coming out. The dead man was the only son of a woman who was a widow, and a large crowd from the town was with her.

7:13 When the Lord saw her, his heart was filled with pity for her, and he said to her, "Don't cry."

7:14 Then he walked over and touched the coffin, and the men carrying it stopped. Jesus said, "Young man! Get up, I tell you!"

7:15 The dead man sat up and began to talk, and Jesus gave him back to his mother.

The resuscitation story at Nain had a profound effect on Jesus' disciples. The early church believed in the words and deeds of Jesus and this inspired them to have faith and act boldly; they told and retold many events like this one with no other purpose than to show new converts who the real Jesus was. This was all a part of the oral tradition that arose after Jesus' death. He was a compassionate, caring person.[15] There was no doubt about his miraculous deeds for early Christians; this was not myth nor fairytale to them. These events took place, according to the scriptures, and were written down by committed believers. It is this testimony that we rely on; it is what the Jesus movement believed. Such events, according to Ratzinger,[16] are crucial because they reveal the Father's profound love of the people of God through the person of Jesus. These and other Gospel stories allow the reader to understand the founder of this new religion and why so many people were committed to his way of life.

Jesus urged his followers to prepare for the coming of the kingdom which He said was imminent. After returning from Egypt (see Matt 2:13ff) he spent most of his life in rural Galilee, a remote outpost in the Roman empire.[17] With his disciples and followers he traveled to Jerusalem to celebrate the Passover, knowing full-well the possible dangers awaiting him. His words and actions offended the Jewish officials and thus they branded him a trouble maker and blasphemer. They seized him one night and delivered him to a Roman official named Pontius Pilate, asking that he be executed for his so-called crimes. These were simply trumped up charges brought by a Jewish lynch mob who represented a very small portion of the total Jewish community, many of whom were living in the Diaspora, that is, outside of their traditional homeland. With the population of the Roman empire approximately 50 million at the time,[18] and Jews making up only about 6% of the realm, it is clear that these 2 to 3 million Jews were not consulted about whether Jesus should live or die. The mob's response to Pilate that "His blood be upon us and on our children" (Matt 27:25) is a flippant comment by Jesus' haters and is not mentioned in the other three canonical gospels.[19] All of the approximately 2 to 3 million Jews living at the time did not affirm or deny such statements. This is clear since we know that by 150 A.D. the majority of the Jews lived in the Diaspora.[20] Certainly a large number of Jews lived in the Diaspora during the time of Christ and this forced migration started in 586 B.C. under occupation of Nebuchadnezzar. Some Jews tried and finally succeeded in having Jesus executed because he offended their religious sensitivities. Not all were a part of this conspiracy. We will see later how the 2nd century charge that the Jews were guilty of "deicide" (the killing of God) is simply a preposterous statement which unfortunately has become a great source of antisemitism in the Christian church and the world for many centuries. The Second Vatican Council (1962-65) rejected the label of "deicide" for Jews and condemned antisemitism; nonetheless, for 1,900 years before this ecumenical council convened, many Christians cultivated an ideology which singled out Jews as Christ killers and a cursed people. Catholic liturgical prayers at Good Friday services in the 1950s (all part of the old Tridentine Mass) were offensive and seemed to imply that the "perfidious Jews"[21] were a lost people with no hope for salvation. That all changed in theory with the insights of Cardinal Bea and the courageous teachings of Vatican II. John Wilkins rightly calls this change the Catholic U-turn toward Jews. [22]

After his death, Jesus' followers were convinced that God raised Jesus from the dead and they proclaimed this belief to all who would listen to their preaching. Many converted to this new Jewish religious sect according to the Acts of the Apostles which has led scholars such as Ehrman to state: "Christianity has been, by far, the most important religious, social and cultural phenomenon in Western civilization and continues to be the largest religion in the world."[23] Christianity numbers about 2.1 billion adherents in 2008. Some believers are more committed than others.

2. The Jesus Movement. Life after Christ's death was scary to most of his followers. The crucifixion had forced the apostles to go into hiding, confused and fearful. John the Baptist had been murdered by King Herod Antipas (son of Herod the Great) some time before Jesus' crucifixion (Matt 14:1-12). Many did not know what to do and were afraid they would be killed as well. This band of men and women gathered on numerous occasions after the crucifixion to pray and console each other; through the experience of Pentecost and the gift of the Holy Spirit they were strengthened and became courageous believers. They believed they were given the power to build the new church. The pouring out of the Spirit inspired men like Peter (Acts 2: 40-41) to preach the good news.

He spoke to them for a long time using many other arguments, and he urged them, "Save yourselves from this perverse generation." They accepted what he said and were baptized. That very day about three thousand were added to their number.

All this was accomplished not by an educated Roman citizen turned religious leader, but rather through the efforts of an uneducated Jewish fisherman from Galilee named Simon Peter. He used his talents well. He attributed such a change of heart to the workings of the Holy Spirit.

Without question we see from the scriptures that Peter was the undisputed leader and spokesperson for the early church. As the apostle who presided over the choice of a successor to Judas, Peter explained the meaning of Pentecost to the crowds, and he healed the lame beggar at the temple (Act 3:1-16). After converting to this new religion, Paul was instructed by Peter in Jerusalem regarding the message of Christ for about 15 days (Gal 1:18-19).

Despite these singular accomplishments, we know that it was Peter **and** Mary Magdalene who became the first witnesses of the resurrection. Peter is referred to as the rock: "You are Peter and upon this rock I will build my Church" (Matt 16:18), according to the New Testament proclamation. This meant that Christ—belief in Him—is the foundation of the Church, which was understood at the time as "the assembly of God's people." It was Joseph Ratzinger (now Pope Benedict XVI) who rightly stated this in his doctoral dissertation that the church is founded on Peter, but not on "his person but on his faith… the foundation of the church is Christ."[24] Some argue that the passage in Matthew 16:18 are not the words of the earthly Jesus (*verba et gesta Christi*) but rather a phrase composed by the Christian community to reflect their confession of faith as to how church structure was to be understood by the followers of Christ.[25] This most quoted passage from scripture comes, of course, from Matthew's Gospel, written between 80-90 A.D. The Petrine text as it is called does not appear in any other canonical Gospel. Most probably the sacred writer drew upon earlier written sources (not Mark) and oral traditions to present these ideas. However, Henry Chadwick reminds us that Matt 16:18 must be understood in its historical context. The Petrine text cannot be seen to have played any part in the story of "Roman leadership and authority before the middle of the third century when the passionate disagreement between Cyprian of Carthage and Stephen of Rome [Bishop of Rome] about baptism apparently led Stephen to invoke the text as part of his defence against Cyprian. But it was not until Damasus in 382 that this Petrine text seriously began to become important as providing a theological and scriptural foundation on which claims to primacy were based."[26]

Peter was important in the early church but we must remember that the leaders of the church were brethren, and the bishop of Rome was seen as the first among equals. After the Pentecost experience Peter traveled to many churches throughout the Roman Empire and was a leader in the Jerusalem community with other apostles: James and John. The Jerusalem community was truly the mother church of the early followers of Christ: it was the headquarters of the first Jewish Christians. Peter's task at first was to proclaim Jesus to Jewish converts who accepted the Risen Lord as Messiah but still felt bound to the law of Moses. Peter also worked in Antioch where he debated Paul concerning whether gentile converts had to accept Jewish dietary laws and circumcision. Paul said "no" and Peter came to realize that he could not put old wine into new wine skins. He followed Paul's lead. They had the power to teach and set policy for the people of God. It was his strong faith mixed with human frailties ("Depart from me, Lord, for I am a sinful man" Luke 5:8) that became a part of the rich tradition of the early church. Certainly today we find there is broad consensus that Peter was in Rome during the 10th year of Nero (65 A.D.), who then burned parts of the city and subsequently blamed Christians for its destruction. As part of Nero's persecution of the followers of Jesus, Peter was singled out and executed sometime around 64-65 A.D.[27] Many historians assert that this marked the first persecution of the Christians by Roman authorities, whose attacks on Christians were sporadic, occasional and regional.[28] No archeological investigation has ever uncovered Peter's remains in Rome, but it is a long standing belief within the Catholic Church and some other traditions that he was martyred and buried in Rome. It is extremely doubtful that he was the sole leader of the church in Rome at any time. We find in contemporary religious literature the general conclusion that "Catholic theologians concede that there is no reliable evidence that Peter was ever in charge of the church of Rome as supreme head or bishop."[29]

Peter and the rest of the apostles inspired the early followers of Christ; this loosely knit group of spiritual men and women took on various roles in ministry: apostles, elders, teachers, disciples, prophets, deacons, etc. (Ephesians 4:7ff). The social background of the new church was clear: they were men and women drawn from the lower classes, for the most part, and their task was to carry on the work of the risen Christ. Jesus proclaimed that the poor were blessed. The twelve apostles are a symbol of renewal: there were twelve patriarchs representing the twelve tribes of Israel. The story of Israel renewed in Jesus can start with no fewer than twelve. These men were fishermen and peasants; the larger group of Jesus' disciples came from the same common stock. Later on, it is not surprising to find that Callistus, Bishop of Rome (217-222 A.D.), was once a slave but eventually became head of the church in Rome.[30] This is great social mobility, indeed.

These early Christians were a marginal group in Roman society and had very little political clout in the empire during the first century. By the 4th century the new religion called Christianity was a major social and political force in the empire. To some degree the first generation Christians had withdrawn from the temporal affairs of the world due to their beliefs regarding the end time. The second coming of Christ was imminent. Nevertheless, things would change. They were a people from the countryside and rural areas as was the case with the prophet, John the Baptist. Peter and Andrew were probably disciples of the Baptist for a time. The early followers of Jesus were not urban for the most part but, later on, Christianity took on a distinctive urban flavor, i.e. the church in Corinth, the Jerusalem church, the church of Antioch. The apostles, disciples, teachers, prophets and prophetesses served the community with spiritual gifts and a desire to perform service for its members. Some women were called "apostles," and they played an important role in establishing the early church in new regions. The term "apostle" means "those who are sent" and one of the most important women apostles was Mary Magdalene, who grew up in the town of Magdala, not far from Nazareth (see map, p. 20). She was a devoted follower of Jesus, having witnessed his crucifixion and death (Mk 15:34ff). She and others stayed with Christ until the very end, and she was rewarded for her faith. "Having risen in the morning on the first day of the week, He appeared first to Mary of Magdala, from whom he had cast seven devils" (Mk 16:9). This way of speaking, in biblical terms, indicates that Mary had some type of ailment which Jesus cured, not that Mary was in sin or controlled by the devil.[31] Jesus called women to his inner circle of disciples and thus showed little support for the patriarchal system of the time (Greco-Roman and Jewish) which was hostile toward women. She was sent by the risen Lord (Jn 20:1-18) to announce the resurrection to the eleven apostles and the other followers, but they would not believe her. This important mission prompted church leaders to call her **apostola apostolorum**, namely, "apostle to the apostles."[32] It is interesting to note that Peter, James, and John did not take Mary off to the side and tell her to stop talking about Jesus this way; she was not told to refrain from discussing the resurrection in the future. The followers of Christ respected each other and did not silence those who were judged to be inspired by faith.

Some writers suggest that Mary was well-to-do and used her resources to support the ministry of Jesus. Despite the misreading of Luke's Gospel by Pope Gregory the Great in 591 A.D., Mary Magdalene was not the penitent sinner in the Gospels who with a jar of precious ointment came to Jesus to acknowledge her need for forgiveness. Pope

Gregory mistakenly labeled Mary a penitent whore. These and other errors by later church leaders helped distort the importance of Mary Magdalene in the mission of the early church. It took a long time before the Catholic church finally clarified these issues for believers in 1969. This is a lesson to all Christians to avoid the tendency of later church members: false adulation of bishops and popes. Because they have made numerous mistakes over the years, we must be careful.

The First Witnesses for Christ: They were All Jews.

It may come as a surprise to modern Christians to realize that all our religious forefathers and mothers were Jews. Jesus and his mother as well as Joseph were Jews; they were faithful observers of the Mosaic law. The first Christmas had three Jews in attendance: Jesus, Mary and Joseph. The child of Joseph and Mary was brought to the Temple to be circumcised on the eighth day. Jesus taught in the synagogue on various occasions during his public life. Those who sought to carry on the legacy of Christ came from the Jewish world of ideas; like Jesus they spoke Hebrew and/or Aramaic. Paul, the first Christian writer, wrote in Greek and he set a language pattern for all subsequent New Testament writers. It is a generally accepted tradition that the entire New Testament (27 books) was written in Greek by Jews who converted to Christianity. By the middle and late 1st century, Greek was the language of the church, and thus we find that all the books of the NT were written not in Hebrew but Greek.

Buildings and Cathedrals?

Christ gave no orders to his followers for the construction of religious edifices or sacred structures. Peter's suggestion that some tabernacles be set up to commemorate the transfiguration was ignored (Mk 9:2). Jesus prayed in the temple and local synagogues; at times he chastised those whom he thought were out of line: the Scribes and Pharisees. They were seen as hypocrites who had received the law but did not obey it (Acts 7:53). Many of these leaders were corrupt and in need of conversion and reform. Jesus, the prophet, said to them "It is written, my house shall be called a house of prayer, but you have made it a den of thieves" (Mt 21:13). After his death and resurrection, Christ's followers met in various homes to console each other and to worship; they prayed, sang hymns, and broke bread together as He had instructed them at the last supper. These were the first house-churches of the Jesus movement. While at prayer in the home of one of the disciples, the Holy Spirit appeared and some disciples spoke in tongues; it was the first Pentecost.

The Jesus movement was first an Aramaic-speaking community centered in Jerusalem after a period of teaching and discernment with Jesus in the region of Palestine near the Sea of Galilee. The new religious group was at times called the Nazarenes,[33] "The Way" (Acts 1), and later on the Jesus movement. The second coming of Christ was a central theme of their witness. The kingdom of God was near. Such apocalyptic/eschatological ideas go back to the book of Maccabees in the second century B.C. Jesus worked in this Old Testament climate and urged his followers to be ready since they did not know when the day of judgment would come. The first generation of disciples was deeply influenced by Jesus' teachings about the "coming of the kingdom"; they expected the world to end soon. This mentality affected their way of life, conversations, marriage, plans for the future, and so forth. Jesus, it was proclaimed, sits at God's right hand, until he comes in glory and judgment. Later on, the Jerusalem community came to speak of itself as "ekklesia" or church. In the Hebrew tradition this meant the gathering of God's people.[34] Thus we have this fledgling group's first understanding of itself, namely, the church is the **gathering** of God's people brought together by Christ. That is the first Christian understanding of the Greek term "ekklesia."

Various writers have found it useful to call the early Christians a Jewish sect. That is, a group of Jewish followers of Christ who had "broken off" from traditional Judaism, and set up its own unique way of relating to God, following Jesus' example, His direction, and teachings. They considered Jesus the Messiah and Son of God, but most Jews at the time did not accept this way of thinking. The newly formed religious group was at odds with established secular society, its norms and institutions. Christians refused to pay homage to the various Roman gods at the time and many died for their beliefs. Jesus was seen by the new sect as the longed-for Messiah, but the Jewish religious power structure refused to accept this view of reality. The term "sect" was not used in antiquity but is a useful concept to describe what was going on in the early life of the Christian community. The sect begins rather small, has a charismatic leader, rejects the prevailing views of the dominant religious group and substitutes the new standards (the new wine) of the founder.³⁵ It is from these roots that the Christian community evolved and took shape in the first century. Looking back on the early struggles of Jesus' followers, one can see them trying to build an organization that would be worthy of Christ's example and courage. Their attempts to become a strong movement were organized by charismatic leaders (Peter, James, John, Mary of Magdala, and especially Paul) who wanted to spread the good news and promote church growth. They had to move quickly because in their view the end was near. One of their famous prayers was "Marana tha" (an Aramaic expression) meaning "Our Lord, come."³⁶ Traveling and establishing new churches was a central focus for the first generation Christians. Today we would call the group a "flat" organization with limited hierarchy, and shared decision making, as well as commitment to creativity and equality. The Apostles were the main leaders; their mission was to serve (diaconia) others and go forward with the program to establish new faith communities. The followers of Jesus held that the Spirit was at work in the community; they had to listen and read the signs of the times. Only later, toward the end of the first century, did the followers of Jesus organize a formal structure that could be called a church as we understand it today, namely, the people of God characterized by "the monarchical episcopate."³⁷ These organizational ideas were derived from the Old Testament (e.g., King David) and the governance model at the time: the Roman empire. Such structured church ideas were not a part of the first generation of the Jesus movement; they represent a major shift by early Christians into the world of bureaucracy, hierarchy, and social control. Early Christianity's social construction of reality was very different from models of church around 110 A.D. Later on, the Christian church developed a rather "tall" organization, namely, one that had various levels of authority: bishops, priests, deacons, laity. The term hierarchy arose around the 5th century.

It is clear from reading the Acts of the Apostles and many New Testament letters that three religious concepts kept the reality of Jesus' death and resurrection alive in the early church: the preaching of the Gospel, baptism, and the celebration of the Lord's supper. The first ten years of the Jesus movement may have been nurtured by an Aramaic oral tradition dealing with the sayings and deeds of Christ. At the time of Jesus' public ministry "very few Jews could speak, read, or write

Hebrew."[38] He left no written documents with his followers and so members of the Jesus movement decided to tell and retell stories of the life of Christ: his words, sayings, and deeds had powerful meaning to them. Many of these stories "were likely in Aramaic, the language of both Jesus and his first followers. Only later were they translated into Greek, and later still collected into what we call the Gospels."[39] The first communities were made up of Jewish believers for the most part. Later on, with the preaching of Paul, many Gentiles joined the Jesus movement and so the oral tradition became a recalling, in Greek, of the sayings and deeds of Messiah. Skilled story-tellers and believers with extraordinary memories (think of the Homeric tradition) most probably had a prominent role in worship services at house-churches which kept alive the memory of Jesus' life. They were communities of joy that inspired new converts. Baptism marked the new convert's initiation into the community of believers; indeed, it announced one's entrance into Christ's spiritual kingdom. Peter testifies that baptism must be "in the name of the Lord Jesus Christ" (Acts 2:38). Raymond Brown notes that "we are not certain about procedures in the earliest baptismal practice; but most likely 'in the name of' means that the one being baptized confessed who Jesus was...."[40] Paul makes clear the role of baptism in Romans 6:3-4 when he asks "Do you not know that all we who have been baptized into Jesus Christ have been baptized into his death? For we were buried with him by means of baptism into death, in order that, just as Christ has risen from the dead through the glory of the Father, so we also may walk in newness of life." The Gospels proclaimed the good news that Jesus died and rose so that His followers might be saved. Baptism sealed the new covenant. With this in mind, some have called the four Gospels passion narratives with long introductions. Moreover, they tell us what the preaching of the NT was about, namely, what Christ did to save all those who believe, by giving his life for their salvation. The third key element of early Christian life was the celebration of the Lord's supper which recalled the death and resurrection of Messiah; this sacred meal renewed the group's new covenant with God and with each other. We find Paul's account of the institution of the Lord's supper in 1 Corinthians 11:23ff:

> [11] For I received from the Lord what I also handed on to you, that the Lord Jesus, on the night he was handed over, took bread,

24	and, after he had given thanks, broke it and said, "This is my body that is for you. Do this in remembrance of me."
25	In the same way also the cup, after supper, saying, "This cup is the new covenant in my blood. Do this, as often as you drink it, in remembrance of me."
26	For as often as you eat this bread and drink the cup, you proclaim the death of the Lord until he comes.

This is the oldest preserved Eucharistic prayer that we have.[41] All three synoptic Gospels (Matt, Mk, Luke) record a similar account of the Lord's supper but Paul's version was penned around 54 A.D.—several decades before the canonical Gospels were written and 20 years after the death of Jesus. According to White,[42] the words "I received…what I also handed on to you" are a rabbinic formula used for passing on oral tradition. If this insight has validity, Paul is drawing on practices that were present in the Christian community years before the writing of this letter, namely, the community celebration of the Lord's supper. He is telling the Corinthians about practices in the early church prior to writing this letter. The church in Corinth was a mixed group of Jews and Gentiles which Paul had converted some 5 to 10 years previously, and he now writes to them about his concerns.[43] The Eucharist was a source of great hope and consolation for the developing church and the letter encourages them to celebrate with reverence. Paul drew upon an oral tradition as he writes the epistle but it is unclear how old these sayings, prayers, and stories are. It is quite possible that he drew upon oral traditions from 40-49 A.D. and thus we have a glimpse of the early church's religious practices and rituals. After Paul left Corinth to continue his missionary work elsewhere, we do not know who led the Eucharistic celebrations which usually followed the Agape meal. Paul most certainly trained leaders to take over religious services in his absence and many writers speculate that some women probably had the authority to lead the Eucharistic celebration. Women held important positions in the early church. Who were these women leaders? Priscilla could have easily taken such a role. She was not only Paul's colleague but was the teacher of Apollos as well (Rom 16:3-5, Acts 18:24-28). Phoebe was a church leader as were Syntyche, Euodia

(Phil. 4:2-3) and Lydia (Acts 16-14-15, 40). The new religion utilized all the committed believers—men and women. Thus, the church grew in numbers through the work of Paul and his new theology.

In summary, three key features of early church life (baptism, the Gospels, the Lord's supper) were the center of their fellowship; they were a community of believers and these three religious experiences gave them a sense of solidarity.

Hellenistic Tension

During the early period of the infant church, we find rapid growth in the Mediterranean area (see map) and the surrounding environment.

This religious group emerged from Palestinian Judaism to a universal mission to all people looking for spiritual enlightenment. At a certain point in church development (viz., the Council of Jerusalem, 49 A.D.) more and more converts to Christianity had come from a unique group called Hellenist Jews. This was the **second** phase of Church growth. These were Jewish immigrants who came from all parts of the Roman Empire (the Diaspora)[44] and eventually some chose to settle in Jerusalem. They spoke Greek and used the Greek version of the Old Testament called the **Septuagint.** They were faithful to their basic Jewish traditions but over the years mixed more easily with Gentiles than traditional Jews living near the Sea of Galilee and took on some of the new ideas of the Greek culture. Of course, it goes without saying that Jews were a minority in the Roman empire. In our modern parlance we would say Hellenist Jews had become secularized to a certain degree. It is not surprising that such diversity in the early church led to tension and conflict: Hellenists versus Hebrew Christians from Palestine. A very human problem arose with these followers of Christ regarding the issue of caring for widows (see Acts 6:1-5). It is clear that some Hellenist believers complained that certain of their widows were being overlooked by the church's charitable services to widows. The Twelve—not just Peter—created a council of seven Hellenists (Stephen was one of them) to help oversee such distributions for widows. Even the most devoted followers of Christ needed a structure to avoid bias and discrimination. Key: early Christians spoke up and let their needs be known to the community. Groups were formed to decide what to do and how to carry out the will of God for the community. No one person gave orders or ruled over others. Conflict was resolved in community. It was essential that **Koinonia** (fellowship, community) be preserved. As one studies the activities of the early church we find the practice of turning to groups or councils to resolve differences; it was a distinct social pattern. They did not turn to one man, e.g. Peter, to solve conflicts. There was no cult of personality here. Today the Catholic church is very centralized and looks to Rome and the pope to solve complex problems. It should be added, all dioceses around the world are actually *forced* to do this by the Vatican power structure. This was not the way early Christianity operated. Thanks to the Protestant Reformation the early church model of organization was given new life as Luther pushed for decentralization and reform.

Summary and Conclusion (Introduction, Chapter 1). The following points are crucial in understanding the first years of the Jesus Movement.

1. Women played a key role in the ministry of Jesus both before and after his death and resurrection. Jesus broke from the traditions of patriarchy and was seen talking with women, eating at their homes, inviting them to be in his company.
2. The first followers of Jesus came from the lower classes for the most part. Peter was married and had a house which is mentioned in the Gospels and Acts. These first followers of Christ were not wealthy by any means. Some women supported the ministry of Jesus and they had some influence and wealth. Mary Magdalene was one of the women who supported Jesus from her own means.
3. The religious movement Jesus started was an informal organization, and it lacked buildings or offices; Jesus taught in the local synagogues in rural Galilee, and did not have his own place of worship. This informal structure continued after his death and resurrection; Jesus' followers met in what we call today "house-churches." This was a charismatic group and the twelve drew upon the gifts of the many followers; they were open to the Holy Spirit for guidance.
4. The followers of Jesus wanted to gain new converts for the church and stressed missionary work. This was very different from the ministry of Augustine and Ambrose (4th and 5th century), for instance; they had church buildings and people came to them for the most part. The first and fourth century were very different indeed.
5. When the followers of Christ had problems (e.g. service to widows) they spoke up and let the community know what the difficulties were. The early Christians solved problems by meeting in groups and no one person took control. This was a participatory process; the elite disciples of Jesus did not take over and dictate policy.

CHAPTER TWO:

The Pauline Churches

If Jesus were here today there is one thing he would not be--a Christian.

Mark Twain's **Notebook**

As the early Church grew in numbers there arose a group of Jewish elders, scribes, and Pharisees who began to harass and at times even imprison the followers of Christ (Acts 8:2ff). The persecution centered primarily on Hellenistic Jewish Christians; a major thorn in the side of these believers was a man named Saul of Tarsus (he was from a city north of Jerusalem). He even led attacks against the Nazarenes and was a witness to the stoning of Stephen: "Saul for his part concurred in the act of killing" (Acts 8:1). This act of violence (about 36 A.D.) followed a fiery speech in which Stephen, a Hellenist preacher in the Jesus movement, spoke out boldly against the Scribes and Pharisees who had not accepted Christ as their Messiah and savior. The church had its first martyr. Later on, James the Son of Zebedee was killed by King Herod Agrippa I ca. 41 A.D.[45] The persecution of the Hellenist group of Christians caused many new converts to flee Jerusalem and later establish new churches in Antioch, Damascus, and elsewhere.

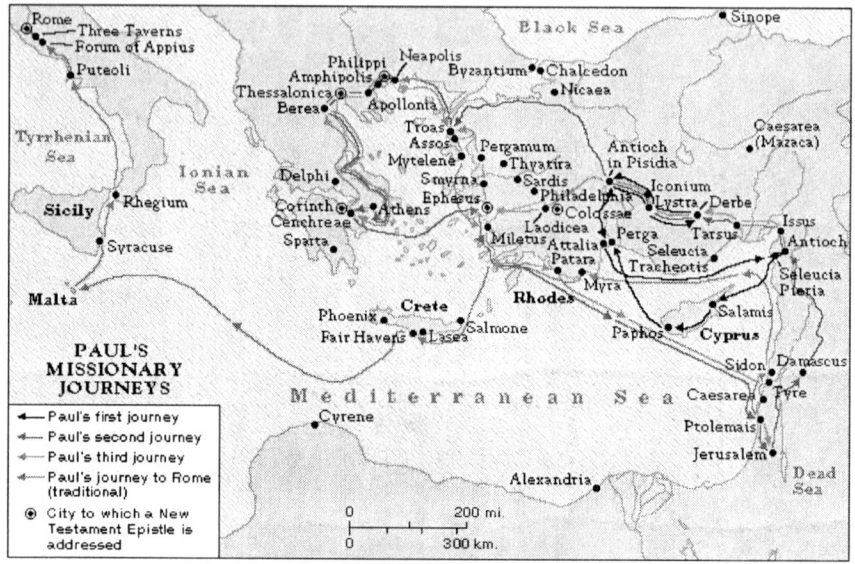

Thus a new era of church growth emerged: the evangelization of the Gentiles. This was the **third** phase of Church growth, starting as a Jewish Christian sect, then appealing to Hellenistic (Greek-speaking) Jews who converted to Christianity, and finally continuing as the Pauline mission to the Gentiles. St. Paul was the true architect of this latter program—hence he was called the apostle to the Gentiles. It was in Antioch—a city of about 500,000—that Jesus' followers were first called "Christians" (Acts 11:26).[46] This is how the followers of Jesus would henceforth be known. The Acts of the Apostles was written ca. 90 A.D. and thus the name "Christian" arose before the turn of the first century, though Paul never uses the term in any of his letters. The earliest recorded use of the term "Christianity" is attributed to St. Ignatius of Antioch who died ca. 107.[47]

Saul, after his well known encounter with the Risen Lord on the road to Damascus, became the new man of faith. He heard the words (Acts 9:4) "Saul, Saul, why do you persecute me?" The mysterious voice from heaven could not be ignored. After much prayer and his subsequent baptism, Paul built a new life for himself and claimed to be an apostle by the will of God. He said he was chosen to be a leader of the church by the order of the risen Christ. He received a special call in a revelation; he had been given a mission from God and a special Gospel to be preached to the gentiles. Thus he joined Barnabas in Antioch after spending three years in Arabia and 15 days working with Peter in Jerusalem. The church could never have advanced in numbers and vision without the contributions of Paul. Through his efforts Christianity began to flourish in the non-Jewish world. During the years 40-46 he selected Antioch as his base and probably served the numerous house-churches there. In a short period the early Christian church grew from being a small Jewish sect to a significant multi-cultural religious force in the Roman empire, including Hebrews like Peter and James, Hellenist Jews such as Stephen (d. 36 A.D.), as well as Gentiles who embraced Christ as their savior, as evidenced in the conversion of the pagan, "God-fearing" man named Cornelius (Acts 10:1ff). He was Peter's convert who was baptized without undergoing circumcision. It is clear that Paul and Peter shared similar views on the treatment of gentiles. The apostle to the Gentiles began work in earnest and labored for about 25 years in the Mediterranean area. Paul's first missionary journey took him to Syria and Cilicia ca. 46-48 (modern day Turkey and Greece) where he preached his Gospel to the gentiles, that is, a message that did not impose Jewish dietary laws nor circumcision.

No man shaped early Christianity more than Paul. The early church fathers simply refer to him as "the apostle." Of the 27 books comprising the NT canon, 13 were either written by him or attributed to Paul. His story dominates another book: the Acts of the Apostles. Anyone who wishes to depart from the authentic truths enunciated by Paul, does so at his own peril.

Several factors helped Paul to successfully preach the Gospel in the Roman empire. Of course, he was a holy and committed man of God, but he must have loved to travel; he used this gift to benefit the church throughout the Mediterranean region. Some historians claim that Paul's missionary travels covered some 8,000 miles.[48] In those days that was an adventure. The cost to travel by ship from Alexandria to Athens, for example, was just two days wages (two drachma) so people could move about the Roman empire with relative ease.[49] There were dangers, nonetheless, and Paul encountered a few ship wrecks in his day (Acts 27:1ff). He traveled by sea to the island of Cyprus where he converted Sergius Paulus, a high-ranking Roman Proconsul. Paul had a way of contacting and interacting with important leaders in Roman society and the mission of the Church obviously benefited. He probably was a skilled horseman (a talent not likely found in Galilean fishermen), and as a Roman citizen,[50] he was free to move about on various Roman roads as a protected traveler. Many writers overlook the fact that the Roman Emperors made it a point to build roads throughout the entire empire and thus Paul was able to take advantage of highways built by pagans to promote his new religious program. Lionel Casson notes: "A planned network of good roads gave him [Paul] access to all major centers, and the through routes were policed well enough for him to ride them with relatively little fear of bandits."[51]

By defining technology in the very broad sense[52] one can understand that Paul utilized 1) horseback riding skills, 2) Roman roads, 3) shipping routes and 4) tent making (leather works) to further the message of Christianity. His father apparently made tents for a living and such a background proved useful during Paul's missionary journeys, as he was often without a place to stay. At times Paul engaged in manual labor (tent making, leather goods); he did not want to be a burden to the Christian community. This practice allowed him to set up contacts in a new city and led to conversions and new churches. In short, he paid his own way.

From the beginning, the social structure of the church reflected considerable diversity in language, ethnicity, religious background, and social class; it had to alter some of its practices to accommodate this multicultural reality. In studying religious groups and other organizations over the centuries, sociologists have talked about such changes as "the social construction of reality."[53] In essence this means the process whereby people creatively shape reality through social interaction. Applied to the Christian experience, it means individuals and groups grow, adapt and take on new features because they want to survive and promote the original principles of their religious heritage and founder. This idea captures the notion that culture shapes the lives of people and their religious beliefs; there is reciprocation as well. Groups, like the early church, can influence culture and society as was evident with Constantine's reign (see chapter 10). The formidable challenge for Christians was not to abandon the "first principles" of the leader, Jesus; that was the mission of the early church. The notion of "social construction of reality" has to be understood in the context of religious values, however. The early Christians maintained that they were guided by the Holy Spirit and thus they prayed for help in constructing each new reality of church life as it strove to come into being. For instance, they prayed for help in selecting Matthias (Acts 1:26) to be one of the Twelve after the betrayal of Judas. They prayed to understand how to better serve all widows in need (Acts 6: 1-6); they then acted as a group. There was no cult of personality in the human followers of Christ, at least at this early stage of church development. The one person they devoted their lives to was the Risen Christ (see Paul's writings, Romans 13:13). As conflict and confusion arose in the early church, we find some interesting practical methods used by Paul and others to resolve their differences.

Council of Jerusalem

Between 48-49 C.E. Paul, Barnabas and Titus traveled to Jerusalem from Antioch (a trip of about 300 miles) to discuss the Gentile question.[54] During the previous few years Paul had already established new house-churches in at least three regions: **Galatia, Macedonia and Achaia**. Church leaders were appointed there and he also ministered to mixed groups of gentiles and Jewish Christians living in Antioch. Some authors state that the majority of the believers residing there were gentile Christians.[55] Do the new Gentile converts have to accept Jewish norms regarding circumcision and Hebrew dietary rules? Paul, an educated Pharisee, a skillful writer, and a Jew, did not want to impose on the new Gentile converts his own Jewish traditions derived from the old Mosaic law (old wine) if this was not absolutely necessary. He asked: is this what the risen Christ (Messiah) wants? Does the New Covenant require old Jewish norms? His answer was a categorical "no." In fact, he was actively preaching this new doctrine before 48 A.D., namely, a Gospel without Jewish observance for gentiles (new wine) and his actions caused some to question his orthodoxy. Was Paul jumping the gun?

The Council of Jerusalem (Acts 15:4ff) was convened to deal with this festering problem; some have argued that this assembly was "the most important meeting ever held in the history of Christianity...."[56] Hence Church historians examine the actions of this conference closely to gather insights into early Christian life. Many Jewish Christians grew up in Hebrew families and were taught: "Unless you are circumcised according to the custom of Moses, you cannot be saved" (Acts 15:1).

Major religious norms were being challenged by Paul at this time; the circumcision party strongly opposed his teachings, and James tended to support that group of conservatives who wanted to keep things as they were. This is a classic case of what a conservative really is. They felt circumcision was the Godly thing to do since it was the ancient law of Moses. Peter was open to more discussion on the matter since he had been instrumental in the conversion of the gentile centurion Cornelius. Socialization in the Jewish tradition helped one appreciate this religious ceremony, but as Gibbon observes, outsiders looked upon circumcision somewhat differently: "The painful and even dangerous rite of circumcision was alone capable of repelling a willing proselyte from the door of the synagogue."[57] Paul, Barnabas and Titus (an uncircumcised gentile) as well as other leaders in the Antioch church opposed any doctrine that required circumcision and the observance of Jewish dietary laws for new Gentile converts. So the apostle to the Gentiles traveled south to Jerusalem to discuss this issue at a formal council. There was no small dissension and debate on this matter in the early church, and the controversy had to be resolved: what was necessary for salvation? The discussion in Acts (15:7ff) is quite sketchy but it is clear that this problem was dealt with by 1) calling a meeting, 2) discussing the issue in an open forum, 3) and issuing a statement or accord about the conclusions arrived at during the conference. We should note that the New Testament canon had not yet been set (27 books of the NT) and would not be finalized until the 4th century. Hence we have here a group of believers, reflecting on their own religious experiences through prayer and then making a decision for the good of the whole church. They were the first who raised the question: What would Jesus do (WWJD)? It was the community in prayer that determined, as best they could, the will of God and not the New Testament which was nonexistent at the time. They knew the words and deeds of Christ through oral tradition and their own experience; they were guided to action by the inspiration of the Holy Spirit. The early Christians decided what was necessary for salvation. Nothing could have been more important for the council participants. They did not open their bibles and find a text which solved their particular problem. At the end of the Jerusalem meeting we read in Acts: "It is the decision of the Holy Spirit, and ours too, not to lay any burden beyond that which is strictly necessary" (Acts 15:28). The leaders of the early church ordered all to "abstain from food sacrificed to idols, from blood, from the meat of strangled animals and from illicit marriages" (15:29). The apostles could agree on these principles, apparently, and so the church moved on. The key element of the conference was that Paul and Barnabas would "go back to Antioch with the good news that freedom from circumcision had been recognized....The Jerusalem conference preserved koinōnia [fellowship] about the essential for conversion: Gentiles do not have to become Jews."[58]

These are important lessons taught us by the first generation Christians. The early church experienced great conflict and it took bold steps to resolve these matters. Paul's focus was clear: stress the essentials of Christianity and all the rest will fall into place. The other apostles, the "pillars of the church" agreed. Note too that at this time the mother church was Jerusalem and not Rome; Peter speaks to the whole church from Jerusalem around 49 A.D. which was some 15 years after the death of Christ. Rome was not yet the center of Christianity. James, the brother of the Lord, was head of the Jerusalem church and surprisingly, he gained this high ranking position without being one of the original twelve apostles chosen by Christ.[59] In short, you can be a "pillar of the church" and not be one of the twelve. The community of believers said so.

Paul and his followers returned to Antioch carrying a letter (Acts 15:30) stating that the new gentile converts did not have to observe the Jewish dietary laws nor circumcision. Everything appeared to be settled. But radical traditionalists from Jerusalem visited the church of Antioch and tried to alter the message of the Jerusalem conference (Gal. 2:14). Peter came for a visit as well and probably wanted to know how the community was getting along. Conflict was brewing in this mixed Christian church of both Jews and Gentiles, even after the pillars of the church had made it clear: no circumcision is required for Gentile converts. Paul writes about this conflict some years later in his letter to the Galatians (ca. 54 A.D.):

Galatians 2:11-14 [11]But when Cephas came to Antioch, I opposed him to his face, because he stood self-condemned, [12]for until certain people came from James, he used to eat with the Gentiles. But after they came, he drew back and kept himself separate for fear of the circumcision faction. [13]And the other Jews joined him in this hypocrisy, so that even Barnabas was led astray by their hypocrisy.

For Paul there could not be two churches but one regarding this important matter and there must be mutual respect for all. Peter was not helping matters by compromising on the principles laid down by the Jerusalem conference. After this blowup Paul left Antioch for a long missionary journey, never again to return to the city of his first missionary work. He never wrote a letter to the church of Antioch. His friend and co-worker, Barnabas, could not deal with this continued conflict any longer and separated from Paul to become the companion of Peter. No more fighting; Paul moved on, but everyone knew his views and what had been previously agreed upon in Jerusalem. Basic fellowship was preserved and the church managed to survive despite major differences. Paul's teaching carried the day. The future church was to be a Gentile church. The next time we hear from Paul is through his first known letter: Thessalonians, ca. 50-51; this letter is the first document to fill the pages of the Christian scriptures. Here is a brief summary of Paul's first 15 years as a Christian[60]:

Table 1. Paul's First years in Ministry.

Event	Date	Scripture
Conversion/calling	35-36	Acts 9: 1-8
Trips to Arabia Jerusalem	36-38	Gal. 1:15
Antioch Base	39-46	Acts 5:23
First Mission journey	46-48	Acts 13-14
Jerusalem Conference	49	Acts 15
Return: Antioch	49	Gal. 2:14
Letter, Thessalonians (1)	50-51	Thess. 1:2

Another significant contribution of Paul to church history and doctrine is the notion of the **Pauline privilege**. Because of his concern for God's people and their newly found faith in Christ, Paul was concerned for converts with marriage problems. How could he help Christians live in peace? Here are his reflections on marriage to the church in Corinth:

If any brother has a wife who is an unbeliever but is willing to live with him, he must not divorce her. And if any woman has a husband who is an unbeliever but is willing to live with her, she must not divorce him. For the unbelieving husband has been sanctified through his wife, and the unbelieving wife has been sanctified through her believing husband. Otherwise your children would be unclean, but as it is, they are holy. But if the unbeliever leaves, let him do so. A believing man or woman is not bound in such circumstances; God has called us to live in peace (1Cor 7:12-15).

Paul's teaching on marriage is unmistakable and his theology is clear. He wants his people to adhere to Christ and not lose faith. His writings reflect a desire to find new ways, in line with Gospel values, to help people deal with family problems and live their faith. One application of the doctrine outlined in Corinthians is easily summarized: two non-baptized persons marry and later on one of them decides to become a Christian.[61] After baptism, the non-baptized person finds he or she cannot live in harmony with the baptized person. The marriage can be dissolved when the baptized person enters into a marriage with a baptized Christian. This is the Pauline privilege which makes remarriage possible. Paul was open to change in order to help Christians live their faith life. But Paul's progressive pastoral theology raised eye brows in some circles and a proto-orthodox faction in the church ignored his writings for some time.[62] He was considered a bit too liberal for some and his special knowledge received in an encounter with the risen Christ on the road to Damascus sounded dangerously Gnostic(see chapter 7). His views on women in the church caused considerable controversy in his day as they do in 2008.

Paul and the Role of Women in the Church

We find conflicting statements in the Pauline corpus about the place of women in the church. In certain of his letters St. Paul writes that all Christians are equal through baptism. Such statements are recorded in his undisputed writings (these letters were written between 51 and 58 C.E.) where he argues from the doctrine of baptismal equality that there can be no discrimination in the churches.[63] His classic statement on baptismal equality occurs in the letter to the Galatians (3:27-28):

For all of you who were baptized into Christ have clothed yourselves with Christ.

There is neither Jew nor Greek, there is neither slave nor free person, there is not male and female; for you are all one in Christ Jesus.

The total number of Paul's undisputed letters are seven and there is a great deal of scholarly consensus on this point. They are Romans, 1 and 2 Corinthians, Galatians, Philippians, Thessalonians 1, and Philemon. Here we find the true thoughts of Paul without compromise. Paul states that men and women are equal before God and the church. At other times, e.g., in the pastoral epistles, we see a different picture regarding the role of women (e.g. 1Tim 2: 9-12). These "other" letters bearing Paul's name do not enjoy the same scholarly esteem as the undisputed corpus. They were most likely written in Paul's name by his disciples, according to most biblical scholars. Three of these "other" letters are called "Deutero-Pauline epistles" (Colossians, Ephesians, and 2 Thessalonians) because there is no strong consensus as to whether they are authentic letters written by Paul himself or epistles written by disciples in his name—a practice well known in antiquity. We are not sure that they are authentically Paul. This practice is acceptable unless the disciples depart from the true Pauline legacy. If they do, then we must revert back to the doctrine in the undisputed letters for his true teachings. The authorship of the three pastoral epistles (Titus, 1 and 2 Tim) are greatly disputed and are thought to be pseudepigraphy, i.e., writings that are attributed to Paul but not really written by him. For a long time (2nd to 19th century) many scholars thought Paul was the author of the letter to the Hebrews, but now almost all biblical scholars agree that the author of this epistle is simply unknown. Our understanding of Pauline literature has changed over time. In summary, we can state today's general consensus in Table 2.

Table 2. Authorship of Paul's Letters.

Key NT Letters	Paul Author?
Rom, Gal., 1 & 2 Cor, Philip, Phil, 1 Thess	Yes
Col, Eph, 2 Thess	Maybe
Titus, 1 & 2 Tim	Not likely
Hebrews	No

Because of the general high esteem Paul had in the early church, his over-zealous followers wrote several documents that were representative of his religious views and attitudes, but when all is said and done, Paul was the true author of only 7 undisputed letters. His disciples presented some of their own ideas when crafting certain letters included in the Pauline tradition (Titus, Tim 1,2). L. Michael White reminds us that in the ancient world there was generally a positive attitude toward the practice of disciples writing in the name of some long-deceased person. Plato, Socrates, Diogenes, and Crates come to mind.[64] Two points are relevant here regarding such pseudepigraphy. First, material written in the name of the master that does not contradict his known authentic writings are fine. Second, when disciples alter the teaching of the master and try to present him in a new light, then we should make clear what is happening; that would be negative pseudepigraphy. Such disciples in the "school of Paul" felt their editing was good for the church. It allowed the church to make adjustments and to move forward with changes in the church that were needed at the time. In the case of major disputes, however, one must always rely on the doctrine of the undisputed seven letters of Paul. In the six "other letters" we find perplexing statements regarding the conduct of men and women during worship services. For example, Paul allegedly says: "I do not permit a woman to teach or to have authority over a man. She must be quiet" (1Tim 2: 12). In Col 3:18 we read: "Wives, be subordinate to your husbands, as is proper in the Lord." This does not sound like baptismal equality or the thoughts of a man who put women in charge of house-churches. What is the true message of Paul? Are women equal to men in the Christian church or not? Do women have a major role in leading the church based on Paul's actions? The answers given below are complex and will not satisfy everyone.

Answer #1: There is little doubt that Paul allowed women to hold major leadership roles in the early church.

It is clear that both men and women held important leadership roles in the Pauline churches between 50 and 62 A.D.[65] Over a dozen women were instrumental in spreading the message of the Jesus movement, according to Paul's letters. The women were:

Phoebe: she was the head of the house-church near the port city of Cenchreae (near Corinth) and Paul considered her a co-worker in the Lord. As one of Paul's patrons, she supported his ministry out of her own resources and later was selected by Paul to deliver his longest and most important letter: Romans (16:1-2). Paul calls her diakonos, that is, "one who serves." There were half a dozen house-churches in Rome at the time and she must have known Greek to be able to read and explain Paul's letter which was being sent through her. This was a major assignment given only to a special disciple and head of a house church. Origen and St. John Chrysostom wrote that Phoebe had been officially ordained.[66]

Prisca: Aquila and his wife, Prisca, lived in Rome and supported a group of Christians that met in their home (Rom 16:3). Prisca and Aquila were also instrumental in establishing a house-church in Corinth and Ephesus (1 Cor 16:19).

Mary: she worked diligently to spread the Gospel to the Romans and they were eager to know about Jesus.

Persis was a co-worker for the Gospel (Romans 16:6) together with Tryphaena and Tryphosa.

Julia: she was the mother of Rufus and the sister of Nereus. Paul named her as one of the leaders in the Christian community of Rome.

Junia was a very talented woman and together with Andronicus (her husband?) are "prominent among the apostles" (Romans 16:17). Junia was one of the first to preach the Gospel in Rome. Note that Paul here applies the term "apostle" to a woman.[67] Here we see the use of the term apostle in a much broader sense than the traditional meaning, namely, a member of the twelve apostles chosen by Christ. Paul is an apostle (not one of the twelve) and so are many others who 1) have seen the risen Lord, 2) preached the Gospel, and, 3) have established new churches.

Lydia: she was a woman of considerable means (Acts 16:11) whom Paul met while in Philippi, and he later converted her to Christianity.

Lydia and her whole household were eventually baptized and Paul says he was invited to her home. Later on, she became head of a church that met in her house.

Euodia: Both she and Syntyche were co-workers with Paul and he says the two women "struggled beside me in the work of the Gospel" (Philippians 4:2).

In summary, no one can deny that Paul appointed women to high status positions in the early churches, and their contributions were crucial for the growth of Christianity in this early period. Why have some stated that Paul maintained women should be quiet in church and not be allowed to teach men? How could they teach and lead the church if they were supposed to be silent? This is a complex problem and will not be easily resolved.

In the first place, we must invoke the essential doctrine of Paul in his undisputed letters: there is true baptismal equality among all Christians. As a Jewish visionary and new convert to the Jesus movement, Paul asserted ideas that were similar to those of Christ: women were important in the ministry of God's Son, viz., Mary Magdalene, women who traveled with Jesus, the woman at the well. Women will be important in the Pauline churches as well. For Paul the Kingdom of God was already operative in the world and this kingdom must reflect God's divine plan and will; that is, all are equal before God. In the struggle to build the kingdom Paul preached a doctrine of peace through justice and not the dogma of the Roman empire: peace through victory and submission. No one group should dominate another. In his dozen or so years of missionary work before he wrote his first known letter (1 Thessalonians, 50 or 51 A.D.), Paul consistently questioned what people considered normal in Roman civilization at the time. He opposed the imperial Roman Way—an unjust society, a society of oppression. Centuries later we find that Augustine had a different view of the Roman empire; he cooperated with government officials in suppressing heretics and served as judge in some civil cases. We understand what Paul was up against when reading A. N. Wilson, who tells us that Rome was "the first totalitarian state in history."[68] The doctrine of Paul, when clearly understood, always sought to challenge the world in which Christians lived. In short, Paul argued there is no distinction, before God, between male and female; we are all one in Christ. Why shouldn't we behave that way here on earth? St. Paul writes: "There is neither Jew nor Greek, there is neither slave nor free, there is neither male nor female; for you are all one in Christ Jesus. And if you are Christ's, then you are Abraham's offspring, heirs according to the promise"(Gal 3:28ff).

Paul challenged the standards and norms of the time. But he did not live long enough to personally teach his views about Christ's revelation to large numbers of people. He probably died during the persecution of Nero around 64 C.E. Only a small number in the Jesus movement heard him preach or had the privilege of studying his letters which were sent to communities of house-churches for the most part. As the story of Christianity unfolded, we find the second generation of Christians rewriting the doctrines of Paul to suit their own religious preferences and needs. They found it necessary to "domesticate" some of the teachings of Paul.[69] Twenty years after the great apostle's death, his disciples wanted to bring Paul into the mainstream of what they considered orthodox Church thinking. The so-called orthodox Christian group was making its presence felt with a vengeance. This perspective is what many scripture scholars observe in 1 Tim: 2-11ff and the other pastorals which were probably written by a sympathetic follower of the Pauline tradition circa 90 A.D.—thirty years after the apostle's death.[70] Thus we get the word "pseudepigraphy," a word scholars use for forgery. In the early centuries of Christianity it was common to attribute writings to a great teacher if the document was generally in line with the leader's point of view. It would appear, however, that the authors of the pastoral epistles and Colossians took some liberties and added ideas that were not really part of the true Pauline tradition. Some felt Paul was too radical. The early church's not too subtle movement to sanitize Paul was to reflect an increased "accommodation to the world after the apostle's death."[71] Many ask today: did we make a wrong turn in the road here? Do we have to rediscover the real Paul? The pastoral epistles, which have been attributed to Paul, e.g. 1 Timothy etc., illustrate the revision of Paul made by his followers. The letter to the Colossians is another good example of how the church tried to "rehabilitate" Paul so that he would be more acceptable to church leaders and some new believers. But which Paul do you want? The Paul of history or the revisionist Paul who has been modified by clerics who had their own agenda? I'll take the unvarnished Paul any day.

What evidence do we have that there are really two Pauls presented to us by the New Testament? Textual analysis shows that "roughly one quarter of the vocabulary in the Pauline pastorals does not appear in the other Pauline letters...."[72] The "other" letters include seven of Paul's undisputed letters such as Romans and 1 Corinthians. The true spirit of Paul is lacking in the pastorals. The letter to the Colossians is an illustration of what we call late first century redaction[73] by clerics unwilling to accept the radical Paul and desirous of adapting Paul to fit in with Roman Empire norms. Here we find 87 words in the letter to the Colossians that do not appear in the undisputed Pauline letters. According to Raymond Brown, the majority of critical scholars contend that Paul did not write the letter to Colossians.[74] Likewise, Paul probably did not write 1 Timothy which appeared around 90 A.D.; his disciples put this document together and thus some call it a forgery. It was not truly written by Paul who died around 64 C.E. These aberrations were tolerated in early Christianity for the good of holy mother church. We have to read the scriptures with these insights in mind. Modern biblical research helps us resolve disputes when we find contradictions in the writings of Paul: women and their role in the church. Col and 1 Tim do not reflect the authentic teaching of Paul regarding women as handed down in his undisputed writings. Brown thinks that later NT writings (circa 80-90 C.E) are a corruption "reflecting an increasingly authoritarian patriarchal church order."[75]

But what about 1 Cor 14? This epistle was definitely written by Paul, but it contains negative statements about the role of women in the church. They contradict his basic doctrine of baptismal equality. Is this the true Paul? The text in question is:

As in all the churches of God's holy people, women are to remain quiet in the assemblies, since they have no permission to speak: theirs is a subordinate part, as the Law itself says. If there is anything they want to know, they should ask their husbands at home: it is shameful for a woman to speak in the assembly (1 Cor 14: 33-35).

This seems to settle the issue: Paul sees men as superior and that women should conform to the man's directives. Yet, a closer look at 1 Cor 14 shows what many authors have been saying for some time: this section of Paul is an interpolation.[76] That is, a copyist has inserted words in the sacred text that were not written by the principal author of the letter.

We must realize that in reading the New Testament (1 Corinthians is just one example) we are not dealing with the original texts of St. Paul. The vast majority of scripture scholars agree that we have a copy, not the original document produced by St. Paul. In fact, all of our new testament documents are copies; the original Greek texts have been lost.[77] We have in 1 Corinthians a document that was handed down to us by copyists. It is our responsibility to evaluate the text with the help of scholars and determine what part of the scripture is the real message of Paul and what are manipulations by highly motivated scribes. This is the very essence of the historical-critical method which "has been in use in Catholic theology ever since the door was opened for it by the encyclical *Divino Afflante Spiritu* in 1943...."[78] The general conclusion regarding 1 Cor 14: 34-35 is that it is not the work of Paul but the views of later Christian teachers.[79] *The HarperCollins Study Bible* states this is a non-Pauline addition to the letter.[80] The field of textual criticism has as its goal to present past texts so that they are as close to the original as possible. Obviously, this involves much controversy and all decisions need to be based on solid evidence. It is true that all texts are innocent until proven guilty, but we have to listen to biblical scholars as they work to give us the best interpretation of any suspect text. The *New Jerome Biblical Commentary* views 1 Cor 14 "as a post-Pauline interpolation"[81] and reflects the misogynous views of 1 Tim 2:11. In the discussion of Paul and the role of women, it is essential that we come to a solid understanding of what Paul's authentic views were. It is clear that Paul promotes radical equality, but his followers had another view of what the church should be. We must remember: only Paul was given the special revelation on the road to Damascus, not his editors.

The late 1st century leaders of the church wanted women to be subordinate to men.[82] This was the way the Roman Empire worked and church leaders wanted to fit in; patriarchy was the norm. The second coming of Christ had not yet occurred and Christians needed to adjust to the dominant culture. The Christian community was becoming institutionalized. We have to understand what was going on in the early church and then try to determine what the real message of Paul reveals to us. Hans Conzelmann sees this passage from Corinthians (1 Cor 14) as an attempt to bind the church to general custom regarding women.[83] Do we want the true Jesus and the unvarnished Paul or the second generation version of faith in Christ? I think we know the answer. These examples show us the folly of fundamentalist approaches to biblical studies: simply believe the words as they were written! That cannot be the policy of the informed Christian. One must understand the culture, background, and idiosyncratic processes at work in the development of the scriptures. This is not an easy task.

The educated reader of the scriptures must ask: what version of reality do I want? Do I want the true Paul who encountered the risen Christ and was told how to conduct his life or do I want a latter-day cleric's version of Paul that his boss told him to serve up so that the truth of the Gospel would be less offensive to some church leaders at the time? Clerical mischief occurred in the church long before the sex abuse scandals of the contemporary Catholic church. We have nice words for these past practices: redactions, interpolations. There are two Pauls in the scriptures; the choice is yours.

This discussion of Paul and the role of women shows the evolution of church thinking and how serious conflict was at the center of early church life. Ideas did not simply evolve in some organic growth model for the better. People ripped key ideas out of Paul's teaching and practice; then they replaced them with doctrines more palatable to second generation believers. Thus we see conflict theory[84] (a.k.a., social reform theory) operative in the early church; the concept is a much more accurate portrayal of church activities than an "organic growth" model that Küng and others seem to espouse.[85] Those latter concepts are too kind for people who have presented their version of reality as the truth, using deception and coercion. Clerics with power asserted what would be true and believable. This does not happen all the time, but it occurs enough so that the reader must be careful.

Later apocryphal writings and archeological findings underscore other gender disputes evident in the early church. The **Acts of Paul and Thecla** (an apocryphal document) show that there was a close working relationship between this saintly woman (never mentioned in the NT) and the apostle Paul. This document was written in Greek sometime during the second century and was known to Augustine, Origen, and other church scholars. The author describes events that took place in the missionary life of Paul (45-62 A.D.) and some argue that 1 Tim was written to counter the Paul/Thecla oral tradition.[86]

Thecla, a saint of the Catholic church and whose feast day is celebrated on September 23, traveled with Paul on occasion and was even called "female apostle" and "equal to the apostles."[87] Yes, women had a prominent role in Paul's theology and ministry, and the life of Thecla illustrates this point.

Ehrman points out that in the *Acts of Paul and Thecla* we find Paul seeking to convert women to a life of strict asceticism and sexual renunciation.[88] He says "Blessed are those who have wives as not having them, for they experience God." That is comparable to Paul's ideas in 1Cor 7:2-9, namely, that he "would like everyone to be as I am myself." That would mean without a spouse, and, of course, practicing abstinence. This is seen by many as an "interim ethics" since the second coming of Christ was believed to be imminent. Paul's preaching converts Thecla to a life of virginity, much to the chagrin of her fiancé, Thamris. The unintended consequence of this directive by Paul to his followers had a tremendous impact on his counter cultural message against patriarchy. By choosing a celibate life, women were set free from the real or potential domination of their husbands. They were free to devote their lives to the Jesus movement and many did just that. A significant number of these women became heads of house-churches. This is a remarkable lesson in the sociology of religion taught by the apostle Paul, namely, the unintended consequences of preaching asceticism for the Kingdom of God: he helped women avoid the rule of patriarchy.

In addition to the above story about celibacy for the Kingdom, there is considerable evidence to date that a group of Christians in the 6th century viewed Paul and Thecla as a powerful spiritual force, and that together they contributed to the growth of the early church. In a small cave near Ephesus, Karl Herold uncovered images of both Paul and Thecla painted on the stone walls.[89] Interpreting these images found in 1906 is problematic, but one approach mentioned by Crossan gives the following set of observations. Both Paul and Thecla are seen as leaders in the church. The images are of equal height and so the icon may be saying that the two images are of equal importance to the artist and maybe to others in the church at the time. The fact that the right hand of both figures is raised can be interpreted as a teaching gesture. This could mean equality in power or shared authority. One image in the cave was damaged by later iconoclasts: the face and hand of

Thecla were disfigured, but the image of Paul was not harmed. Clearly someone or a group of people rejected the importance of this woman leader in the church and made their views known in the cave. The cave has come to be known as Paul's Grotto which is indicative of our early 20th century tendency: give the man a lead role.

It is evident from this brief discussion that Paul held to a radical doctrine of baptismal equality whether one places much credence in the **Acts of Paul and Thecla** or not. Generations after Paul's death, we find his disciples watering down his legacy to fit their view of ecclesiastical and social reality. They probably thought this was for the good of the church. We must rediscover and reassert Christianity's basic roots and let the true story of Paul be told.

Answer #2. The pastoral epistles sought to diminish the role of women in the early church because leaders felt this would be good for the church.

With the destruction of Jerusalem by the Roman army in 70 A.D., religious groups were fearful of more persecution by Roman authorities. Soldiers had just killed 700,000 Jews and anyone who looked radical to the emperor would probably suffer the same fate. Peter, Paul, and James were killed in the early '60s A.D. and this left the first Christians reeling. The early church wanted to survive and so they made accommodations to the Roman culture. One can say they were almost forced to do this by their environment: change or die. They had little choice. Second, some philosophers and religious thinkers such as Montanus, used women e.g., Maximillia and others, in leadership roles and the proto-orthodox church probably wanted to avoid any association with these groups and their practices. They were heretics! Thirdly, as the church grew in numbers, the Christian communities moved from private space (houses) to public space (church buildings) and this was the realm of men, not women.[90] Ecological theory, using concepts such as habitat, environment, and population would suggest that the church organization adjusted to the times.[91] Since patriarchy was the dominant cultural norm for Romans, men gradually took over most of the leadership roles in the new public church by the beginning of the 2nd century. In short, we can see that this is a cultural-deterministic model of change, which now can be re-examined, given our new norms of what is a just society. The early church made adjustments; so can the church of today.

Garry Wills' recent essay on St. Paul highlights some of the controversy surrounding the work of the apostle.[92] Scholars in the early church questioned Paul's orthodoxy. For some it was an issue of doctrinal purity. Had Paul gone too far? The Gnostics, later condemned by church fathers as heretical, saw Paul as a great leader. This did not help his cause, however. Because of the Gnostic emphasis on having "special knowledge" of God and the spiritual world, they loved Paul's religious orientation. First, he claimed a special encounter with the Risen Christ on the road to Damascus which led to his calling to be an apostle. Second, he stated that he was swept up into the 3rd heaven[93] (a mystic) and this is the kind of role model the Gnostic sect loved to emulate. If we have this special knowledge, according to Gnostic preachers, we may not need the church. These individualistic tenets and other factors led to the condemnation of Gnostic leaders by proto-orthodox Christians in 144 A.D. Some orthodox church leaders did not like Paul because of his views on circumcision. There was a vocal group of Jewish Christians (Paul was a Jew) who resented his opposition to circumcision and the skirting of dietary rules for the sake of his Gentile converts. They did not like his views on women. For some, Paul had gone too far. Paul was martyred ca. 64 and his words in the letter to Timothy reveal his anguish, namely, "that all in the province of Asia have turned away from me, among them, Phigelus and Hermogenes" (2 Tim 1:15). Nevertheless, when the canon of scripture was finally set toward the end of the fourth century, it was obvious that Paul and his message had a central role in the early church's understanding of revelation—and for all church history. He was vindicated by the church in later years. Garry Wills tells us why: "His letters stand closer to Jesus than do any other words in the New Testament."[94]

CHAPTER THREE:

The Post-apostolic Church:

Increase, Multiply, Defend

> *By 300 A.D. there were millions of Christians living in the Roman Empire*
>
> *(Rodney Stark)*

The period after 70 A.D. is usually considered the post-apostolic age of Christianity. Almost all of the apostles were now dead (John the Apostle, the lone exception, died at Ephesus around 100 A.D.); the followers of Christ were being led by a second generation of disciples. As the story of early Christianity unfolds, we find that the people of God are called "Catholic" (meaning "universal") for the first time by St. Ignatius of Antioch in a letter (ca. 107 A.D.) to Smyrnaeans. ***Catholic*** teaching eventually came to mean that which was believed always, everywhere and by all.[95] This was a huge development in our understanding of Christianity. Other changes include the notion of church governance wherein men, not women, were given the title of "bishop"; we also see the increasing claims to primacy by the bishop of Rome over all Christian churches. Many were uneasy about this Petrine development.

Some argue that Christianity was going through a spiritual explosion in the first century and that this trend continued for two hundred years. Paul's missionary work was bearing fruit. The church began to plan for the future and was less and less concerned about the end of the world and the Second Coming of Christ. They had work to do here on earth. One of their chief accomplishments during the last third of the 1st century was the writing of the canonical Gospels.

Period of the Evangelists

Between the years 70 to 110 A.D. the early Christians saw the need to write a detailed account of the words and deeds of Jesus for their communities and posterity. During this time the well known Gospels of Matthew, Mark, Luke, and John were written, but other accounts of the life of Jesus took shape as well, e.g., gospel of Thomas, gospel of Mary, gospel of Philip, etc. These three documents and several others were probably written around 140 A.D.; we will focus our attention, for now, on the four canonical Gospels.

Jesus was certainly a real, historical figure (see Tacitus, 117 A.D.), but he wrote nothing that we know of and so his followers took on the daunting task of preserving his memory and teachings, first orally and then in written form. There is no question that the Gospels were shaped by the social context and audience of the time. For example, 1) Luke, a co-worker with Paul, wrote for Gentiles, 2) while Mark (a.k.a. John Mark) developed his Gospel for Greek speaking Christians who did not know Aramaic but had some knowledge of Jewish Christian traditions. Obviously, the life of Jesus was written down some 40 years after his death, and some details are recalled differently. Nonetheless, the point here is that an enormous task was undertaken by the early church to solidify the new religion's first principles. There were some oral and written sources to draw on and so the author of Mark began his work. The following model expresses how this first Gospel took shape.

Oral history=> Some Written documents => Mark's Gospel 72 A.D.

Mark's sources came from an Aramaic tradition which later was translated into Greek. The Christian liturgies were the setting where the memories of Jesus were told and retold to strengthen the community's faith. This social mechanism (group prayer meetings) provided the incubation period needed to refine the Christian truths that were so vital to the Jesus movement. It is clear that the Gospels are not "histories" (recording and interpretation of significant facts) as we understand the discipline today, but rather they are in the tradition of "lives" written about great people, e.g., Homer, Moses, Plato, Socrates. We know that in this genre the writers may at times embellish events and order things differently to make a point to their audience. The Gospels tell the story of the good news of salvation in Christ seen from different perspectives. That was the main point of the four evangelists.

Mark's Gospel came at a time of great turmoil and fear. Peter, Paul, and James were all killed in the early '60s; with the fall of Jerusalem in 70 A.D. and the killing of close to 1 million Jews by the Roman army, times called for meditation and reflection. How could the Gospel help Christians deal with their troubles? This new religious group studied and prayed; after about 40 years they had their religious "constitution." The whole process of writing the Gospels was an expression of faith by the early Christians.

Jesus' everyday language was Aramaic which was common to residents of Judea, but he probably used some Greek as the son of a carpenter who in all probability worked in the prosperous city of Sepphoris—some four miles from Nazareth. The first oral tradition about Jesus' words and deeds would have been in Aramaic, and later these stories were told in Greek to new converts. Gradually, the bits and pieces of Jesus' life were written down and these documents have been labeled "Quelle" (source) by biblical scholars. The community needed a permanent record of the life, death, and resurrection of Christ which had been preserved by telling and retelling these events during numerous liturgies at house-churches. It was almost 15 years later when Matthew produced his Gospel (85 A.D.) and Luke's work came later. John's "spiritual Gospel" took its final form about 110 A.D.[96] This period of growth allowed Christians to assert, in their view, the true message of Jesus; later on we will see that these ideas would be challenged.

Our focus here is on the synoptic Gospels as they are called: Matt, Mk, Lk. This term is used because these three Gospels can be viewed together, seen side by side, for comparison, viz., the call of the disciples (Text: New American Bible).

Mark 1:17	Matthew 4:18	Luke 5:10
Come after me, and I will make you fishers of men.	*Come after me, and I will make you fishers of men.*	*Do not be afraid; from now on you will be catching men.*

Here we see Matthew depends on Mark, who wrote first, while Luke generates his own wording of the call of the disciples. Events are ordered differently as well: the call is in the very first chapter of Mark, whereas Luke and Matthew place this crucial event 4 or 5 chapters after their introduction. Why do the synoptic Gospels seem to have the same ideas and share direct quotations? What is their relationship to each other? Did they take material from one another? How do we explain the dependence of these Gospels on one another? This in essence is the synoptic problem, namely, the difficulty biblical scholars encounter when dealing with the origin and interrelationship of the above three Gospels. The widely accepted solution to this problem is called the two source theory, which is accepted by the majority of biblical scholars (figure 1). There are other competing theories, but we will focus on the less complicated approach to this problem for now.

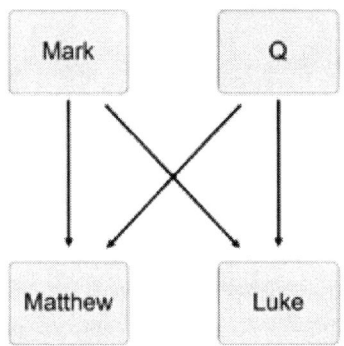

Figure 1. The origin and relationship of the three synoptic Gospels.

The best way to approach the two source hypothesis is to remember five basic points: 1) The Gospel of Mark was written first (ca. 72 A.D.) and the author relied on oral tradition and probably some written documents developed by the Christian communities between 33 and 65 A.D. 2) Matthew and Luke, who wrote their Gospels 15 years later, depend on Mark for some material (see figure 1) but draw on other material that the proto-Gospel did not contain. 3) This dependence on Mark is obvious according to Brown's summation: 80 percent of Mark's verses are found in Matthew and 65 percent of Luke comes from Mark.[97] 4) But there is independence as well, namely, Matthew and Luke have verses of similar or matching material, but these items are not in Mark.[98] For instance, the "Our Father" appears in Matt and Luke but not in Mark. 5) Hence, scholars posit a Q document that Matthew and Luke draw upon, but Mark was probably unaware of; it was developed later or unknown to Mark, who was not an eye witness to Jesus' earthly life. Hence we conclude that the above three Gospel writers 1) have material in common, 2) they have unique material, 3) and they move events around when it fits their purposes. The majority of scholars adhere to the two source hypothesis which appears to be the most plausible theory for explaining the synoptic problem.

Clearly the early Christians spent some 40 years writing and editing the four Gospels. This was a key period for building the foundation of the Jesus movement. They use cultural and social experiences to tell the story of Jesus. The evangelists shaped their material somewhat for their unique audiences. This is but another stage in the growth of the early church.

As the church evolved, the task of building and expanding the church became paramount; the period between 70 A.D. through 300 was considered the time of Catholic Christianity. The term "catholic" is never used in the New Testament but became a way of describing the church at a later date. The first to use the term "Catholic" was St. Ignatius of Antioch (ca. 105 A.D.) It meant that the church was universal and not local; secondly the term meant that the church was indeed "orthodox", namely, it accepted the fullness of God's revelation in Christ. Obviously, many in the Christian churches have forgotten the true significance of this word. Later on, officials of the Roman Empire had Ignatius arrested and tried to make an example of him; he was executed in the public arena in hopes that his murder would dissuade people from joining the Christian church. Roman torture and murder had just the opposite effect.

Church Structure

Another important development in the life of the church had to do with organizational structure. From the time of Jesus' public life until the second century, the people of God organized themselves in various ways. Table 3 shows the progression of organizational structure in the first 3 decades of the early church; change would be a hallmark of this transitional period.

Table 3. Early church structure before 64 A.D.

30-33 A.D.	Pauline churches 40-60 A.D.
JESUS	RISEN CHRIST
APOSTLES	APOSTLES
DISCIPLES	PROPHETS
FOLLOWERS	TEACHERS
	COMMUNITY

In the beginning of his public life, Christ selected the 12 apostles, added 72 disciples, and hundreds from Judea followed Him as He preached to them on mountain sides and at times in the local synagogue. Jesus called for a New Covenant and made it clear that his way of life was different. He even abolished certain norms of the Old Testament. Review this example from Matt: 5:38ff.

On an Eye for an Eye:

[38] You have heard that it was said, 'An eye for eye, and tooth for tooth.' (Ex.21:24, Deut.19:21, Lev.24:20)

[39] But I tell you, Do not resist an evil person. If someone strikes you on the right cheek, turn to him the other also.

[40] And if someone wants to sue you and take your tunic, let him have your cloak as well.

[41] If someone forces you to go one mile, go with him two miles.

*[42] Give to the one who asks you, and do not turn **away** from the one who wants to borrow from you.*

Jesus repeated the old law (Moses) and then gave His followers new norms to follow.[99] He asserted: "Moses told you, but I say....." (Mk: 10) Christians were asked to build a whole new world on earth, and a heavenly kingdom was prepared for those who followed the new way of life. This is obviously the creation of a new religion, a new covenant.

Through His words and actions, Jesus involved the women of his time in the proclamation of the kingdom. He talked to women, depended on their support and service to proclaim His Gospel values. Mary Magdalene was a prominent figure in the new religious movement and was the first person He appeared to after the resurrection (Jn 20: 1-18). She proclaimed the good news of his resurrection to his other disciples. Referred to as the "apostle to the apostles"[100] in early Christian writings, she demonstrates the totally new approach Jesus used to confound the so-called "wisdom of this world." St. Paul later would stress this point to the church in Corinth: "For the wisdom of this world is foolishness with God" (1 Cor. 1:19).

The loosely knit group of leaders and followers of Jesus is contrasted in Table 3 with Paul's Christian communities developed during his missionary work (45-60 A.D.). The Pauline communities, the church of Antioch, church in Corinth, etc., exemplified a model of organization that was charismatic and informal.[101] There were numerous statuses and roles in this group of believers as we can easily note from reading the New Testament and reviewing Figure 2.

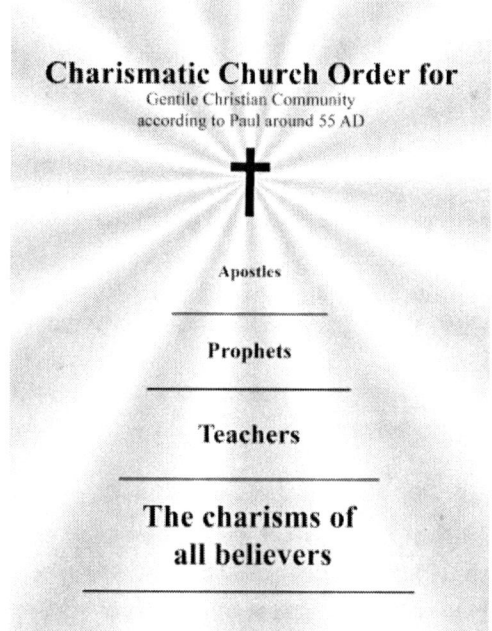

Figure 2. The Pauline Church Structure.

Despite the belief in the imminent coming of Christ, the Jesus movement had provisional church structures.[102] At the center of church order for Paul was the risen Christ. The apostles were the pillars of the church (the twelve) but Paul expanded the meaning of the status, "apostle," to mean anyone who was sent to establish a new church. Thus women were given the title of apostle in some instances. By status we mean the person's position in the community's social structure and in this case the early church —the people of God. In the Pauline churches it was clear that the apostles were the major force at work but many other people such as prophets and teachers assisted in ministry. Women held both these latter statuses in Paul's house churches. The **Didache,** or "teachings" of the Apostles, written sometime around 100-110 A.D., notes that prophets and teachers led the Eucharistic celebration. This ancient document was considered sacred by the church because it contained the teachings and directives of the twelve apostles. Everyone in the assembly had gifts (charisms) which were to be utilized to build up the church; Paul advocated a charismatic church structure. The biblical foundation of this conception of church order is from St. Paul, 1 Cor 12:28ff.

28   Now you are Christ's body, and individually parts of it.

29   Some people God has designated in the church to be, first, apostles; second, prophets; third, teachers; then, mighty deeds; then, gifts of healing, assistance, administration, and varieties of tongues.

30   Are all apostles? Are all prophets? Are all teachers? Do all work mighty deeds?

31   Do all have gifts of healing? Do all speak in tongues? Do all interpret?

Strive eagerly for the greatest spiritual gifts. But I shall show you a still more excellent way.

When Christians met, they worshiped in house-churches and various devout members would be asked to lead the Eucharistic celebration. Who presided at the liturgies? The apostles took this role when present, no doubt, but others led the celebration of the Lord's supper in their absence. Raymond Brown, arguing for a later date for the Didache, observes: "About the turn of the first century the **Didache** (10:7) depicts a situation where prophets celebrated the Eucharist, and that may have been the custom earlier as well."[103] We should keep in mind that women exercised the role of prophet in the Pauline churches. Hence the function of Eucharistic leader could easily have been taken by the head of the house-church, its teachers, and prophets. It is true that Justin Martyr (d. 165) states that the "president of the brethren" officiated at the Eucharist.[104] But he lived at a time when the church had developed a more formal structure that had excluded women from most leadership roles. Paul's experience was different. We can use the term "role" in the Christian community to mean the behaviors associated with one's status in the community. The apostles, for instance, would be the obvious leaders of the Eucharist, but others who were subordinate could take this role as well. Many different people could take the role of celebrating the Eucharist.[105] Some argue that women performed this role at times in the early church. This custom was lost when second generation Christians decided to take on the patriarchal norms of Greco-Roman culture.

What factors allowed women to take leadership roles in the early church? First, Jesus took the lead during His lifetime. Women gave important instructions to the Eleven after the death and resurrection of Christ. Jesus conversed with women and ate with them; He considered Mary Magdalene a key leader. St. Paul depended on women leaders as he traveled throughout the Roman empire, preaching the Gospel. Ten women are mentioned by St. Paul in his epistles as prominent members of the church in proclaiming the Gospel. Phoebe's title "diakonos" indicates that she was the leader of a house community. She is mentioned in the letter to the Romans 16:1 as the person who would deliver the epistle to the Christian communities in Rome. L. Michael White notes that "the emissary delegated to carry the letter…and to present it in each church was one of Paul's most trusted co-workers from the Aegean mission. Her name was Phoebe, the house-church patron from Cenchreae, the eastern harbor of Corinth."[106] Paul needed a trust-worthy disciple to carry his letter to the five or six house-churches in Rome.[107] With so many Christian cells in the city it is likely that certain members of those house-churches were chosen to celebrate the Eucharist; Paul calls Phoebe "diakonos" and this role may have qualified her to lead the Eucharistic celebration. Junia is described by Paul as distinguished among the apostles. The woman Prisca, mentioned several times in Paul's letters, was a missionary and founder of a local church. These would have been likely candidates to celebrate the Eucharist in house-churches. A second factor that led to the utilization of women was the development of house-churches and not public buildings for worship. Women supported Christ's ministry and had the role of family and house coordinator in the Jewish community. The early followers of Jesus did not own church buildings and so they met in homes and other facilities for worship services. Women were in charge of the home for the most part; that was their role in the Jewish family structure. Clement I says in his letter to Corinth that women "should manage their household affairs becomingly, and be in every respect marked by discretion." The Christian community could not overlook and ignore the women whose homes they were using for worship, and women were naturally invited to participate in church services and ministry. This was a natural evolution of shared authority and responsibility contained in the house-church concept and Paul's theology. As this relatively small group of believers grew and flourished, there is no question that they were fully equipped to carry on the work of Messiah: baptism was essential as is evident when Paul was baptized by Ananias soon after his conversion; they had the oral tradition of the Gospels and communities celebrated the Lord's supper. The fundamentals of Christianity were in place.

Nevertheless, the Pauline churches were not the only structure of church to be found ca. 55 A.D. Figure 3 illustrates a structure operative in mostly Jewish Christian settings.

Figure 3. Structure of Jewish Christian Communities.

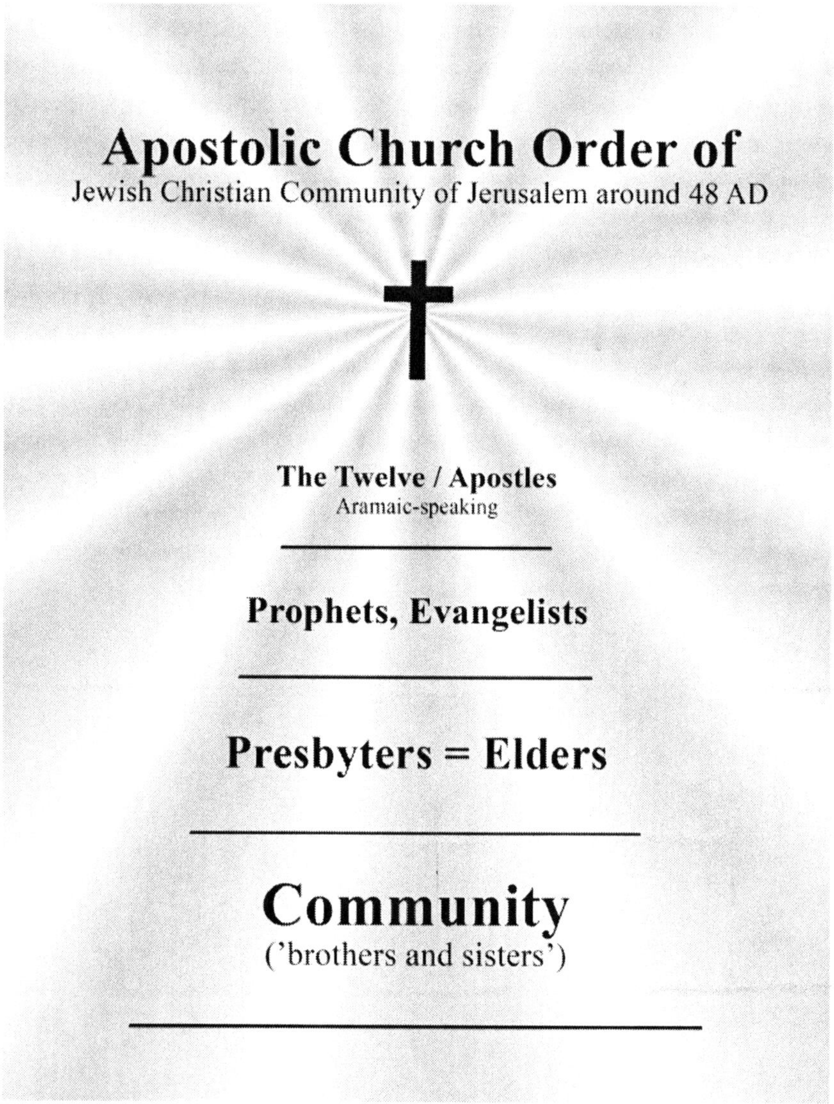

Apostolic Church Order of
Jewish Christian Community of Jerusalem around 48 AD

The Twelve / Apostles
Aramaic-speaking

Prophets, Evangelists

Presbyters = Elders

Community
('brothers and sisters')

As in the Pauline churches, Christ (Messiah) who is risen and alive, takes center stage. Peter, James, and John led the Aramaic-speaking community, with James, the brother of the Lord; James was head of the Jerusalem community even though he was not one of the original twelve. Paul came to these leaders to discuss the issue of circumcision for gentile converts. He wanted this powerful group to extend fellowship to the gentile churches; they acquiesced at the conference of Jerusalem. In addition to apostles, prophets played a key role in church structure. We note in Acts 11:27: "At that time some prophets came down from Jerusalem to Antioch...." These religious leaders came not in the OT tradition to call God's people back to their sacred traditions but to actually predict that there would be a famine in the area; alms were needed to assist those in need. What happened next was a true sign of Christian fellowship (koinonia).

29
> So the disciples determined that, according to ability, each should send relief to the brothers who lived in Judea.

30
> [7] This they did, sending it to the presbyters in care of Barnabas and Saul.

The collection was sent to "presbyters" using the good services of Barnabas and Paul. The term "presbyteroi" indicates this role would be performed by older more experienced men (hence elders is implied).[108] The Jewish synagogue structure had groups of elders who performed various religious tasks and the Christian presbyter's status was influenced by that model. This view of church leaders involves service to the brothers and sisters in need. A similar example is found early in Acts when the "Seven" were appointed to help serve Hellenist widows in the community. Leadership has its duties. The notion of "charisms" and the importance of women leaders are played down in this Jerusalem church model.

As we move to the year 100 and beyond we note how the church changed dramatically in terms of its organizational characteristics. Figure 4 illustrates this profound change.

Figure 4. Church structure 80 years after Jesus' death.

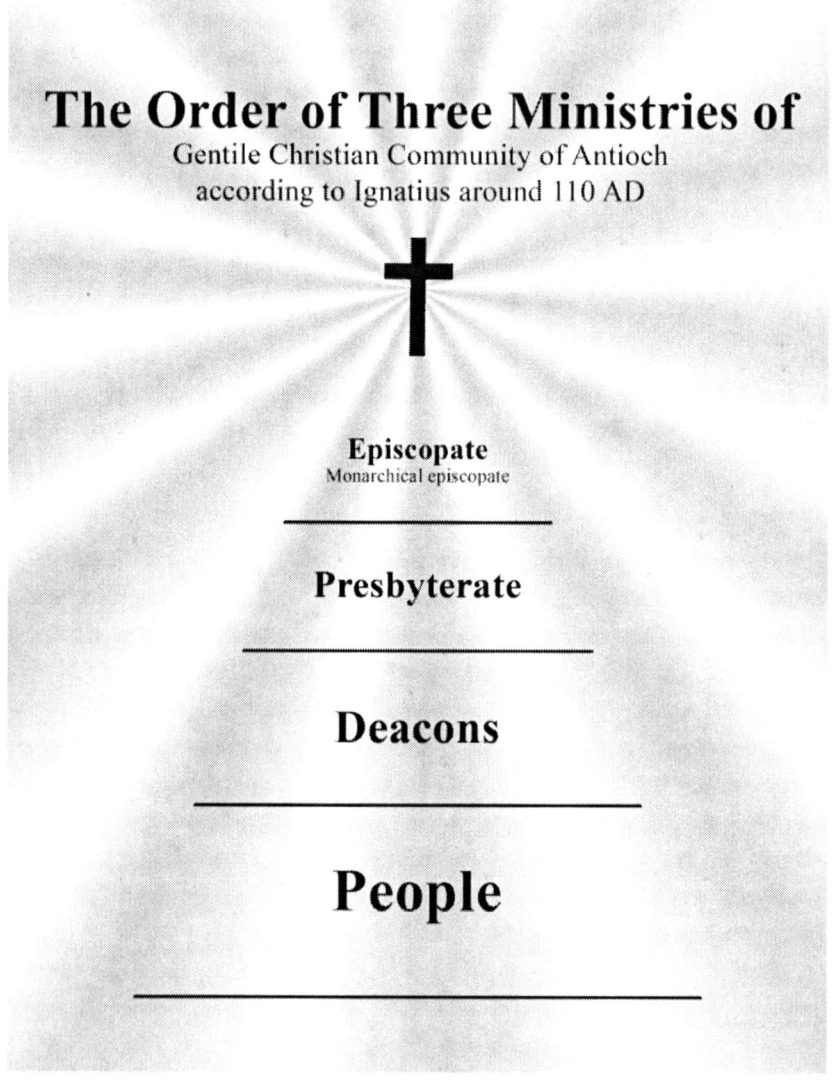

In the pastoral epistles (written ca. 80-90 A.D.) we find the concept "overseer/bishop" (episkopos) which is another title for presbyter.[109] Later on in the 2nd century the status of "episcopate" emerged as one who was superior and distinct from the presbyter. Bishops were in charge of certain cities and/or regions. By the 2nd century the status of bishop was defined as monarchical, that is, as a successor to the apostles, he was in charge and ruled the flock until death. Nonetheless, the leaders of the church in Augustine's time removed certain bishops for misconduct and so their tenure in office was not absolute. Thus, the notions of bishop, presbyter, deacon and the laying on of hands became an important feature of life in the church by 110 A.D.—about 50 years after the death of Paul. Women served as deacons until about the 5th century, and so this practice could be restored immediately to the Catholic church, given its century's old custom.[110] The only thing stopping such action are the senior clerics running the Vatican today. Church institutionalization increasingly favored men over women, in imitation of the Roman culture, which sought to control large numbers of people with male-dominated policies and structures (patriarchy). Paul Hoffmann finds these church developments perplexing since they have led to 1) male dominance in church leadership, 2) the repression of charismatic gifts, 3) authoritarian policies of bishops 4) loss of the prophetic role, and 5) an overemphasis on uniformity when such rigidity is not necessary.[111]

What led to this drastic change? The destruction of Jerusalem by the Romans was a catastrophic event in 70 A.D. beyond all comprehension and may have influenced Church development for decades thereafter. Jewish leaders were fed up with the dictatorial practices of their Roman occupiers, not to mention the high taxes. The Jewish army took control of Jerusalem and the surrounding area in 66 A.D. due to the work of zealots challenging the validity of the Roman occupation.[112] The future emperor Vespasian, together with his son, Titus, and several legions eventually took control of the city in 70 and killed at least 700,000 rebellious Jews in the process. The temple was completely destroyed as the Romans sought to teach a lesson to all those who would oppose Caesar. With Christians numbering less than 10,000 at the time, many leaders in the Jesus movement probably felt it was important to face reality and conform to principles of an authoritarian government (see Fig. 5). Their survival was at stake. The Roman plunder of the Temple with all its gold and silver could well have been worth millions of dollars at today's prices for the conquering soldiers. The pillaging of the temple, its total destruction and the burning of Jerusalem with terrible suffering and loss of life wiped out about ten percent of the Jewish population.[113] The church in Jerusalem was weakened and some Christians looked West to find a center of power and influence. Rome was a logical choice since Paul had already founded many house-churches in the city. Gradually the new religion began to look like a typical group in the Roman empire. When in Rome, do as the Romans do.

Figure 5. Sack of Jerusalem: Arch of Titus, Rome, 81 A.D.

Church buildings became a reality toward the middle of the 2nd century. The patriarchal system, in contrast to the example of Jesus and the practices of the Pauline churches, began to take hold; men took control of the more formal church building program and its religious services. House-churches became less important, and the church began to look more like the structures of Roman society than the models of church envisioned by the followers of Jesus and Paul. Assimilation into Roman customs made Christianity resemble a typical organized group in the empire.

Two leaders in the church clearly point out this change. The first letter of Clement I shows a dramatic moment in the history of Christianity. For the first time we find the distinction of "clergy" and "laity." Here roles are clearly specified. St. Ignatius of Antioch goes even further and tells the laity to revere and obey the bishop "as if he were God."[114] St. Paul never took this view of himself and he was certainly an important leader. Why such a shift in church thinking?

First, one must realize that the New Testament canon had not yet been established and hence the second generation of leaders had no foundational documents to depend on. Obedience to church authority was the next option. Certainly, the four Gospels were written (Matt, Mark, Luke, John) by 110 A.D., but there were many other Gospels in various forms to attract Christians. Which ones were central to the teachings of Jesus and thus the supreme guide to church growth? The early church had developed new structures that seemed to go beyond any biblical directives. Leaders had to appeal to their authority as direct descendants of the apostles to bring about conformity to the new changes. Moreover, the writings of Paul were viewed with suspicion by some, and his doctrines had not been sufficiently sanitized by second generation church leaders to be accepted by the whole church. The radical Paul seemed dangerous. As the early church moved to the period of the Patristics (Fathers of the church), we find that these men laid out principles which many felt were proper for governing the church at the time. If the bishop and his words were to be viewed as God's words, women had very little chance to redress any of their grievances. Hence a new direction in the church became clear. Authority emerged from the top down. Men were in charge. Certainly not all bishops were authoritarian leaders but this tendency had its day. Augustine confronted Pope Zosimus in the 5th century when Pelagius appealed to the bishop of Rome and gained his support. But Augustine was brilliant and not many could challenge his teachings or his debating skills, including the bishop of Rome. Pelagius was eventually condemned and Augustine's North Africa group won out over the bishop of Rome. However, the average Christian simply followed the local bishop's lead. The charisms of the faithful had to submit to the men in charge.

In the early part of the 2nd century, we find that each city usually had its own bishop and thus he would lead the Eucharistic celebration when he was in town. Otherwise, this task fell to the presbyter. The bishop and presbyter were selected by the community and these roles were designated by the "laying on the hands" which later was called ordination by church leaders. Thus, it is improper to say that Jesus ordained the apostles at the last supper. Ordination, the notion of bishop and presbyter were concepts that had meaning only later in the early church. In the new, organized, hierarchical church, women played a subordinate role; for various reasons they were downgraded as we have already pointed out. It is clear that the actions of Jesus and the charismatic communities of Paul were less important to second and third generation Christians. The church thought it was on the right track. In fact, the church of 110 A.D. was moving away from its founding principles. Some have claimed that today's churches must rediscover the teachings of the early church and distinguish "man-made" structures which can be changed for the good of the whole, and "God-revealed" principles that cannot be altered.[115]

Besides focusing on the changing church structure, we want to continue our discussion about the major reasons for church growth at this time. In his classic book on the Roman Empire, Gibbon[116] spends a great deal of time detailing the causes of the church's rapid growth during the 1st to the 3rd century. His observations are reasonable and persuasive.

Christianity's epic struggle to survive in a hostile environment reminds one of the David and Goliath story found in the bible. By 300 A.D. a significant portion of the Roman empire was Christian, even though there were periods of great persecution and hardship. According to Roberts, by "the year 300 Christians may have made up only about a tenth of the population of the empire."[117] In contrast Ehrman thinks Christians comprised only about 7 percent of the empire at that time. For most observers this was evidence of great progress since the total population of the empire was about 60 million.[118] Christians moved from a modest group of about 1,000 members in 40 A.D. to over a million in two hundred years. In fact many estimate that there were about 4 to 6 million Christians as the Council of Nicaea assembled in 325 A.D. Sociologist Rodney Stark[119] has developed a growth model of early Christianity that shows how quickly the early Christian church grew in the first three centuries. Here is a summary of his findings:

1) Stark argues that there were about 1,000 Christians by the year 40 A.D. We read in Acts that 120 followers of Jesus met in an upper room after Jesus' death (Acts 1:15). In another place we find a statement that there were 5,000 believers in Palestine ca. 36 A.D. (Acts 4:4). The first number is quite low and may have been a group of Jesus' closest followers. The latter number is thought to be an exaggeration which many feel is a characteristic of Luke, the author of Acts. In general it

is fair to say that the numbers in the Jesus movement were small at first. Origen (185-254 A.D.), the only real genius in the early church after Paul, attests to this when he states that "only a very few" had joined the Christian movement.[120] That comment, of course, must be understood relative to the whole population of the Roman empire at the time: about 50 million.

2) Each decade, Stark reasons, this new religion grew by about 40 percent. This is not implausible, and he uses the growth of U.S. Mormonism in the last 100 years as an example: a growth rate of about 40 percent per decade. By the end of the first century, Stark maintains, there were about 8,000 Christians. Table 4 below shows the 1st century numbers according to the Stark model of growth.

Table 4. Growth of Christianity: 40 to 100 A.D.

Year	Number	Increase
40	1000	-
50	1400	400
60	1960	560
70	2744	784
80	3842	1098
90	5379	1537
100	7531	2152

3) The number of Christians by 300 A.D. If one continues the calculations above, he will arrive at a reasonable estimate of the church's size by the beginning of the 4th century, even before Constantine gave Christianity special favors. That figure, according to Stark, would be 6,299,832 or about 10 % of the Roman empire.[121] The following graph illustrates a more conservative estimate (5% of the Roman Empire); this is still an amazing growth curve for the rise of this new religion called Christianity.

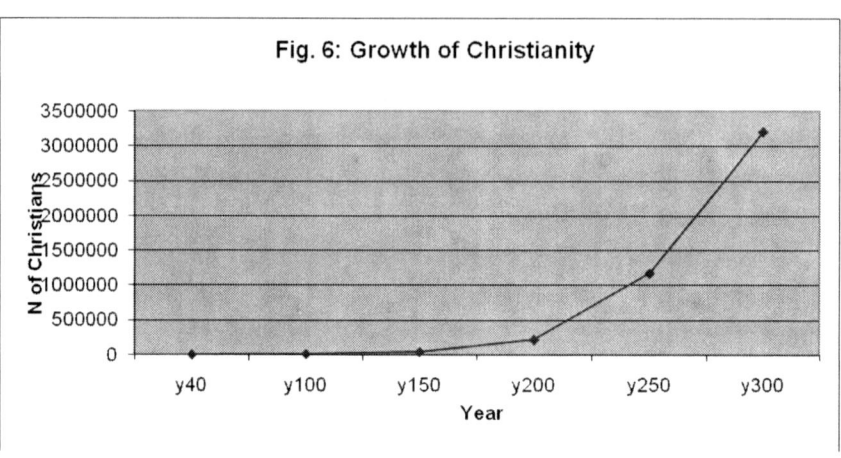

Fig. 6: Growth of Christianity

Of course one must consider four factors related to church growth: new births and converts, minus deaths and those who left the church for whatever reason. How much did the church grow between years 40 and 60 A.D.? Hypothetically, with 400 births plus 800 conversions minus 100 deaths and 140 leaving the church, we have a membership of 1960 [1000 + 400 + 800 - (100 +140)]. This was the number of believers 30 years after the death of Jesus.

Using an alternate approach allows us to obtain a number many accept as plausible and hence partially explain the growth of Christianity 250 years after the resurrection of Christ. We know from numerous sources that there were about 60 million people in the Roman empire in 300 A.D. and many scholars state that about 7 to 10 percent of those were Christian. Many of these estimates were made long before Stark made his calculations and the probability model for Christianity's growth. This second approach would give us roughly 3 to 6 million Christians ca. 300 A.D.; even if we take the more conservative view, i.e., 3 million, we can see that this new religion gained a tremendous following and certainly made an impact on society. Thus, through the work of modern demographers we have been able to determine approximately how many Christians there were at the beginning of the 4th century. We also have some idea of what the growth rate might have been: about 40% per decade. Little wonder that Constantine chose this rapidly growing religion to solidify his power base in the Roman empire. They were an emerging force in the realm. Through the 313 Edict of Milan, Constantine declared general freedom of worship and mentioned Christians by name as the favored religion. Several decades later, Christianity became the official state religion under Emperor Theodosius I (347-395 A.D.) Such a move could only increase Christianity's numbers.

At first the followers of Christ simply wanted to be tolerated and left alone. There were numerous God-fearing people in the empire, and many writers assert that these people were prepared to receive the Christian message if only asked; some of these God-fearing people responded to the preaching of the apostles. Growth in the early church came about because young families socialized their children to become members of the new religion and, second, there were numerous converts to the faith: some Jews, some Gentiles. Some pagans had spiritual aspirations as well. The majority were polytheists (believed in many gods), and not monotheists, like the Israelites and the early Jewish Christians. Thus, the Gospel found root in the Jewish and non-Jewish community—two groups with very different backgrounds. The Christian community saw themselves as the New Israel (a New Covenant was proclaimed by Jesus in the Gospel) and so this teaching made it easy at first to appeal to Jews throughout the empire. The message of Jesus was the fulfillment of Old Testament prophecies. With the fall of Jerusalem in 70 A.D. we find many Christians migrating to cities such as Antioch—the 3rd largest city in the empire. By 305 A.D. this city in the eastern part of the Roman empire had a population of about 500,000; fully half its population were said to be Christians. Growth in church membership was remarkable and needed new organizational strategies and skills to deal with such growth. With the expansion of the church, we see a move to the western part of the empire, and Paul's missionary journeys helped to prepare the way for this development; the Gospel was preached in what is now Turkey as well as the city of Rome. Paul had plans to travel to Spain and preach the Gospel, but apparently that trip never materialized. A letter written by Trajan notes in 112 A.D. that there had been a rapid growth of Christianity. This concerned Roman officials such as Pliny the Younger who worried that pagan shrines might be ignored and maybe even deserted. By the year 250 A.D. according to the modern scholar Adolf Harnack, there were no less than 80,000 Christians living in Rome.[122] Some say the number of Christians could have been as low as 50,000. With the total population of Rome about 700,000 at the time, we see that Christians made up about 7% of the population.[123] It should be noted that we still find the same observation about the Christians and social class in the mid third century: the Christians were drawn primarily from the lower classes. This is the conclusion of scholars who note that early Christians spoke Greek (koinē), the common language of the time,[124] whereas the true Roman upper classes spoke Latin. Cornelius, Bishop of Rome (251-253A.D.), gives us some valuable information about his church in a letter dated 251 A.D.[125] The church in Rome had 46 priests, 14 deacons and subdeacons, an additional staff of 94, plus a total of 1,500 beggars and widows who depended on gifts from the church of Rome to survive. Cornelius gives no data on total church membership in Rome at that time, but in order to support so many employees and various charitable works, a large number of active church members was required to support such ministries. A total of 50,000 to 100,000 church members in the city of Rome (total pop. about 900,000) seems reasonable with roughly 1 priest per 1,000 Christians. Certainly the church took root in the imperial city, Rome, but it was not the mother church of Christianity from the beginning. The church in Rome took on, during later years, some of the wealth of the city, and this factor helped Rome assume a major leadership role in the Christian community. The church in Rome was said to be "first in charity"; it gave to others in need.

Certainly the church expanded beyond Rome. We find that there is evidence of the Christian church in Gaul (France) by 150 A.D., specifically in the city of Lyons. Bishop Irenaeus (d. 202) wrote letters from this part of the empire. Moreover, the church grew in Britain and Spain, especially in the area of North Africa (present day Algeria). A document from Carthage notes that every town had its own bishop and that Latin was spoken there—a sign of some upper class movement by the Christian community, although Rome's leaders considered this area somewhat backward. Some writers have stated that by 300 A.D.(before the rule of Constantine) no area in the Roman empire was without a preacher of the Gospel. Most say that the rural areas were less evangelized, but that was to be expected due to lack of interior roads and other travel problems. Later we will see how the Christian church was made the religion of the empire—a fact that helped solidify, for a time, the social structure of the Roman empire.

Of course, the church had its detractors. An outspoken critic of the church named Celsus stated that Christians were a worthless group and that its membership was comprised of the lower classes, slaves, women, and the poor who willingly joined the Catholic church.[126] Over the years Christians gradually moved up the social ladder and became a significant part of the dominant social structure. Nonetheless, we see that this early lower class experience made Christianity mindful of the poor—the Gospel is preached so that its message is tilted toward service to the poor. Christians could not forget their original social status nor the preaching of Jesus regarding concern for the poor.

To answer detractors like the philosopher, Celsus (circa 150 A.D.), and others, the church moved into a somewhat defensive mode; it developed what is called the genre of Christian apologetics. During the period from 120 to 210 Christianity needed a movement that would defend the faith from external attacks. Names such as Justin, Athanagoras, Tertullian have been associated with this period of church history. This group, and others, felt the church was on trial; it had to prove to critics that its doctrines were valid and deserved the public's respect. The writings at the time may have been addressed to the emperor or enemies of the church, but the real audience was the Christian community itself. Apologists wanted to train the ordinary church member so she could defend the faith against detractors. Justin Martyr provided leadership in this area and his book ***First Apology*** exemplifies the tone of this literary genre. He is one of many "Church Fathers" who emerged to lead the Christian community through rough times. He defended the teachings regarding Jesus' resurrection; after all, myths about Roman gods included accounts of their death and rising, he said. Egyptian writings about the god Osiris speak of his death and later rebirth.[127] Moreover, Justin took issue with slanderers who would say that Christian prayer services were nothing more than sex orgies and cannibalistic rituals. He argued that these charges were simply made out of ignorance and jealousy. Justin founded a Christian school in Rome and records for us the nature of Christian worship services at the time (130 to 160 A.D.). The lower class Christians had to use rented apartments above Roman bath complexes to meet and pray. L. Michael White states this is "indicative of Christian practice at Rome in the mid-second century before there were formal church buildings."[128]

Tertullian (b. 150), one of the early church fathers (Patristics), wrote numerous books on the fundamentals of Christianity. We find that 31 of his books written in Latin have survived. He was the first to use the term "Trinity" in his discourse on the nature of God; later on, the Council of Nicaea in 325 A.D. elaborated on the teaching of three persons in one God. He also wrote a tract on the persecution of Christians and posited that such policies were irrational; Catholic Christians were doing no harm to the empire.

What were the precise causes that led to the spread of Christianity? The followers of Jesus attributed such growth to the workings of the Holy Spirit. But writers such as Gibbon[129] have outlined some of the human factors that helped advance the cause of Christianity. One was the burning desire and conviction that Christians displayed regarding their religion. They demonstrated zeal for the faith. They were tenacious in their Christian beliefs. For them Christianity was the fulfillment of their life. They were given the good news and were transformed and inspired to live a moral life patterned after the teachings of Jesus. They wanted to spread this message to their families, friends, and all peoples. Their basic message was that men and women have been redeemed. There was a promise of immortality: life after death. In addition, the new religion grew, in part, because it met basic human needs. It was not a branch or offshoot of Stoicism, which taught suppression of carnal desires while letting the will turn man's action into virtue. They saw all grace (the source of Christian virtue) as the active love of God who worked miraculous deeds among his people. God made their lives meaningful. Tertullian offers us another reason for the growth of this new religion. It was their extraordinary virtue. He said pagans observed: "See how they [Christians] love one another."[130] This was the kind of group outsiders wanted to join. Their charity impressed people in the empire. Christians cared for the poor, widows and orphans. Christians visited those in prison. In short, they were active members in their church community. Lastly, it is fitting that Christians honor their dead. Such practices reflect a belief that all men and women are sacred; hence they must be given an honorable burial. St. Paul's preaching did not fall on deaf ears: the body is a "temple of the Holy Spirit" (1 Cor. 6:19). In the first century Christians did not have their own cemeteries and many resorted to using common burial plots where pagans too were buried. In the second century Christians began burying loved ones in underground catacombs and so today we have tours of these ancient burial sites in Rome which reveal early church practices. My visit to the catacombs in 2007 showed me the great care early Christians took in remembering their dead. There are some 15 kilometers of underground tunnels in Rome, initially excavated in the 2nd century, that attest to their concern for burying the dead. By 150 A.D. some Christian churches had their own burial grounds and historians claim that the oldest Christian cemetery was along the Appian way.

Early church writings tell us that the lives of Christian martyrs must not be forgotten; they had offered the Christian community a witness to the faith. Thus, many shrines were erected to honor the memories of Christian Martyrs. Many people were converted after having experienced such tragedies. Women who suffered because of the death of their husbands were known to the community. Children were orphaned and people had compassion for them. Some pagans converted when they witnessed the brutal but heroic deaths of Christians. These courageous deeds helped spread the faith. We have, therefore, the paradox: the death of Christians led to expansion of Christianity. It is the Christian explanation of this modern saying: addition by subtraction. "The blood of martyrs is the seed of Christians" (Tertullian).

Summary and conclusion (chapters 2-3):

Principles 1-5 see above, end of chapter 1.

6. The Pauline churches drew upon the talents and gifts of all its people, both male and female, to build a charismatic Christian community.
7. The blood of martyrs inspired others to join the church. Many died for their faith as did modern heroes such as Fr. Maximilian Kolbe, the saint of Auschwitz.
8. Paul was by far the greatest apostle in terms of missionary work and zeal for establishing new churches. He helped to bring tremendous growth to Christianity. His epistles play a seminal role in the formation of the NT canon and make up the bulk of the Christian scriptures after the four Gospels.
9. The early church was multicultural, drawing converts from numerous religious, racial, and ethnic groups; many languages and regions of the Roman empire were represented. By 300 A.D. there were at least 3 million Christians in the empire.
10. The social construction of reality for the Christian meant a

break with the past: rejection of forced circumcision and the Jewish dietary laws. Such actions caused great conflict and turmoil. Leaders of the Jesus movement changed the very laws that Jesus and his parents obeyed! This social adjustment was not called the "dictatorship of relativism," but rather the apostolic innovations needed to deal with the diverse cultural needs of new converts.

11. By the end of the Apostolic era the Church of Rome was not yet the chief church for the Christian people. They did not see Rome as the center of Catholicism.
12. Whenever possible Paul tried to find ways to help people live their faith despite family and church conflict. He did not want to lay heavy burdens on the Jesus movement if these norms were not the will of God as revealed by Christ(Messiah).
13. Christianity was clearly a group religion and demanded community involvement when deciding important matters.
14. The focus was on church growth, how to expand the church and spread the good news. There was a clear move away from 'end of the world' mentality. They began to see that Christians must build the kingdom of God here on earth.
15. Women had been asked to take on leadership roles in the church, but after about 70 A.D. they were more or less relieved of their duties, despite the example of Jesus and Paul who championed women leaders. Those who wish to improve the role of women in Christianity today must point to the practices of the early church.
16. Growth of the church was aided by a tenacious religious spirit which refused to relinquish the faith. Members shared the faith with others. By 150 the Gospel was being preached in all parts of the Roman empire.
17. House-churches were the norm at least through 120 A.D.
18. Converts came from diverse families: Jews, pagans, gentiles; later the church was comprised mostly of gentiles.
19. After 110 A.D. we see growth of the church as a bureaucracy with men taking almost all leadership roles.
20. Christians were still being drawn from the lower classes in 150 A.D.
21. Justin Martyr was the most prominent apologist of his time and taught others how to defend the Christian way of life.

CHAPTER FOUR:

THE BLOOD OF MARTYRS

> "Allow me to be eaten by the beasts—that is how I can reach God; I am God's wheat and I am ground by the teeth of wild beasts that I may be found pure bread of Christ.... Pray to Christ for me, that by these means I may become a sacrifice."
>
> —*Ignatius of Antioch to the Romans.*

Christians were ready to die for their religious convictions and in 36 A.D. Stephen continued the remarkable story of this band of believers by becoming its first martyr, only a few years after the death of Christ. James, the son of Zebedee, was executed on trumped up charges around 44 A.D. After thirty years of church growth, Peter and Paul along with many other Christians died in Rome during the persecution by Nero. Polycarp, the student of John the Apostle, became a casualty at age 80 during one of the many persecutions in the middle of the 2nd century. Some followers of Jesus were burned at the stake, Peter was crucified, others were beheaded and still others were thrown to the lions and other wild beasts. In general, though, historians tell us that the persecution of the Christians was half-hearted before 200 A.D. This may be true, but many followers of Christ died, nonetheless, and left numerous families without a husband or father or mother. They were church heroes and heroines; their names were added to a new Christian book called the **Martyrology.** Shrines honoring the martyrs were erected throughout the empire and visitors paid homage to their fallen brothers and sisters. At this point in history (33-400 A.D.) there was no evidence of any devotion to the Blessed Virgin Mary and no shrines were built in her honor. In 431, however, the Council of Ephesus proclaimed the divine motherhood of Mary and conducted the official council meetings at the church built there in her honor. Marian devotions and practices would emerge later in the middle ages. But why were there so many martyr shrines? Why were Christians persecuted so much?

The reasons Roman officials gave for killing many Christians were numerous. First and foremost, Christians would not pay homage to the emperor by offering sacrifice to him. The Jews likewise declined the practice of emperor worship because of their long standing belief in the one, true, God: Yahweh. Their reluctance to honor Caesar was often overlooked by the empire. James Carroll rightly points out that they were given a legal exception from emperor worship:[131]

"Jews and Christians were equally determined to refrain from participation in the cult rituals of Rome's pagan civic religion. But going back to the first century B.C.E., Jews had been exempted from the requirements to offer sacrifices to and utter blessings in the name of pagan gods. When the Church grew apart from the synagogue, Christians lost that exemption...."

Christianity was a new phenomenon and not an ancient religion like Judaism. They were viewed by Roman authorities as something quite novel —a superstition rather than a religion. That did not deter the early Christians who sought to convert all who would listen to the good news: Jews, Greeks, Romans, pagans, etc. But the zealous heirs of the apostles' faith appeared dangerous to the power structure of the Roman empire. The gods of the Romans were many: the god of the Sun, rain, harvest, birth, war; most of all they held emperor worship in high esteem. Christians would not go along with such blatant acts of idolatry and thus many martyrs were created through this holy dissent.

After the persecution under Nero, we find Pliny the Younger (d. 112 C.E.) starting his own campaign against Christians in the province of Bithynia (modern day Turkey). He writes (*Letters,* 10.96ff) to the Emperor Trajan:

Meanwhile, in the case of those who were denounced to me as Christians, I have observed the following procedure: I interrogated these as to whether they were Christians; those who confessed I interrogated a second and a third time, threatening them with punishment; those who persisted I ordered executed.

For Pliny and his cohorts, just to be labeled a Christian was worthy of death. Trajan in reply to Pliny's letter said, in effect, "good job." But he offered this advice:

You observed proper procedure, my dear Pliny, in sifting the cases of those who had been denounced to you as Christians....But anonymously posted accusations ought to have no place in any prosecution. For this is both a dangerous kind of precedent and out of keeping with the spirit of our age.

Such a callous exchange was typical of Roman officials. Killing innocent Christians became a matter of course. It took about 200 years to move from this brutal practice of Roman law, to the Edict of Toleration in 313: religious freedom was accorded to all. In the meantime brutal attacks continued against the members of this new religion. Emperor Marcus Aurelius followed this line of reasoning and executed Justin Martyr and others in Rome ca. 165 A.D.

One of the most cherished stories of martyrdom discussed by Ehrman[132] and others, is the execution of St. Perpetua in 202 C.E. This third instance of persecution occurred in North Africa during the reign of Septimus Severus; he published his first anti-Christian decree[133] in 202 and soon after he ordered renewed attacks on Christians who were living around the North African city of Carthage. Clement of Alexandria wrote that at this time "many martyrs are daily burned, confined, or beheaded, before our eyes."[134] Still nursing her young son, Perpetua was jailed for treason with several other Christians. The Romans would kill anyone: the old man Polycarp at age 80 and a poor woman who had just given birth. Perpetua refused to offer sacrifice to the Roman gods. It became clear that this group of Christians was going to be executed for their beliefs and refusal to perform emperor worship. According to her own prison diary, which has survived, Perpetua's father came to the jail and begged his daughter to go along with the Roman pagan ritual.[135] "Daughter, pity my white hairs. Pity your father...." The pleadings of her pagan father went unanswered and Perpetua refused to renounce her faith in the Christian Savior by offering sacrifice to the Roman emperor. She was eventually executed by the sword of a reluctant gladiator.

The fourth tragic episode of Christian martyrdom occurred under the emperor Decius. This was the first universal and organized attack on Christian believers that we know of. In 250 A.D. he issued an edict that all members of the Roman empire must offer sacrifice to the emperor in the presence of a Roman official. The act of homage earned the Roman citizens a certificate (libellus) which proved that the bearer had performed his yearly religious duty. This policy proved to be quite unpopular and ceased in 251. Many Romans admired the brave Christian martyrs and some converted to the new religion because of their heroic example. Due to the persecutions of Decius, an internal problem in the church arose because a good number of Christians gave in to the Roman threats and subsequently offered sacrifice to the emperor to save their own lives. They were called "lapsed" Christians by a significant number of bishops and when they tried to return to the church, some clergy refused their pleas for mercy. Bishops like Cyprian argued initially that such apostasy could not be forgiven by the church and thus all lapsed members had to be excluded from the community. Other church leaders such as Cornelius (later elected bishop of Rome in 251) were more lenient and allowed lapsed Christians back into the fold after a period of sincere penance. This group led by Cornelius asserted that the church was not just for saints but for sinners as well. Augustine in the 5th century likewise treated alienated Catholics with compassion. This is another example in the story of Christianity wherein the moderating forces within the church were able to carry the day and reject radical hardliners who wanted to punish weak people whose only crime was the inability to give their lives for church beliefs. The failures of the first apostles were not forgotten.

Lastly, we want to study the well-known policies of Diocletian and how they led to the slaughter of many Christians. A firm believer in the Roman gods, Diocletian was told that his oracles could not see favorable omens for the empire's future. This negative state of affairs was blamed, of course, on the Christians. So, in 303, he issued an edict against Christians: he closed churches, burned their scriptures and destroyed their sacred vessels; no one was allowed to assemble for

Christian religious services. Moreover, all Christian civil servants and soldiers had to offer sacrifice to the gods. In 304 he ordered all citizens to offer sacrifice under pain of death. The harassment of Christians lasted for almost 10 years with about 3,000 martyrs dying for their faith in the first part of the 4th century.[136] Given the fact that there were 3 to 6 million Christians in the empire at the time (see R. Stark, chapter 3 above), these losses were modest, according to Meeks and others.[137] Nonetheless, people died unjustly, and that was the real crime. With the Edict of Milan, 313 A.D., Constantine and Licinius agreed to the principle of religious toleration and freedom. They made a significant effort to restore all confiscated property to Christians, both private homes and the property of local churches.

The story of Christianity during this period was told by brave martyrs who died for their faith. This time of their epic struggle for survival demanded that enemies **external** to the church be confronted bravely, and some died in the process. The next centuries saw the need to deal with internal threats: heretics from within the church. Thus, the story of early Christianity is one of great conflict.

It did not help that Christians set themselves apart from social and political life. They considered themselves different and morally superior to the Romans. The followers of Jesus were holy and courageous; they were dedicated to a higher Being. Those with ties to the empire considered this behavior suspicious, and furthermore, the Christians condemned the pagans' way of life. St. Peter called the Roman social and political milieu "a perverse generation." In addition, the Christian ethic and way of life made them different. Their very lives were a condemnation of the pagan culture. Because Christians condemned the pagan way of life and rejected the Roman gods, the followers of Christ were treated with scorn. They would not attend social and political events because these occasions usually began with prayer and sacrifice to the pagan gods. Their refusal to be a part of the social life of Rome was considered rude. They saw themselves as different, as followers of a unique way of life. They would not go to events where gladiatorial combat was part of the program. These strong moral stands made it difficult for Christians to obtain work, and the famous theologian Tertullian said he did not want Christians to be teachers in Roman schools. There they would have to tell stories about the powers of pagan gods and this would violate the Christian ethic. Their faith was a pure religion without compromise—at least in the first decades of Christianity. To the Romans and others as well, Christianity was seen as a revolutionary way of life. Before 170 A.D. Cadoux asserts that "there is no trace of the existence of any Christian soldiers…."[138] Some soldiers left the Roman army upon their conversion to Christianity during the 2nd century. Between 200 and 400 A.D., however, the just war theory, which permitted military service for Christians, emerged in religious thought and writing. As a religion favored by Constantine and his family, Christians came to the conclusion that they were obligated to defend the empire and its people against the barbarians. They had to adjust to the realities of Roman society and view the words of Justin Martyr as an idealized way of life:

"And we, who were formerly slayers of one another, not only do not make war upon our enemies, but, for the sake of neither lying nor deceiving those who examine us, gladly die confessing Christ."[139]

For a time, Christians made a unique contribution to Roman society according to church documents; they were a people who espoused non-violence. This tradition is preserved today in the Mennonite religious teaching since most members are pacifists and oppose violence and war. Very few Christian denominations today espouse such a radical nonviolent lifestyle which is modeled after this early Christian tradition. Some individuals or groups practice nonviolence in their particular denominations. As far as slavery was concerned, Christians were similar to their Roman counterparts; they had slaves but as Eusebius tells us, Christians were kind to their slaves whereas the Romans abused them and even killed their slaves when they were no longer useful.[140] In a remarkable turn of events, Callistus I, elected bishop of Rome in 217, had grown up as a slave and then achieved a high position in the church. Pius I who also was bishop of Rome (d. 155) may have been a former slave as well.

The unique Christian ethic was also demonstrated in the way children were treated. Romans and other pagans would take weak and sick children into the woods and leave them to die, but because of the Christian belief that each person is sacred and a "temple of the Holy Spirit" (1 Cor 6:19), this practice of child euthanasia was condemned by the early church. All these ethical differences bolstered the Christian claim to moral superiority but unfortunately made them a despised group in the empire.

Certain emperors, particularly Nero, used Christians as scapegoats for his well known devious behavior. He had Christian men and women executed for starting the fires that burned Rome. Years later historians punctured this myth by pointing out that Nero started the fires himself so he could rebuild sections of Rome to his own liking. He drove his chariot around the burning city observing the execution of men and women who had nothing to do with these fires. Despite these tragedies we find numerous scholars stating that the killing of Christians was not a typical event in the 1st and 2nd century. Nevertheless, they were singled out from time to time on spurious charges. Although a minority in a predominantly pagan world, they were generally tolerated by Roman authorities.

The followers of Christ were often singled out for harsh treatment because of false stories and lies. Slander was one of the minor sins of the Romans, given their propensity for high crimes and murder. They spread rumors about Christian celebrations and feasts, claiming that these events were sexual orgies. The problem was that Christians were secretive about their liturgies which were not open to the public. Barring nonbelievers from their sacred rites bred a sense of suspicion and distrust in the secular society. One of the Christian gatherings was named the Agape feast, and at a certain point in the service there was a time for a "holy kiss of peace." Romans thought this was some sort of love orgy, and they made derogatory comments about Christian morals because of it. There is some truth to the report that these services, at times, may have gotten out of hand; the early church almost abandoned this kiss of peace at one point. Unfamiliar with Christian theology and traditions, the pagans heard that church members observed the last supper of Jesus and that they ate the body and blood of Christ. Thus believers were accused of cannibalism. Pagans said they could not allow such transgressions of the Roman law. Even Pliny the Younger, a Roman magistrate, thought that simply being labeled a Christian was enough to be punished. No human rights advocate, he had many killed during his tenure in Bithynia, 111-112 A.D.(modern day Turkey).[141]

Ironically, the charge of atheism was leveled against Christians from time to time. Because the followers of Jesus insulted the gods of the state by refusing to worship them, they were seen as nonbelievers. Romans claimed that natural disasters etc. would erupt, if people did not worship the gods. Hence the Christians were considered dangerous.

They did not perform their civic duty and this may have angered the gods. At the time the saying was, "If the Tiber floods, throw the Christians to the lions." That made a lot of sense to the Romans but not to the Christian church.

Finally, it is clear that above all else, the failure to compromise about emperor worship caused Christians the most problems in the second and third century. White puts it this way: "It's their refusal to sacrifice before the emperor or even to offer a little incense on behalf of the emperor. Because they won't, they are then treated as if they are treasonous...."[142] The Roman empire was huge—from the Euphrates to the Irish sea—and there had to be some way to unify that diverse group of people and cultures. At first Roman leaders thought that emperor worship would do the trick. To accomplish this quest for Roman solidarity, they tried to disallow the worship of any other deity save the Roman gods. The emperor Decius (249-51) made Caesar worship universal and compulsory. Once a year all citizens of the realm had to proclaim that "Caesar is Lord." It was a test of loyalty. Those who refused were considered traitors. This was obviously a big problem for Christians. During this period when the Christian ethic conflicted with the Roman cultural norms, the followers of Jesus were seen as disloyal and stubborn. They did not compromise, and so the church added many to its list of martyrs.

CHAPTER FIVE:

RELIGIONS IN CONFLICT:

CHRISTIANS AND JEWS

> *Saint Jerome (d. 419 A.D.) denounced Jews as "Judaic serpents of whom Judas was the model."*

The new religion, Christianity, met opposition from the Roman Empire, the pagan majority, and from the ancient belief system of the Jewish people. Almost from the beginning the Jesus movement was on a collision course with the older and more established religion, Judaism. Besides the many years of conflict with the leaders of the Roman empire (Christians would not worship the Roman gods), there was always the continued bickering between Jews and the new sect of believers called "The Way" (Acts 9:2). Life was complex: there was conflict with the state (King Herod Agrippa had James the son of Zebedee killed c. 44 A.D.) and there existed animosity with religious rivals which continued for centuries. Flannery states that Christian anti-Jewish sentiment probably reached its apex with an assault on a synagogue.¹⁴³ Led by the Bishop of Callinicus (Mesopotamia), a Christian mob burned down the local synagogue in 388 A.D. What we call today antisemitism has its roots in the early church.

Causes of Conflict

Scholars give a number of reasons for such religious animosity; most list four major factors that led to confrontations between Jews and Christians.

1. Sacred texts: the Gospels.

One Gospel in particular, Matthew, records numerous disputes between Jesus, a Jew, and the Jewish religious establishment. Brown points out that Matthew's hostile critique of the Jews "is not untypical of the harsh criticism of one Jewish group by another Jewish group in the 1ˢᵗ centuries BC and AD—a criticism that at times crossed the borderline into slander."¹⁴⁴ Jesus' comments regarding his Jewish brethren were clear and succinct (Matt 23: 1-20). He points out, among other things, their proud behavior and love of titles; moreover, he utters seven "woes" against the Scribes and Pharisees. Here is a well-known example: "Woe to you Scribes and Pharisees, hypocrites! Because you are like whitened sepulchers, which outwardly appear to men beautiful, but within are full of dead men's bones and of all uncleanness. So you also outwardly appear just to men, but within you are full of hypocrisy and iniquity" (Matt 23: 27-28). Stinging criticism of the Jewish people was a fairly common occurrence in the Old Testament (Jeremiah 2:1-6). Jesus uses the words of Isaiah to describe his adversaries, the Pharisees and scribes: "This people honors me with their lips but their heart is far from me" (Is. 29:13).¹⁴⁵ Louis Feldman gives his perspective on the confrontations: "Matthew's Gospel is particularly antagonistic to the Jewish establishment. But when Jesus refers to Pharisees as 'hypocrites' (Matthew 23:13) and a 'brood of vipers' (Matthew 23:33), he is berating *fellow Jews*. Jesus undoubtedly regards his violent language as following the tradition of the prophets when they castigated fellow Jews of their day. In other words, it is a *family quarrel*. Jesus looks upon himself as continuing the

Jewish tradition of self-criticism."¹⁴⁶ Presumably, the sacred writer was inspired to use strong language to denounce those who violated the sacred covenant. Jesus followed this tradition in his public ministry, and during the period after his death, these sayings were recalled/read in house-churches throughout the Roman empire before the final form of Matthew took shape about 85 A.D. As the Jesus movement, with the help of Paul, converted more and more Gentiles to the new faith, it was only natural for church members to become hostile to Jews; there were fewer Jewish Christians to tone down the rhetoric. New converts learned quickly. Even though Matthew was simply trying to record in detail the sayings of Jesus, his main point was that the true followers of Christ should not take on the attitudes of the scribes and Pharisees. Jesus said so. He was a devout Jew who was upset with the religious leaders of his time. But tragically, some Christians took these sayings and used them as a battleaxe against all Jews. Some even asserted that Christianity was a balanced religion whereas Judaism was a superficial one. The NT scriptures and how they were interpreted led to great turmoil between Jews and Christians for many years.

2. The killing of Stephen.

Soon after the death of Christ, hostility between two groups of Jews led to the attack and the death of Stephen (Acts 7:54ff). One of the groups, called the Hellenists, were Jews who for the most part spoke Greek. They tended to come from areas where Greco-Roman culture was dominant and some of their leaders even had Greek names. The other group, which could be characterized as traditional Hebrews, were brought up according to strict Jewish standards. The Apostle Paul came from such a background as did Jesus. The twelve apostles were clearly "Hebrew Christians" but their faith in Jesus did not stop them from worshipping in the Temple after the resurrection (Acts 2:46). Conflict between these two groups arose when Stephen, an outspoken Hellenist leader, asserted that the Temple no longer had meaning for him. His speech, recorded in Acts, centered on the importance of the risen Christ and a condemnation of those who refused to believe in Jesus. He accused his audience of murdering the Just One, Jesus. His words infuriated the Hebrew community, so their leaders had Stephen stoned to death. Paul stood by and consented to the death of this bold Christian preacher(Acts 8:1). Ironically, after his conversion, Paul faced similar treatment. While preaching in the synagogue Paul was accused of blasphemy. He writes that "Five times I have received from the Jews forty lashes less one" (2 Cor 11:24). Such harsh treatment toward the leaders of the early church could only add to the animosity that had grown between Christians and Jews. It would not be long before formal action would be taken against this upstart religious movement.

3. The Council of Jamnia.

Convened around 90 A.D., this famous Jewish council met to consolidate Judaism and formally expel heretics from the synagogue, including the followers of Jesus. The conflict between those who believed in Jesus as Messiah and the leaders of the Synagogue (Priests, Scribes, and Pharisees) had reached a boiling point. This group issued a decree against all "Jewish Christians" that they could no longer be allowed in the synagogue. The following words document such action:

> For apostates may there be no hope.
> And the arrogant kingdom uproot speedily in our days.
> May the Christians and the heretics perish in an instant.
> "May they be blotted out of the book of the living,
> and may they not be written with the righteous" (Ps 69:29).
> Blessed art thou, O Lord, who humblest the arrogant.
>   …'Birkat ha-Minim' (Benediction against Heresies)

The Gospel of John (16:2) is apparently referring to this event when John says the followers of Jesus were "put out of the synagogue."[147] The new church was denounced as heretical. Coffman states what such exclusion meant at the time: "This was a penalty dreaded by every Hebrew, meaning loss of social acceptability, employment, and all access to the religious life of the community. Excommunicated persons were held to be worse than pagans and were the object of total rejection and hatred."[148] This pain and embarrassment gave Christians good reason to plan for revenge. By the late first century the line between Jews who did not believe in Jesus as Messiah and faithful Christians was drawn in the sand. The followers of Moses let it be known that they had denounced the heretics and considered the case closed. This was a bitter pill to swallow for many in the Jesus movement who had Jewish roots, yet for the Gentile converts, this was probably a non-issue.

4. Jews accused of murder.

It was not surprising that years later Christians decided to retaliate against those who ordered them out of the synagogue and denounced them as heretics. In the second century Justin Martyr (d. 165) was one of the first bishops in the church to label the Jews as "Christ killers"—they were guilty of murdering "the just one" he wrote. In his famous work **Dialogue with Trypho** (written ca. 135 A.D.) Justin asserted that the Jews had murdered Christ and this sin could never be forgiven. Other comments in this famous dialogue show a famous Father of the Church very antagonistic toward the Jewish people. 1) He states that the Jews are no longer God's chosen people, but rather Christian believers are now the chosen people of God. 2) He states that circumcision does not bring the Jews salvation and righteousness, but rather is used by God to single them out for punishment. "The purpose of this [circumcision] was that you and only you might suffer the afflictions that are now justly yours."[149] Readers of this document were not unfamiliar with the fall of Jerusalem in 70A.D. and the second rebellion and defeat of the Jews in 135 where the Romans crushed the revolt of Simon Bar Kochba. With about 580,000 Jews killed in the war, some Christians saw in this the wrath of God; He had withdrawn his favor from Israel, according to Justin. 3) He claims the Hebrew scriptures as his own for Christians; that is, the OT foretold the coming of Christ and this revelation was ignored by Jews. In Genesis man and woman are made in the image and likeness of God who would later be revealed in Jesus. Moreover, the Paschal Lamb sacrificed at Passover is a symbol of Christ: he would be the paschal lamb sacrificed for the sins of all nations. These assertions naturally heightened antagonisms with Jews. Justin, a church Father, is very harsh with the Jews for rejecting Jesus: "But you Jews are ruthless, stupid and blind, and lame people, children in whom there is no faith."[150] These and other statements helped to fan the flames of antisemitism. Out of love of Jesus, Christians hated the Jews. They had forgotten that Jesus forgave his enemies and so did Stephen when he was dying.

The Epistle of Barnabas (apocrypha) gives us another opportunity to gauge the animosity between Christians and Jews. Written ca. 135 A.D. this letter was highly esteemed by many church leaders and was read at some liturgies throughout the empire. The document is attributed to the companion of Paul but most scholars say the authorship is anonymous. He tells his readers that the Jews had a covenant with God but because of their sins of idolatry, they proved to be unworthy. Moses found that the Israelites had made a golden calf and worshipped it while he was receiving the ten commandments on Mount Sinai. Thus, the sacred covenant was broken and was never reinstated, according to Barnabas. The Jews proved to be unworthy and so Yahweh offered a New Covenant to the followers of Jesus. This is rightly called the supercessionist doctrine by James Carroll and others; the Christians had replaced the Jews as God's chosen people.[151] Barnabas claims the Jews failed to understand God's message in many ways. For example, the dietary law banning pork was not to be taken literally. God did not want his chosen people to associate with people who acted like swine, i.e., they squeal when not fed and are quiet when eating or are full. People are like swine when they forget God as they fill their bellies with food and think everything is going right. They only call upon God when they need something, e.g. food, water, etc. The message is clear: do not associate with people like that. Pork chops and a ham sandwich are fine. Christianity is superior to Judaism, according to Barnabas, because the Jews broke the OT covenant but Christians were faithful to God through the new covenant secured by Jesus. In his letter Barnabas calls Jews a wretched people because they put so much stress on buildings (Temple) and not on faith in God. But these attacks against Jews are mild compared to remarks made by Bishop Melito of Sardis who in the latter part of the 2nd century gave an inflammatory sermon against the Jews on the feast of Easter. The bishop and his flock lived in Asia minor but this small town in the Roman Empire became famous because it was here that the Jews were charged with the crime of deicide; they had killed God. We have now the complete sermon wherein Melito says that "God has been murdered" by the sons of Israel, the Jews.[152] It is Ehrman's view[153] that this is really the first time a Christian ever charged the Jews not simply with the death of Jesus, but with deicide—the murder of God. Later on, Origen (d. 254) and St. John Chrysostom (d. 407) repeated the charge. The latter was perhaps the most tactless "saint" in the history of Christianity. Chrysostom wrote eight sermons denouncing Jews as "pigs", and described the synagogue as a place worse than a brothel. As if this was not enough, he stated that he hated the synagogue and hated Jews. After a thousand plus years we find the Nazis using Chrysostom's words to justify their persecution of the Jews during

World War II. By saying that there was no possible pardon for such an act (deicide), these early fathers of the church laid the ground work for a Christology reeking with antisemitism. Augustine's statement that "Jews may survive but they cannot thrive"[154] helped push the Christian church into a huge black hole of antisemitism. The charge of deicide was the theological turning point in Christian-Jewish antagonism. Much later, at the Second Vatican council (1962-1965), the Catholic church rejected the very concept of deicide as well as the doctrine of supercessionism. The Jews and Christians are God's people according to Vatican II documents. Many Protestant churches have followed suit.[155]

"Since the spiritual patrimony common to Christians and Jews is thus so great, this sacred synod wants to foster and recommend that mutual understanding and respect which is the fruit, above all, of biblical and theological studies as well as of fraternal dialogues."[156]

And again we read in this council document:

Although the Church is the new people of God, the Jews should not be presented as rejected or accursed by God, as if this followed from the Holy Scriptures. All should see to it, then, that in catechetical work or in the preaching of the word of God they do not teach anything that does not conform to the truth of the Gospel and the spirit of Christ.

But a thousand plus years of hatred and killing made it difficult to heal old wounds. Prayers said in all Catholic churches on Good Friday during the 1950s referring to the "perfidious Jews" were dropped through the orders of Pope John XXIII (1959-1963) who convened Vatican II.[157] Nevertheless, the damage had been done.

Conclusion

It is clear that during the first centuries of Christianity, this period of virulent hatred of Jews saw no head of the Church of Rome ever condemn such words and practices (Clement I did speak out on abuses in the church of Corinth). Thus, no leadership from that part of Christianity could be counted on to preach the Gospel of love for all people as Jesus had taught. Jesus had forgiven his enemies, but his followers could not bring themselves to follow the master's superior virtue. Their love of Jesus led them to hate those who were judged responsible for his death. During the first 300 years of Christianity, the bishop of Rome had a very modest social agenda. Speaking out against hatred of Jews was not one of them.

Summary and Conclusion (Chapter 4 and 5)
22. Christian martyrs multiplied because they refused to participate in emperor worship; there were no exemptions like those given to Jewish believers.
23. Many Christians felt they maintained higher moral standards than their pagan neighbors. Secretive liturgies led to grave misunderstandings about Christian worship services.
24. Antisemitism began early in the Christian church and the term 'deicide' helped to galvanize church members to hate the Jewish people. Augustine and the bishop of Rome were no help in stemming the tide of hatred toward Jews.

CHAPTER SIX:

THE BISHOP OF ROME

And so I say to you, you are Peter, and upon this rock I will build my church, and the gates of the netherworld shall not prevail against it.

I will give you the keys to the kingdom of heaven. Whatever you bind on earth shall be bound in heaven; and whatever you loose on earth shall be loosed in heaven." (Matt 16:18-19)

The story of early Christianity is about preachers, prophets, martyrs, apologists, and evangelists. There is one feature of the Jesus movement, however, that has taken center stage over the years: it is the rise of papal power and control over all church affairs. No other element of Christianity has caused more conflict and divisiveness for the people of God. Ironically, the office of the papacy was to provide church unity, according to Cardinal Avery Dulles; however, just the opposite has been the outcome for the last ten centuries. The first appearance of some kind of centralized leadership in the new Jewish-Christian sect occurred rather early.

Peter was the spokesperson of the Twelve and a principal figure in the decision made at the Council of Jerusalem, 49 A.D. Eventually this small sect would develop into a church, following the principles laid down in the work of Ernst Troeltsch.[158] But in the beginning the informal structure prevailed. Paul reported his meetings with Peter for 15 days, and then moved on to preach the Gospel to the Gentiles. He was basically on his own. This small group of committed believers voiced its criticism of the Roman culture (Peter: "a perverse generation"), and the corruption they observed in their own Jewish faith. The new religion rejected a great deal of existing norms and values; at the same time Jesus and his followers laid down new principles (Sermon on the Mount). The members of the new sect were rather poor and drew their first members from the lower classes. One joined this marginal community by conversion (call) and not all were interested or could qualify. The community was led by passionate men and women who had little education; most were illiterate. Nevertheless, this was an inclusive group and members shared their gifts with one another; they all participated in the affairs and decisions of the new religion.

But gradually the Jesus movement grew into a church with very different characteristics, which Troeltsch states is typical. The size of the new religious group went from a few thousand to several million by 300 A.D. This kind of growth required changes in structure and coordination if the church was to survive. The church became more tolerant of the so-called "lapsed" Christians and after 170 A.D. permitted church members to be soldiers in the Roman empire. Heretics saw the church develop an orthodox view of reality and all members were asked to adhere to certain key beliefs. Rejecting war and violence was not considered a prime concern. The Jesus movement had long before abandoned the Jewish dietary laws and circumcision. After Constantine and his policies favoring Christianity, the church accumulated great wealth, new churches, and gold vessels; members took part in the governance of the empire. Scholars emerged such as Origen, Tertullian, and Justin who helped articulate the basic principles of Christianity. A distinct area of Christian literature developed including the NT scriptures, works of apologists and important documentation regarding church decision-making (Nicaea, 325). The church took its place as an important part of the Roman Empire.

This drastic change from sect to church was certainly evident in the office of the bishop of Rome, later to be called the papacy. By studying how this office emerged, we can appreciate why this new religion took its place as one of the most important factors in the development of Western civilization.

Peter was head of the Apostles and the undisputed leader of the new religious sect that broke off from its Jewish roots after the death of Christ. He presided over the choice of Judas' successor, and with prodding from Paul opened the church to the Gentiles who were not required to undergo circumcision and observe Jewish dietary laws. Nonetheless, it is doubtful that he was ever in charge of a Christian community in Rome, but probably died there as a martyr during Nero's persecution around 64 A.D. Who was his successor? Those waters are rather murky.

One tradition, grounded in the writings of Tertullian (d. 225) as well as St. Jerome (d. 420), argues that Clement I was Peter's immediate successor. If this is true, then the list of Popes in *Liber Pontificalis* containing the names of Linus and Anacletus as subsequent successors of Peter would be incorrect. A second century document from St. Irenaeus, stating Linus was bishop of Rome has proven to be a forgery.[159] Given these historical realities, we continue our discussion with the importance of Clement, Bishop of Rome, who governed the church some time after the death of Peter.

Clement I (88 – 99 A.D.) demonstrated a strong personality during his years of church service and was highly thought of by many Christian leaders. He was most likely the Clement mentioned as a co-worker in Paul's letter to the Philippians (4:3). It appears that he was head of one of the house-churches in Rome during the late 1st century; he had the task of communicating to various churches.[160] The First Epistle of Clement (usually called 1 Clement) was an important church document (circa 96 A.D.) and at times communities read this letter at Eucharistic services. Some have argued that it is the most important 1st century document outside of the NT; it was included in a few early church canons. The letter was carried by three emissaries from the church in Rome to the church in Corinth which was experiencing considerable discord at the time. The intervention of the Roman church was a case of *fraternal correction* and not an action by a bishop making an authoritative stand regarding the affairs of another church.[161] It would be hard to argue that during the tenure of Clement I that there was a united and coordinated leadership role in the church of Rome. For some, at least, the bishop of Rome operated in a modest way after the death of Peter; the "monarchical episcopate had not yet emerged there, and it is therefore impossible to form any precise conception of his [Clement's] constitutional role."[162]

A younger group of presbyters in Corinth had deposed the elders of the church and taken over church governance. Clement asked that the community reinstate the elders to their former roles. There is no information available to determine if his letter brought about the desired change requested in Corinth. White states that the "decision of the Roman church to dispense such advice and the form in which it was presented are modeled on the prerogatives of the capital, specifically the Senate and the emperor of Rome, to manage the affairs of its provinces and cities."[163] This theme will be evident as we study and observe the behavior of the early church leaders, and specifically the bishop of Rome. McBrien sums up the situation quite well: "When some Catholic theologians and historians today suggest that the hierarchical structures of the Church, including the papacy, owe more to the Roman Empire than to Jesus, they do not exaggerate."[164] There is no solid historical evidence that Clement died a martyr as recorded in Liber Pontificalis (5th century) but traditions like this show how early Christians tried to embellish the saintly resumes of leaders to inspire new converts, among other things. Hero tales got in the way of history.

Anicetus (155-166) was the next important bishop of Rome whom we have chosen to consider, and he ruled for 11 years. During that time he concerned himself with heretics like Marcion who some proto-orthodox believers called the "first son of Satan." These early believers did not mince words and their practice of name-calling was part of the process of making villains out of church enemies. His predecessor, Pius I, had already expelled Marcion from the orthodox community in 144. The most notable event that history records during his time was a visit from Bishop Polycarp to Rome. The aging disciple of St. John pointed out that the churches in Asia celebrated Easter in a special way: the feast took place in the spring, on the 14th day of the Jewish month of Nisan. Why not have the church of Rome do the same, asked Polycarp? Anicetus declined to act on this recommendation and said that the church in Rome celebrated the feast of Easter (Christ's Resurrection) every Sunday. Anicetus wanted also to follow the custom of his predecessor—a familiar theme of church leaders throughout the ages. It was not proper according to some, to act contrary to the actions of the previous Pope. You have heard of the race card. This is the "C" card and it is the conservative card. Maintain and conserve the customs of your predecessor. This was a dangerous pattern since it caused considerable cultural lag in the church's policy structure, which like other societal institutions, was biased toward maintaining traditional values. One thing is clear: around 100 A.D. the church did not celebrate Easter in the West as a separate feast, and certainly not in Rome. A second point is that some authors[165] see in Anicetus' behavior (circa 160 A.D.) a clear sign of the monarchical episcopate, namely, one bishop in charge of a region with various presbyters and deacons under his jurisdiction. They had power to set policy and others obeyed.

With **Soter** (166-174) as head of the church in Rome, we find a break with the past: Easter was celebrated as an annual liturgical event. Some argue that this was the most significant change during Soter's tenure in office. The interesting twist is that the celebration day was to be the Sunday following the day of Passover, the 14th day of the month of Nisan. Such an arrangement would not go unnoticed in the eastern part of the empire which celebrated Easter on the day before the Jewish Passover. Tension between the East and West began early.

Victor I (189-198) became the first African to hold the position of bishop of Rome. Hence leadership of this important see was not restricted to those born in and around Rome. McBrien[166] states that through his guiding hand, synods in Rome advocated the celebration of Easter throughout the entire Christian church. In 190 A.D. Victor ordered that every church observe Easter as do the churches in Rome. The feast would be celebrated, following the lead of Soter, on the Sunday following the Jewish Passover. When the churches in Asia minor refused to change the day of their Easter celebration (14th day of the Jewish month of Nisan)—it could fall on any day of the week—Victor proclaimed that such churches were not in communion with the universal church. He ordered them excommunicated.[167] Such authoritarian tactics did not sit well with Bishop Irenaeus of Lyons; through his intervention the pope lifted the sentence of excommunication and peace was restored. These actions indicate that already in the latter years of the 2nd century, the bishop of Rome claimed privileges and power that were superior to other bishops in the Christian church. But other Christians agreed to disagree. He was the successor of St. Peter, but was not without his limitations and needed fraternal correction.

Victor is known for a number of "firsts" while serving as Bishop of Rome. He was the first to have dealings with the imperial household. The emperor's mistress Marcia, a Christian, secured the release of some Christians condemned to the mines of Sardinia. He was the first bishop of Rome to have masses said in Latin, not Greek, which had been the customary language before Victor's arrival. As the first African born bishop of Rome he brought diversity to the imperial city. He did not suffer a martyr's death as some early writers have claimed.

Urban I achieved the position of bishop of Rome (222-30 A.D.) while Alexander Severus was emperor. This was a period of some tranquility for the early church. The schism of Hippolytus, who tried unsuccessfully to become bishop of Rome, continued to plague the church, but there is no evidence that Urban had any contact with such dissidents. Nothing really noteworthy emerged during his time as bishop.

Stephen I (254-257) had a relatively short reign as bishop of Rome, but important decisions were made by him which solidified the power of the Roman See. During the persecution of Decius (250-251) a certain number of Christians—including priests and bishops—committed apostasy by agreeing to offer sacrifice to the Emperor, and thus their lives had been spared. Cyprian of Carthage and numerous other bishops in North Africa voiced their concern about apostates who wanted to return to the church; there was to be no rehabilitation for them, they said. Admittedly apostates had denied the faith under duress, but in his document "On the Lapsed" Cyprian argued that no human power could remit apostasy.[168] Later on, after the persecution of Decius subsided, Cyprian changed his stand, asserting that bishops had the powers of the keys and thus could remit such grave sins.[169]

On the issue of baptism by schismatics, many bishops in North Africa joined Cyprian in maintaining that such administration of the sacraments was invalid. Cyprian and his colleagues advocated a policy of rebaptism in such cases. Many church officials objected to such extreme measures and appealed to the bishop of Rome, Stephen, and asked him to intervene in the case. Stephen declared that there should be no rebaptisms and that there should be some leniency for apostates so that with some penance they could return to the church. Stephen sought to impose his view on Cyprian and all the Christian churches. During this time Rome was considered the last court of appeals in church disputes. Stephen "was in fact the first pope, so far as is known, to find a formal basis for the Roman primacy in the Lord's charge to the Apostle Peter cited in Matt 16:18."[170] This is a perplexing statement because 200 years had already passed since the Petrine doctrine was recorded in Matthew. One would think this argument should have been used much sooner.

Many authors debate the merits of Matt 16: 18 as a scriptural foundation for the primacy of Peter and the power of the pope. Küng states that this "is not a saying of the earthly Jesus but was composed after Easter by the Palestinian community, or later by Matthew's community."[171] This famous quotation "Thou art Peter…" is not found in any of the other canonical Gospels and that is troubling. A doctrine so central as the primacy would presumably be found in all the Gospels. Raymond Brown has his own reservations regarding the text: "The unusually heavy Semitic background of the phraseology makes it likely that this was not created by Matt but drawn by the evangelist from an earlier source. Many would deny that it was spoken by Jesus himself, e.g., on the grounds that it was missing from the presumably older account of the scene in Mark, and that it contains a reference to 'church' (meaning 'church' at large) that is unique in the Jesus tradition."[172] It suffices to say that the primacy of Peter as a doctrine arose based on some shaky testimony by the author of Matthew. The tradition developed later but the earthly Jesus probably did not authorize it. That is reasonable, but can our understanding of the primacy of Peter change, now that we have more information about the role of Peter? Some think we have a distorted view of the papacy based on new insights about the words of Jesus. The whole issue needs to be reevaluated.

Sylvester (314-335) served as bishop of Rome for almost 22 years but "seems to have played an insignificant part in the great events that were taking place...."[173] It was Constantine who called all the bishops in the civilized world together for the Council of Nicaea in order to resolve church disputes concerning the nature of the Trinity and other matters. The council was attended by about 220 bishops with almost all of them Greek.[174] Less than 10 came from the Latin west, including the 2 presbyters sent by the bishop of Rome as his personal representatives. After the council, all the decisions were submitted to Rome for approval and thus showed some deference to Sylvester by this action.

Siricius (384-399) was unanimously chosen to be the bishop of Rome by his colleagues and this choice was confirmed by Emperor Valentinian II. He was the first bishop of Rome to use the title of "Pope" exclusively, much to the consternation of Eastern Bishops. Throughout the early church the name "Pappa" was a term of endearment for all local bishops, but Rome would have it otherwise. Now, according to Siricius, only the bishop of Rome could be called "Pappa" or Pope. He was the first to issue "decretals" which were papal letters which had the force of law. Thus, we begin to see the unilateral nature of papal authority. Siricius was the first to claim the title "Pontifex Maximus," a designation always claimed by the Roman emperor in previous years. A distinctly religious office under the ancient Roman republic, it was the most important position in ancient Roman religion (pagan). Historians say that the emperor Gratian (d.383) dropped the title from his imperial status and possibly gave it to the bishop of Rome.
In summary one can see in figure 7 how the small sect of Jewish Christians grew into a church with great power claimed by the Bishop of Rome.

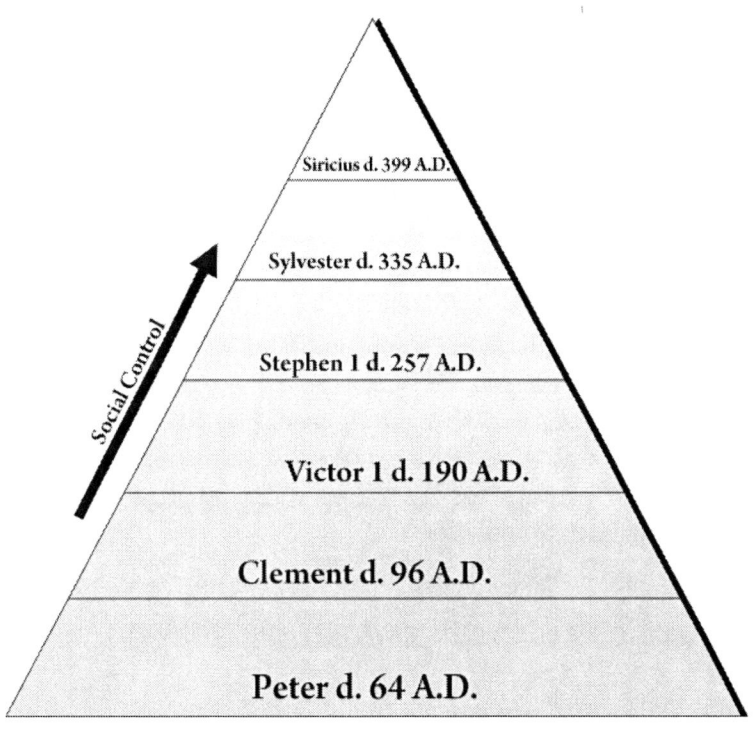

Fig 7 Centralization of Bishops of Rome

At first Peter took charge of the Jesus movement but never operated in a dictatorial manner. Clement offered fraternal correction to the church in Corinth but did not order, as bishop of Rome, any changes in the structure of that community. He recommended, he urged people to act. The first century of Christianity was marked by decentralization. By the end of the second century, Victor gave orders from Rome regarding the celebration of Easter, and he felt everyone should obey him. Stephen resolved disputes about apostates and rebaptism; his office was viewed as the court of last resort. Sylvester approved the canons of Nicaea but failed to attend this important meeting, as did many clerics in the West. By the end of the 4th century, Siricius asserted his power and authority by claiming unique titles of Pope and Pontifex Maximus. There was no question that he felt the bishop of Rome was in control of the entire Christian church. Augustine would clarify this assumption.

It is clear that the Bishop of Rome had gradually strengthened his hold on the power structure of the early church. He was head of the Christian community situated in the imperial capital and well-known for its charitable activities. St. Ignatius said that the Christian community in Rome had the "primacy of love." Since Rome claimed to be the undisputed location of the tombs of Peter and Paul, it was only natural, some argue, that this center would be held in high esteem. We will revisit this topic when discussing the contributions of St. Augustine; the "primacy" of the bishop of Rome plays out in varying degrees in the early 5th century.

TIME LINE FOR BISHOP OF ROME (33 -399A.D.)

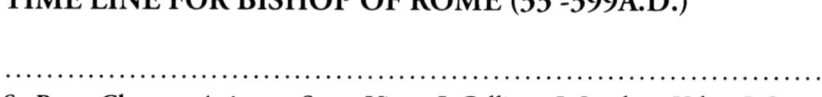

St. Peter Clement Anicetus Soter Victor I Callistus I Stephen Urban I Siricius

CHAPTER SEVEN:

THE GNOSTIC CHRISTIANS

> *Gnosticism operated "as a kind of elitist and secretive spirituality movement within Christian circles."*
>
> L.Michael White

As the early church grew in numbers and diversity, leaders were concerned about how to preserve the orthodox teaching of the apostles and felt that it was their duty to root out false prophets who could lead believers astray. Thus we come to a confrontation with some of the **internal** forces that threatened the new Christian religion. What was the true message of Jesus and how could the church avoid distortions of the Gospel? Given the diversity of the followers of Jesus, this question was particularly difficult to answer: there were Hebrew converts, Hellenists, and Gentiles with pagan backgrounds. Converts brought their old belief systems when they joined the Jesus movement. How does one express in human terms the revelation of God given such a multicultural religious setting? Answer: only with great difficulty.

The 1st and 2nd century orthodox Christians encountered what they considered false notions of Christianity, and their leaders felt compelled to correct their sisters and brothers (see Paul's letter to the Colossians, 2:18). He admonishes against the worship of angels, which is taken by some as a reference to certain Gnostic beliefs in the community.[175] One of the major doctrines that needed clarification was that Jesus was not only the Messiah, but that He was also God. Another key belief, that Jesus died and rose from the dead, had to be proclaimed. Jesus was fully human as well as divine. He was not just an apparition from God; He was God and man.

The Ebionites (a Jewish Christian group, many of whom first followed John the Baptist) challenged these doctrines early and often. This first century set of believers held that Jesus was a mere man but by his faithful observance of the law was justified and had become the Messiah. He was not God, but the Ebionites did accept him as the Messiah. Such ideas were rejected by leaders of the early Christian church; these strong reactions showed the convictions orthodox Christians had developed about the nature of Christ and how they must oppose those who do not hold to proper Christian beliefs. Over the years, from 110 to 160 A.D., there was a fight to see which faction would win out. Orthodox Christians had the teachings of Jesus, the letters of Paul, the Gospels, and the beliefs of the apostles. They felt equipped for the challenge.

As if this theological fight were not enough, the doctrines of Docetism arose to challenge the Ebionites and others. Docetists held that Christ was not really a man, a human being, but had only appeared to suffer and die on the cross for sin. They argued that Simon of Cyrene was crucified instead of Jesus; Docetists came to this conclusion because God, in their view, cannot die.[176]

In addition to these challenges, there arose a formidable opponent in Gnosticism, which for many years battled the leaders of the church for the right to state what were the essentials of Christianity. *Gnosticism* is a philosophical and religious movement which originated in the eastern part of the Roman empire (viz., Egypt) before the time of Christ.[177] Brown argues that Gnostic strains were rooted in Judaism and that Christian Gnosticism "appears as a secondary development."[178] Henry Chadwick agrees, but notes that the Gnostics depend not only on Jewish traditions (Genesis, the serpent, etc.), but also Platonism (dualism between the realm of ideas and world of experience) and Zoroastrianism (the importance of angels).[179]

The name "Gnosticism" is derived from the Greek word *"gnosis"* which literally means *"knowledge."* This religious group tried to mix its ancient views with the doctrines of early Christianity (a process called "syncretism") around the 1st and 2nd century; they challenged many of the fundamental apostolic teachings. Gnostic teachers such as Valentinus traveled from Alexandria to Rome (circa 140 A.D.) in order to win over new converts and debate religious issues with anyone who would listen. Unlike Marcion of Sinope (d. 160), Valentinus utilized the Old Testament in teaching the importance of special knowledge to achieve one's eternal destiny.

The Gnostic view of religion and the world is complex and at times contradictory.[180] One of the first principles of Gnosticism is the concept of enlightenment, that is, we need knowledge to overcome ignorance and thus achieve salvation. This requires a spiritual guru to help us on our journey to true knowledge. Jesus provided this special knowledge to his disciples. The spark within one's soul must be aroused. He/she will have the knowledge to guide us. Some contend that Gnostics were very open to the idea of women as leaders and perhaps this tendency may explain why many women followed the teachings of this group. It is clear that Polycarp (a disciple of John the Apostle), who died a martyr in 155 A.D., worked hard to combat the teachings of Gnostics. Later on, Irenaeus joined the battle from far-off Gaul (modern day France).

A second principle of the Gnostics was that the Christianity they observed needed to be purified from corrupt practices. Basing their doctrine on a fundamental principle of dualism of the world, they held that two forces are operative in the cosmos: good and evil. The spirit is everything and the body is nothing. They admonished married couples not to engage in sexual intercourse and those betrothed not to consummate their marriages.[181] Borrowing their basic ideas from various schools of thought, Gnostics argued that it is evil to be identified with matter. Influenced mightily by Platonism, Gnostics built on Greek philosophical principles and proclaimed that people "must escape the material world and go to their true home in that other world."[182] Above all Gnostics believed that the Supreme Deity cannot be associated with the creation of matter. The Supreme Being is totally other (the Good God) and is removed from matter and the creation of matter. The good God is the origin of the soul. A lower god

(Demiurge) created matter and the world as we know it. How are we then to explain God and his creation?

Creation occurred, according to the Gnostics, through a series of emanations which to some degree were an extension of God's nature. These emanations, willed by God, then produced lesser beings. God sent Jesus (a lesser God) to free humans from the chains of matter. Michael White clearly points out that in this system redemption is "based on releasing the soul from its physical 'prison' (the body) in order to be reunited with the divine spirit."[183] Christ fulfilled his redemptive role by descending into the body of Jesus at his Baptism in the Jordan and left him at the Mount of Olives before the suffering and crucifixion occurred. Some of the Gnostics held that Jesus did not have a body at all but was really a phantom, a Ghost, or an apparition. Hence scholars conclude that this is a doctrine that rejects the true humanity of Jesus.[184] Gnosticism also embraces the doctrine of predestination—an idea that Calvin would develop more thoroughly during the Protestant Reformation. In short, redemption is granted to an elite few from all eternity, through no good works of their own. These special beings have what is called the divine spark. Salvation is certain for them. Heathens and mediocre believers try to achieve salvation, but are unlikely to attain eternal bliss. One can see in this system that there is an upper and lower class of believers; the lower class live by faith, but the elite—upper class—are illuminated and live by a special knowledge given them by God. St. Paul and Mary Magdalene had this special knowledge, according to the Gnostics. They championed St. Paul because he exemplified this special knowledge (revelation) received on the road to Damascus and in a vision where he was taken up to the 3rd heaven (2 Cor 12:2). Besides the spiritual groupings devised by Gnostics, there is a third category which could be called the "spiritually challenged," that is, they do not really understand; they do not get the special insight and they cannot see true spiritual reality. These are predestined not to get it. Thus many writers conclude that Gnostics operated as a "kind of elitist and secretive spirituality movement within Christian circles."[185]

Clearly some Christian Gnostics had a strong aversion to Judaism and the Old Testament (Marcion); their quest for special knowledge and insight regarding salvation became a central focus. Marcion (d. 160 A.D.) claimed that the OT God of the Jews created this miserable world, favored David despite his crimes, and "devised the humiliating method of sexual reproduction....[sic]"[186] Thus, the God of the Jews must be rejected in favor of God the Father revealed in Jesus. Marcion was excommunicated from the church in 144 C.E.; thus Christians used a practice of exclusion that had affected them years before when they were excluded from the synagogue.

Gnostics knew others wanted these special secrets from God but few proved to be truly worthy. Jesus gave special knowledge to the Gnostics but He hid knowledge from others. This belief is alluded to in the **Gospel of Mary** wherein Jesus supposedly shares special secrets with Mary Magdalene, one of His closest disciples, but not with others. Such events irritated the other apostles so that Peter remarked "Did he prefer her to us?"[187]

It is interesting to note that most theologians prior to *The Da Vinci Code* hype, never seriously raised the question of whether Jesus and Mary of Magdala were a couple as Gnostic texts imply. Few early 20th century writers ever suggested this. There is no clear evidence in any early church writings that Jesus took a wife or had any children. In this book's APPENDIX A we will discuss the matter in detail.

Gnostics held that most Jews had rejected Christ as the Messiah and so they do not receive God's special knowledge. A key Gnostic leader, Marcion, rejected the Old Testament altogether and any allegorical interpretation[188] of biblical texts. For example, Isaiah's statement (7:14) that "Behold, a virgin will conceive, and bear a son, and shall call his name Immanuel" cannot be seen as pointing to a deeper meaning than its literal understanding at the time. Marcion did not want to have anything to do with the OT, but other Gnostics were not so exclusionary. Christians like Irenaeus could see in this passage a deeper, allegorical meaning, namely, that of the coming Messiah, Jesus. The OT is worthless, according to Marcion—a view not shared by fellow Gnostic, Valentinus. Taken to an extreme, Gnosticism asserted an antisemitic bias which led to the doctrine that only an elite group of Christians would be saved, while the rest of humanity would be left out of the kingdom. These ideas are not dead and can be found today in Tim LaHaye's *Left Behind* book and series; only true believers will be taken up to heaven in a future special rapture, while the unrighteous will perish.[189] Because the Jews rejected Christ, they cannot be saved unless they convert.

Special knowledge and insight comes from God; some do not receive it—certainly not those who reject Christ. Such insight and knowledge includes knowledge of human nature (the body is a cage of the soul). Second, some are destined to return to the spiritual realm with God; that is their destiny. Third, this special knowledge allows one to understand the origin of the world, creation and how evil came into the world. Lastly, the elite will find their way back home ("we come from God and we return to God") through secret passwords and codes which will allow them to get by those who would try to block their assent to Light.

The "orthodox" Christians responded to the Gnostics by writing the **Apostles Creed** which stated the true doctrines of Christ for all believers, based on the Gospels, Paul's epistles, and correct apostolic teaching. Some argue that because women played a prominent role in the Gnostic heresy, they were punished by having important leadership roles withheld from them in the newly structured church. This seems unlikely, since women lost their leadership roles primarily due to cultural factors like patriarchy in the Roman empire, and not due to theological insights about God's plan for the human race. Another problem has to do with doctrine. The Gospel of Mary asserts that there is no resurrection of the body.[190] This idea, of course, was rejected by the early church fathers (Clement I, Letter to Corinthians), and hence such heretical writings were suppressed. The discovery at Nag Hammadi (1945) of Gnostic texts show that people hid writings that church leaders rejected. Others say the exclusion of women by the church was due to simple bias and prejudice against women which was clearly present in the Greco-Roman culture of patriarchy. Saints Jerome and Augustine provide plenty of testimony for the prejudice argument; mysoginism was alive and well in their writings. Some contend Gnosticism had nothing do with the church's new attitude regarding women. After the example of Jesus and Paul who stressed equality of the sexes, the church in 110 A.D. simply gave patriarchy a free hand in church social structure while leaders became more and more assimilated into the Roman empire. Actually, the church was forced by cultural factors to keep women subordinate to men so as not to appear radical and dangerous to the empire. After all, this was the norm in Roman society. Moving from the reality of sect to church, the early Christians just wanted to fit in and be accepted by the dominant society. Men held all public roles in society. The church simply took on the general attitudes and behaviors of the dominant political and social environment which held women in low esteem. Assimilation has its negative consequences for countercultural beliefs.

The Apostles creed, which responded to numerous Gnostic errors, may not have actually been written by the apostles since it first appeared in second century Rome (a version is quoted by Tertullian ca. 200) to counteract the ideas of Gnostic Christians. These ideas certainly became a major problem only in the 2nd century and not the 1st. Nevertheless, its ideas probably sum up well the central views of the Apostles, according to many church historians. See the "Apostles Creed" below, written ca. 200 A.D.; some argue for an earlier date.

> I believe in God, the Father Almighty,
> creator of heaven and earth.
> I believe in Jesus Christ, his only Son, our Lord.
> He was conceived by the power of the Holy Spirit
> and born of the Virgin Mary.
> He suffered under Pontius Pilate,
> was crucified, died, and was buried.
> He descended to the dead.
> On the third day He rose again.
> He ascended into heaven
> and is seated at the right hand of the Father.
> He will come again to judge the living and the dead.
> I believe in the Holy Spirit,
> the Holy Catholic Church,
> the communion of Saints,
> the forgiveness of sins,
> the resurrection of the body,
> and the life everlasting. AMEN.

First the creed states that Christians believe in God the Almighty. He made heaven and earth (contra the view that matter is evil). Matter is God's creation and can be enjoyed by men and women of all ages; it is God's gift. Jesus said eat and drink this bread and wine (matter). He changed water into wine. He ate the last supper with his disciples. Secondly, the creed states that Jesus was miraculously born to a human couple: Joseph and Mary. God became man which is contra the Gnostic doctrines. God took on our humanity in Jesus. Thirdly, redemption occurs through Christ. We are not redeemed by some secret knowledge that only a special few are pre-selected to receive. The creed says that men and women are redeemed by God's intervention in history. The key event in the Christian's life is not gnosis but the coming of Christ and one's faith in Him. Lastly, the early Christians held that we will rise from the dead (contra the Gnostic view that we are freed from the prison of the body forever at death). We will live body and soul in heaven according to the Apostles Creed, formulated in the 2nd century, long before the Protestant Reformation. This is the testimony of the early church. We do not require a teacher or guru, per se, but rather we need a savior, according to the orthodox school. He has accomplished the task. His disciples must will to be a part of this process. The baptized must be willing to follow him, according to the teachings of the Apostles.

In conclusion, it is clear that the orthodox faction won out over time and Gnostic Christians became a thing of the past. Many of their views (creation, sexuality) did not fit the typical family values of the Roman empire, be they Jewish, pagan or Christian. Hence the Gnostic sect lost and orthodoxy became the dominant force in the Christian church. The average God-fearing person in the Roman empire could not follow the dictates of some Gnostic preachers that "to marry and beget children is from Satan."[191]

Summary and Conclusions (chapters 6 and 7):

25. The bishop of Rome gradually gained power and influence over most Christian churches but not without resistance from those in the East and North Africa.

26. Councils were the chief legislative body for the early church.

27. Bishops and scholars rejected the ideas of Gnostic Christians because they did not correspond favorably with 1) the writings of Paul, 2) the Gospels, and 3) orthodox church documents like the Apostles creed.

CHAPTER EIGHT:

WHAT HATH GOD WROUGHT?

THE NEW TESTAMENT CANON

In the words of Bart Ehrman, the New Testament stands unchallenged, not only as the "'bestseller' of all time," but also as the most important "book—or collection of books—in the history of Western civilization."

There were few decisions more important for the development of Christianity than determining the content of the New Testament(NT). One of the most important tasks of the early church was to establish the rule (canon), the constitution for all Christians. Persecutions and heretical teachings made it difficult to accomplish this task, but the story of the Christian heritage and its survival cannot be told without paying close attention to their search for the true word of God revealed in Jesus. Given the promise to the Apostles that the Spirit would be present to guide the church through all ages, leaders worked feverishly to determine what writings were truly the word of God—revelation— and which ones needed to be excluded from the bible. For instance, the Letter of Clement (1), bishop of Rome (circa 88-99 A.D.), was read at worship services by many churches but never became part of the NT canon of scripture.[192] His letter was read at liturgies in Corinth as late as 150 A.D., so it was highly regarded for a long time by the early church. What was the process whereby the true word of God was determined by early Christians?

First, we know that the four Gospels were considered as scripture early on by the Christian community. After all, these accounts gave believers the words and deeds of Jesus—the way to salvation. The four Gospels (Mt, Mk, Lk, Jn) "received ever-widening acceptance after 150."[193] Second, we know that about 100 years after Paul's death, there was a strong move to have his epistles included in the Christian scriptures. These documents, like the Torah for the Hebrews, formed the backbone of early Christian literature. They were important Christian documents, but Roman emperors felt the Gospels were subversive and wanted these writings suppressed. Book burnings were all part of the plan by pagans and others to limit the influence of Christian believers. These sacred writings inspired martyrs and at the same time were a test against heresy. But what was to be the final version of this document? What was the totality of the Christian revelation? There must be a standard, a constitution upon which to build the Christian community. History did provide some guidelines.

The old testament canon (Hebrew Bible) was finalized to some degree by 200 B.C., but Metzger[194] offers considerable evidence that it was really the Synod of Jamnia ca. 90-100 A.D. that gave the final approval for the contents of the Hebrew Bible. Marcea Eliade calls Judaism the first religion of the book, and by this he means the scriptures were crucial in the formation of the Jewish religion of monotheism.[195] They followed the teachings of the book—or at least tried. The books of the OT are made up of the Torah (first 5 books of the bible), second the prophets, and third, other sacred texts. The early Christian writers and preachers used the Septuagint, the Greek translation of the Hebrew Bible (ca. 300-100 B.C.), and quoted it extensively in the NT. As the Christian church sought to develop its own set of scriptures, the Jewish experience in selecting sacred books provided a model to imitate.

For many Christians today the Old Testament is comprised of 45 books, but some religious groups hold that there are only 39 books in the Old Testament that deserve to be called God's Word. Those who accept 45 books as scripture in the OT list 72 books in their entire bible (NT=27). Hebrew men and women in the past reflected on the various religious texts of the time and finally selected a special set of writings to be included in the OT canon. The new religion of Christianity would do the same.

The meaning of the word "canon" has to do with the concept of measuring rod or ruler. That is, the list of books that belong to the OT constituted a standard or ruler for Jewish believers to follow. It was primarily God's word, His law given to Moses. That is how the OT canon of scripture was formulated. The NT canon would follow a similar pattern: it would be a standard or rule for the early Christian church and all who would follow thereafter. It is God's word given through Jesus.

The Muratorian fragment is a copy of the oldest known list of the first books in the New Testament. This canon is a Latin translation of a Greek original thought to be written circa 170 A.D., but it could have been developed later. Scholars point out that all the 27 books of the NT were written in Greek, but none of the originals have survived. We have copies of the originals written in koine Greek. The Muratorian fragment includes the following texts as canonical beginning with the Gospels:

> Four Gospels (Matthew, Mark, Luke, John)
> Acts, plus 13 of Paul's epistles
> 2 letters of John
> Jude
> Apocalypse of Peter
> Wisdom
>
> Total: 23

Not included in this canon were Hebrews, 1 and 2 Peter, and James; but years later there would be additions and subtractions to the Muratorian document. We should be aware that in the long process of copying texts, scribes made some serious errors that only later have been rectified. Carrier gives a well-known example of the "famous King James line 'Glory to God in the highest, and on earth peace, good will toward men' (Luke 2:14)....[It] is treated as an example of the ultimate moral nobility of Christianity. But not until recent times was it discovered that a scribe long ago had failed to record a single letter (a sigma, "s") at the end of this line. The Latin Vulgate Bible, translated late in the 4th century, copied from a correct edition and thus has preserved the original meaning, which is now correctly reconstructed in more recent Bible translations: 'peace on earth toward men of goodwill,' which is not as noble...."[196] Not surprisingly, copying errors occurred when bringing the written word of the Gospel to the faithful, but through judicious research and study, these problems have been resolved for the modern reader.

We find that Irenaeus provided the church with a list of important Christian texts ca. 177 A.D. He quotes "almost every book of the NT, numerous times, demonstrating that the orthodox canon, though not established officially, was by this time generally accepted in practice."[197] The list compiled by Irenaeus proved to be prophetic.

Some years later, Origen (d. 254), the most influential biblical scholar in the first three centuries of Christianity, gave this list of books acknowledged as scripture by all the churches:

Matthew, Mark, Luke, John
Acts
13 Epistles of Paul
1 John
1 Peter
Revelation (John)   Total: 21

The Codex Sinaiticus is one of the oldest known copies of the NT writings and is thought to be one of the 50 copies commissioned by Constantine (d. 337). It contains 29 books, including the following:

Gospels: 4
Paul's epistles: 13
Acts
Revelation
Various other epistles 8
Letter of Barnabas
Shepherd of Hermas   Total: 29

It is clear that by the time of Constantine the canon was not formally set, and this did not seem to bother the emperor. Nothing official regarding the NT canon emerged during the Council of Nicaea. During the 4th century the following six books (Hebrews, James, II and III John, Jude and II Peter) were added to the NT canon and others lost favor in the early church. By 397 the Council of Carthage, through the influence of Augustine and others, declared that there were 27 books in the Christian scriptures; that is the current number of books in the New Testament. The Christian canon was set. The decision by the council was sent to Siricius, bishop of Rome, for ratification since he chose not to attend the meeting and present his views. This action certainly shows the pre-eminent status of the bishop of Rome; it likewise indicates that the bishops and others worked with the Pope to decide on key issues affecting the church. The pope had no problem with the council's action but it is interesting to note that Siricius became the first pontiff to stipulate that no bishop should be consecrated without the knowledge of the Apostolic See. His legally binding decretals were written "in the style of imperial edicts."[198] More and more the church was taking on the attitudes and characteristics of the empire. In 395 the bishop of Hippo, Augustine, was able to sidestep the Roman church's legal system and joined the episcopate (and the priesthood, I might add) through local acclamation and then ordination by a bishop.

There are a number of critical factors that led early Christians to select certain writings into the canon of the NT. First, the writings had to be addressed to the Christian community; for example, Matthew was written for Jewish Christians living in Antioch, whereas Paul wrote letters to the church in Thessalonia, Corinth, etc. There were some exceptions to this rule, however. These writings were subsequently read at liturgical services such as the Eucharist, and thus decisions by the people of God to cherish certain writings more than others helped to formulate the content of the NT. To this general rule there were some exceptions, such as the Letter to Philemon and Letter of Jude which were included because the authorship was tied to a prominent NT personality. A second reason for inclusion in the canon was that the writer had ties to the apostles. Luke, John, Matthew, and Mark certainly met this criterion. But this rule had to be applied judiciously. The Gospel of Peter was excluded because it seemed to support certain Docetist doctrines, namely, that Jesus only appeared to be a man, but was not really flesh and blood. Thus it was judged to be falsely attributed to Peter and not to be a part of the canon. It was not apostolic. Finally, some writings had a self-authenticating quality, that is, they gave accounts of the life of Christ, his words (sermon on the mount) or his encounters with the apostles, e.g. Peter and Paul. In short, they were the very words and deeds of Jesus. This made such texts important to the Christian community, because they did not violate the rule of faith—they promoted belief. In contrast, other writings were classified as "apocrypha"[199] which meant that, although they may be religious and inspiring to readers, the documents were not considered canonical according to the above-mentioned three criteria. They may be useful but they were not the word of God as defined by the community. Clearly the Christians had special norms to determine what was important and what was not.

Various factors made it difficult to make a final determination about what would be in the NT canon. In the middle of the second century (c. 140 A.D.), a religious leader with Gnostic ties named Marcion wanted to formulate a canon of both the Old and New testament scriptures; he tried to persuade Christians to agree that he and his followers had received a new revelation from God regarding the canonical scriptures. He was a powerful force and caused considerable confusion in the early church. His list may have been the first canon developed by the Christian community. Ultimately, he wanted to reject the Septuagint, and construct a new bible consisting of Luke, Paul's letters, and finally some of Marcion's own work which he called **Antitheses**. Marcion's full canon is as follows:

Gospel according to Luke
Galatians
I Corinthians
II Corinthians
Romans
I Thessalonians
II Thessalonians
Ephesians (which Marcion called Laodiceans)
Colossians
Philemon
Philippians   Total: 11

These ideas proved to be rather self-serving if not totally outrageous to most Christians. Little wonder that Polycarp, the student of John the Apostle, called Marcion "the first son of Satan." Early Christians did not mince words, and name calling proved to be an effective tool in dealing with heretics. His move to formulate a canon spurred orthodox Christians to develop their own set of scriptures which they did in the next 100 years.

A prominent thinker in the 2nd century, Marcion was expelled by church leaders in 144 A.D. for his Gnostic teachings; he died about 10 years later. His ideas about the old testament were unacceptable to those who saw Jesus as the fulfillment of many OT prophecies and the promised Messiah. Jesus and the Gospel writers depended on the wisdom of the old testament to tell the full story of the life of Christ. Marcion's rejection of Matthew and Mark was beyond all comprehension. Finally, the prospect of elevating his writings and so-called revelations to the status of holy scripture was too much for the Christian community. His life is a lesson to all reformers: be careful what you reject; the essentials must stay intact. His movement and others which followed told Christian leaders that not only should some writings be ignored but they should be suppressed. They were considered dangerous. The suppression policies of the early church, and the actions later taken by Constantine, meant that important historical documents have been lost for all time. The Christians had their book burnings as did the Romans. Thankfully, some lost writings were discovered in 1945 near Nag Hammadi, Egypt. This was a rare cache of Gnostic texts, some of them called "Gospels," and this new find generated keen interest among biblical scholars. The Gospel of Thomas (Greek version dated about 200 A.D.) was known to Origen and he referred to it around 233 A.D. The only known complete text of Thomas (Coptic) was found at Nag Hammadi in 1945. These and other writings were apparently suppressed documents thought to be lost for all time. They not only provide great insight into early Christian life, but most of all, make it clear that the church had enormous power to control what documents would be preserved for posterity. Condemning heretics and suppressing books was a common pattern of behavior in the church at this time.

Besides Marcion's heretical activities, we find a religious leader named Montanus who challenged church leaders and helped confuse the issue of canonical writings. He labored between 156 and 170 A.D. and maintained that revelation had not yet closed, even after the Apostles and their disciples had died. He claimed to have "special knowledge" which called the church to a higher standard of discipline and holiness; he promoted, among other things, strict rules of fasting. Montanus preached that the second coming of Christ was not far off and that Christians must be prepared for the end of the world. Some men and women joined this group, and it continued to be active until about the 5th century. Most of his ideas and principles were rejected by proto-orthodox church leaders. By the middle of the second century there were some crude outlines concerning what should be a part of the NT canon. To many Christian leaders the Gospels of Matthew, Mark and Luke as well as numerous letters from St. Paul (but not the pastoral epistles) should be a part of the canon. By 220 A.D. the final 27 books of the New Testament were still not determined, since Hebrews and Revelation were still in question. Eusebius[200] tells us that James, 2 Peter, 2 and 3 John and Jude were not universally accepted ca. 230 A.D. By 367 we find that Athanasius had listed a canon of 27 books—the same list of books accepted in the NT canon today. The Council of Carthage in 397 A.D. settled on the present 27 books for the NT canon. North Africa proved to be a place for important meetings and their leaders had a great impact on early church policy. The Christian community took about 300 years to officially settle on the final contents of the NT canon. By way of contrast it took about 200 years after the death of Mohammad for Islam to confirm the final version of the Qur'an. Finalizing religious texts is a long and tedious process.

In summary, it is clear that the Christian church and its leaders worked together over many years to finalize the NT canon. Tradition has it that this whole process was guided by the Holy Spirit. The church operated without an official bible for many years, but many texts were considered sacred and a source of guidance and inspiration long before 397 A.D. The writings made their authority felt in the local churches and during worship services. The existence of the canon shows that the church, despite its problems, wanted to submit to the teachings of the Apostles which were derived from Christ. Christians believed that the hand of God was at work in this entire process.

CHAPTER NINE:

A CHURCH FOR SINNERS, SAINTS, AND SCHOLARS

> I have made it a rule, ever since the beginning of my episcopate, to make no decision merely on the strength of my own personal opinion without consulting you [priests and deacons], and without the approbation of the people.
>
> — Saint Cyprian, Bishop of Carthage, circa 248 A.D.

In the second and third century two important themes emerge in the writings of the early Christian church fathers. These ideas and controversies reflect the tension and conflict that existed in the early church. First, can the church forgive serious sins that are committed after baptism? Second, can the church utilize the many insights of the Greek philosophers in its role as preacher and teacher of the word of God? Origen (d. 254), probably the greatest theologian in the church before Augustine, as well as Cornelius, the bishop of Rome (251-253), helped the church resolve these important issues.

It was the conviction of many early church fathers that the power to "bind and loose" (Matt 16:19) was given by Jesus to Peter and the Apostles. Some argue that this passage shows Jesus giving the power to forgive sins to the church, whereas others claim that "to bind and loose" signifies the power to teach what is to be observed. Brown suggests that the latter interpretation may be the correct one.[201] This was certainly the contention of St. Paul in his many writings. But in the 2nd century, the church found itself in a new situation: gone were the Apostles who were the unchallenged leaders and teachers of the early church. They of course could have told all believers what they thought and how they read the mind of Christ on key matters. Indeed, they did this to some degree. Without this source of knowledge and wisdom what power did the church have to indicate to believers what the will of God was?

To answer this question we must first look at the early structure of the church so we can determine its modus operandi and how it came to believe that it knew the mind of Christ. For Paul the division of labor in the early church was simple: God appointed 1) apostles 2) prophets and 3) teachers as well as healers, 4) followed by those with charisms which are shared by all believers(1 Cor 12:28).[202] These labels referred to individuals as well as offices that Christians could rely on to get answers to their daily questions about how to conduct their lives.

Note one model of church structure that was used by St. Paul around 55 A.D.:

APOSTLES
PROPHETS
TEACHERS
PEOPLE/MEMBERS

It is evident that in the Pauline communities there was no monarchical episcopate, no presbyterate, and no "laying on of hands"; that would develop about 40 years later in the pastoral letters of Timothy and Titus. Here we find three letters attributed to Paul that were written some time between 80 and 100 A.D. Raymond Brown notes some important characteristics of the new church: 1) in each community there should be appointed presbyters (presbyteroi) which means "elder"(Titus 1:5). Older, experienced men should have this position.[203] 2) The functions of presbyters are twofold, namely, to provide the community direction and guide members regarding true belief and moral practice. Although women were apostles, prophets, and deacons in Paul's time, the pastoral letters reflect a major shift: there is no indication that there were women presbyters, although Origen refutes this.[204] By the end of the 1st century the doors were shut to women who aspired to leadership roles given to them by Paul. 3) Lastly, Timothy and Titus mention the role of overseer or bishop (episkopos); it is another name for presbyter (presbyteros) in the pastorals.[205] This would change as time went on.

By the year 110 A.D. we find an organizational model of church that is quite different from Paul's and somewhat refined by Titus' standards. St. Ignatius writes: "Follow your bishop, everyone of you, as obediently as Jesus Christ followed the Father. Obey your presbyters, too, as you would the apostles; give your deacons the same reverence that you would to a command from God."[206] Scholars point out a radical shift in church structure to a model that is much more concerned with social control, obedience and male hierarchy. The model in Antioch looks quite different from the Pauline churches.

EPISCOPATE
PRESBYTERATE
DEACONS
PEOPLE

The second generation Christians probably took the view that the charismatic free churches of Paul were too unpredictable, radical, lacking in stability, and needing strong male leadership. In short, patriarchy took over. Hans Küng sums it up this way: "Indeed, the question of the status of women shows an increasing repression of the original 'democratic' and 'charismatic' structures at the beginning of Christianity and a process of institutionalization which now ran its course increasingly in favor of men."[207] Gone is the doctrine of equality through baptism; local house-churches submitted to the bishop. We are told that in the days of Ignatius of Antioch (d. 117) each church had its own bishop and that he had presbyters and deacons who helped serve the church's needs. During this period in church history, the popular notion was that God's grace comes to the people of God through the ministry of the church and its ordained clergy. Thus the saying of St. Cyprian (d. 258) arose: outside the church there is no salvation.[208] By the late 4th century Augustine wrote: "There is no salvation outside the church" (Salus extra ecclesiam non est, De Bapt. IV, cxvii.24). Early Christianity's conception of salvation was that grace comes through the church via baptism and its preeminent sacrament which is the Eucharist. It behooves Christians, therefore, to be active in the local church and take part in its sacramental life. The exclusionary doctrine of Cyprian and Augustine influenced church doctrine down through the 1960s. We find their ideas were greatly modified by the Second Vatican Council's **Constitution on the Church**, which taught: "Nor does Divine Providence deny the helps necessary for salvation to those who, without blame on their part, have not yet arrived at an explicit knowledge of God and with His grace strive to live a good life" (#16). At times the Roman church's understanding of revelation makes abrupt changes.

By the late 2nd century the notion of bishop as the unchallenged leader of the church became clear. But Cyprian states that he collaborated with the priests, deacons, and the people as he strove to govern the local church. As needs arose outside major cities, bishops would assign presbyters to care for people who lived beyond the major cities. Alexandria had a single functioning bishop by 180 A.D. and these leaders could, according to some traditions, trace their authority back to apostles.

Some wish to challenge this new type of church structure in that it may be simply a human organizational pattern rather than a divine mandate. How should we deal with this issue of Episcopal power? There are three ways of looking at this kind of church development.

1) Back to the basics. What is in the scriptures? What of the Apostolic church must we keep? Are all structures and policies permanent? Some policies seem to be contradictory. We must keep, according to some, the notion of "elder" as the norm, which includes the concept of bishop. The problem here is that women are not included in this post-apostolic theory of church structure because Paul's practices were abandoned as too radical by Roman Empire standards. But women did hold major roles in the Pauline churches around 55 A.D. The dominant culture of the Roman Empire favored men over women when it came to leadership roles and the church used this model in the early 2nd century. Can we now use a non-Roman,

Pauline model today and still be authentic? Are women to be excluded by divine command or human custom? They certainly played a crucial role in the ministries of Jesus and Paul. The human construction of church reality can be altered if such arrangements would benefit the people of God and are not against the divine plan. That is how the church operated in the past. Norms change as societies and cultures adapt to historical events. The church has changed many rules over the years, but the issue of the role of women today does not really mean the changing of a constant norm but rather a return to a valid Pauline practice. Those who ignore Paul are doomed to failure.

Edward Schillebeeckx and his colleagues follow Paul's legacy when they argue that we must reevaluate ministry in the Christian churches when it comes to the role of women.[209] First, they say, the church was mistaken by connecting the faithful's experience of the Eucharist to some "magical power" of the bishops to ordain, thus disconnecting such an event from the community of the believers. It is clear from the life of St. Augustine that the community selected him to be ordained a priest by acclamation. On a visit from Thagaste to Hippo (North Africa), in order to encourage a young man to join his religious order of brothers, Augustine states that the local congregation "grabbed" him and pleaded with him to be their priest. How did this work? "The leading Catholic citizens of Hippo would have gathered around Augustine, as the bishop accepted his forced [sic] agreement to become a priest in the town."[210] The bishop accepted their unanimous choice and ordination followed. The people spoke, then the bishop ordained. Secondly, Schillebeeckx argues that in today's world we must reconnect the Eucharist with the practice of early church communities, even if such actions may violate current church law. Theirs is a call to return to tradition. Third, to accomplish this, Schillebeeckx and colleagues propose that men and women can be selected to preside at the Eucharist by the local community.[211] The bishop would then be asked to ordain such individuals. If the bishop refuses to ordain community-selected leaders, local churches should move forward, confident that the community's will to act provides all that is necessary to preside and fulfill the requirements of the Lord's supper as well as other priestly functions. The scriptures, especially the Pauline letters, reflect this type of creative thinking and practice. The canons promulgated by the Council of Chalcedon (451 A.D.) support such an arrangement, according to Schillebeeckx.

2) Back to church leaders. The argument here is that church leaders in the community were simply exercising the roles given them by God through the Apostles and their successors. In the absence of any clear divine authorized plan or revelation in Jesus' name, church leaders did what was judged to be necessary and beneficial for the church at the time. The argument completely ignores the possibility that human bias (individual or cultural) could ever enter into the crafting of church structures and the exclusion of women. That creates a problem. The church authority proponents argue that the church felt it was being guided by the Holy Spirit in these actions. Thus we should follow this early pattern. The real reason for excluding women was that the church chose to follow Roman culture. They wanted to survive. We see this theme played out later in the Council of Nicaea (325) wherein the doctrine of the Trinity was formulated and taught. The emperor Constantine wanted peace in the provinces; settle the religious conflicts now, was his order to the bishops. The church seemed to be on the right track there. Leaders continued to develop a governance structure which served a useful purpose for them, but can it now be changed? Change may be needed to meet the needs of a new generation and correct the limitations of the past. We dropped the idea of slavery decades ago, but the early Christians accepted this practice. People in this second school of thought argue that the church is a social (and spiritual) entity, existing in a given culture and time in history. The push for adaptation is clearly evident in this approach. Seen as a derivation of Vatican II thinking, contemporary adherents of this theory say the church should adapt and can respond to changing times. Saturday evening masses, lifting the ban on meatless Fridays, the use of married deacons (men only), liturgy in the vernacular are changes which show that the church has the power to make alterations. Many of these changes are based on a return to tradition and not a totally new line of religious thought. The church's demand for an all-celibate clergy occurred in 1139 A.D. at the Second Lateran Council.[212] This legislation radically altered a 1,000-year-old tradition which followed an apostolic norm: Jesus selected apostles who were married men. Peter was married, and popes for hundreds of years saw marriage as a Christian vocation which in no way diminished the priestly role;

some of their sons were later ordained priests. For instance, Hormisdas (d. 523) was married before becoming pope and had "a son, Silverius, who later succeeded him as pope."²¹³ Was this Lateran Council's move an appropriate change for the church at the time, and if so, should it now be continued or rescinded? Should there be a return to the early practice of the early church? Some argue that there is a period after a change wherein we should look for the seal of God's approval. Is the change blessed by God? Is the new teaching "received" by the people of God? Is there some sign? These questions are reasonable but could such a period of reflection be considered rather subjective? What aspects of the church can change? These issues seem open to much discussion and debate.

3) Back to the Holy Spirit. This final conception of church reality states that the Holy Spirit was intensely present to the early church, and thus, what emerged at the time has a certain divine approbation. What happened in the early church was special, particularly in the area of doctrine and structure. The outcome was the work not of men, but of God (lex divina). So the action of this early period is binding on all. This tends to be the view of conservative Catholics of the 21st century until the argument is turned on them to demand change. Keep things the way they are: no women priests? What of married clergy? The early church was guided by the Holy Spirit and its practices have a certain divine approbation. The teachings and pastoral practices of Paul's churches have a special place in our understanding of the future church. That is God's unique plan for holiness and equality. The monarchical episcopate arose over time in the early church but has limited biblical foundation. Did the change lead to greater holiness? Did it lead to greater church stability and spiritual growth? Is the church—the people of God—better off now than it was when Paul wrote his first letter to the Corinthians? Or, did the church become less a witness to Christ by its patriarchal structure? These are difficult questions to answer in any age.

Aside from these issues of church structure and change, church leaders preached about sin, forgiveness, and holiness; certainly these were prominent topics in the centuries after the death of Christ. Justin Martyr told his people that they must have high moral standards. Persecutions arose from time to time and men and women died rather than offer sacrifice to the pagan gods. Many were so courageous that spectators in the coliseum were drawn to convert to the Christian faith by watching innocents die.

Despite the heroic lives of the martyrs and saints, writers say that between 205 and 220 A.D. there was an ethical and moral decline in the church. There was also a decline in morality among bishops and clergy. In response, preachers began to look down on those who sinned after baptism. Could their sins be forgiven? There arose a perplexing answer to this question. God can forgive grave sins such as 1) sexual immorality 2) murder and 3) apostasy (abandoning the faith), but the church cannot! The church does not have the power to do so—or so some people thought at the time. The "rigorists" took the line that the church could not forgive such heinous crimes and that the sinful person would have to ask God's forgiveness on judgment day. These hardliners stated that those who would commit such sins should be (i) excluded from the community and (ii) denied the Eucharist. In contrast, other views arose on the issue of forgiveness. After all, we are talking about a church in which Peter denied Christ three times! Sinners need the church. Callistus (d. 222), bishop of Rome and prominent leader of the church, was a lenient, compassionate man and was willing to take sinners back to the church. He stated that he was given the keys of the kingdom and thus had the power to bind and loose (forgive and teach). So he argued, as a successor of the apostles, that he and his brother bishops had this special power, and he was going to use it. In this dispute he was implicitly claiming that he held the office which made him chief of the apostles and their successors: he was head of the church.

Not everyone appreciated his claim to such power. Tertullian opposed the bishop of Rome on this matter and said apostates could not be taken back into the church. What had happened during emperor Decius's reign of terror (249-251 A.D.) was tragic: many Christians died for their faith; they refused to offer sacrifice to the Roman gods. The church proclaimed them heroes and called them martyrs; their families were devastated. Of course, there were some Christians who were intimidated by the threat of execution and were not as strong in their convictions as the martyrs were—certainly not strong enough to die for them. They agreed to pray to the pagan gods and were spared. The rigorists and some families of martyrs took a hard line against these lapsed Christians. They had sinned and thus a certain group of Christians wanted them excluded from the church. Apostasy could not be tolerated. With the death of Decius in 251, attacks and persecutions of Christians were less pronounced and a period of tolerance followed. Many of the apostates hoped to be readmitted to the church. Some felt, however, that since these sinners had denied the faith, there was no chance for them to be members of the Christian community again. Rigorists seemed to forget about Peter's failures, and that he was forgiven by the risen Lord. Paul persecuted the early Christians and was forgiven for being an accomplice to murder. The Catholic hard-liners felt that re-admitting apostates would dishonor the lives of martyrs and be an insult to their families. After siding with the rigorists, bishops like Cyprian of Carthage, changed their position, and took the view that apostates and other grave sinners could be readmitted but must do penance for their sins. The argument he used, not considered valid by most theologians today, was that these sinners could draw upon the spiritual treasury of the church: the merits of saints, martyrs and confessors. Thus, their weaknesses could be made up for by the good works of others. This theology was rejected years later by theologians and church councils that reaffirmed the principle of God's unconditional mercy for individual sinners, but it was the "merits" rationale, held by early church leaders, which allowed some apostates back in the early church. The history of the church tells us that a certain hard liner named Novatian, offered grave sinners no forgiveness and told the church to pray for them at the last judgment. Cornelius (d. 253), bishop of Rome, asserted that the church had the power to forgive such sins, and like his predecessor, the former slave-become-pope, Callistus, he proclaimed that Christ's church was a church of saints and sinners.[214] Through penance and forgiveness, grace flows again, according to these early church leaders. Advances in theology begun by writers such as Origen and others helped the church move forward in its ideas about sin and the mercy of God. The rigorists lost the battle and those who followed the message of the Prodigal son won out (Luke 15). This is another example of how the church adopted a more moderate view of reality, and rejected the ultra conservative positions of Novatian and others. Some challenged the policies of the bishop of Rome and lost.

Amid all the turmoil and persecution the church experienced in the 2nd and 3rd century, religious leaders did not retreat from their mission to teach and instruct the people of God. But no comprehensive solution to this educational deficit was presented to the growing church until the plan put forth by the new catechetical school of Alexandria: how to be in the world but not of the world (Jn 17:16)? Could the Gospel be preached to well educated pagans who were schooled in Greek philosophy? Was anyone up to the task of explaining the faith to these pagan philosophers? Clement of Alexandria had studied under the wise man, Pantaenus, for some 20 years and felt he was now ready to bring the message of Christ to those schooled in Greek philosophy. During his tenure at the new catechetical school, he wrote the book **Exhortation to the Heathen** which outlined his arguments regarding the strengths of Christianity. His greatest desire was to be an apostle to the Hellenist intellectuals. He would win the young people to Christ with his convincing rational arguments! His was a message of character formation: the belief that spiritual insight comes to the pure of heart. He wanted to convince his young listeners that all truth and good comes from the Creator. He founded a great catechetical school and developed a strong Christian program, but did not live long enough to see how his preliminary efforts would bear fruit. A new teacher was needed to accomplish that.

Enter Origen. Born in 185 A.D. this man was the only true theological genius in the 3rd century. He and his followers continued the epic struggle of building the Christian church's educational foundation. As the new leader of the catechetical school at age 18 and until his death some 50 years later, he wrote book after book about theology and the scriptures. Some contend that he produced 6,000 written works (scrolls, books, and chapters). A rather independent thinker, he argued about theological issues with his bishop (Demetrius) on several occasions. As a popular teacher he drew people from hundreds of miles away to hear his lectures and sermons. His main concern was to expound upon the meaning of God's word. He said that he wanted Christians to know the scriptures. Not an elitist by any means, he respected the simple faith of the masses but wanted to articulate the faith in such a way as to shape civilizations. One of his more controversial views got him in serious trouble with church officials; he asserted the doctrine of universal reconciliation, i.e., all souls will eventually achieve salvation.[215] Yes, hell would be emptied by the end of the world through the mercy of God, according to Origen.

He claimed to be a strict pacifist and argued that Christians should not serve in the Roman empire's army. This principle was followed in the early church for quite some time according to Gibbon,[216] but as more and more soldiers converted to Christianity, church officials developed principles that allowed for military service (just war theory). This proved to be a major change for leaders in the early church and shows their willingness to adapt to new cultural norms. In his many works on theology, which we have only in fragmentary form, Origen rightly distinguished between "dogmata" (church teaching which had to be maintained) and "problemata" (theological issues that needed to be discussed and resolved). Unfortunately, over the years such distinctions tended to be blurred by warring factions in the church. He felt that he needed to be a Greek thinker, a Hellenist, to win young pagans to Christianity. Like his predecessor, Clement of Alexandria, Origen was living proof that some of the teachings of the Greeks could find a home in the church Christ founded. Augustine vigorously opposed Origen's notion of universal reconciliation, and later, at the Council of Constantinople (543), Origen's universalist teaching was condemned by church leaders.[217] It was difficult for the early church to find a proper solution to the many problems Christians encountered. They needed prayer, discussion and sound leadership to resolve the many difficulties that arose.

Summary and Conclusions (Chapters 8 and 9):

28. Christians read their scriptures at liturgies by the middle of the first century.

29. The final NT canon of 27 books was set in the late fourth century.

30. The early church showed compassion for those who submitted to Roman pressure and worshipped pagan gods. The bishop of Rome showed a willingness to forgive.

CHAPTER TEN:

THE WILL OF CONSTANTINE

In hoc signo vinces (In this sign you shall conquer) [218]

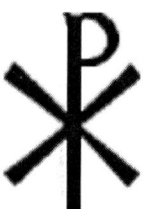

As we study the human condition over time, there are few periods in history that can be called turning points or epoch-making events. Some label these occasions paradigm shifts or new models of thinking and acting. For Roman Catholics the Second Vatican Council (1962-65) qualified as that kind of event.[219] The influence of Martin Luther and the subsequent Protestant Reformation constituted a new era of thinking and believing as well; the Augustinian Monk from Germany helped to revolutionize the Christian church and the world of his time. Another such epoch-making event was the encounter of Constantine with the Christian church; the Age of Constantine (306-337) was a turning point in history. James Carroll calls it the second most important story in the history of Christianity—the first, of course, was the birth of Christ.

Figure 8. The Emperor Constantine

After enduring the savage persecution of Diocletian which began in 303, the suffering church probably expected more of the same in the future. Little did they know that a young Roman soldier named Constantine would come to their rescue and advance the cause of Christianity as well as solidify his warrior aspirations to be emperor. After the death of his father, Constantius in 306, the Roman soldiers stationed in Gaul (France) declared they wanted the young man, Constantine, about 30-years-old, to be Emperor. The future ruler of the whole empire bided his time and finally in 312 he crossed the Alps with his troops. His goal was to capture Rome and become the new emperor in the West. The one man who stood in his way was his hated rival Maxentius. As they prepared for the decisive battle of their lives, each man would have turned to the many pagan gods for help, particularly Mars, the god of war, and Apollo, the Sun God. The two soldiers probably offered the customary sacrifice, and prayed that victory would be in the offing. In a mysterious revelation before he was to encounter Maxentius in battle, Constantine saw a white cross in the heavens near the sun (the Chi Rho symbol, see p. 122 above) and heard the words "In Hoc Signo Vinces" (In this sign you will conquer). Convinced that he would win through the intercession of the Christian God, Constantine prayed for victory. With the cross on their shields,[220] Constantine's inferior forces proved victorious.[221] At a decisive point in the struggle for Rome, the two leaders met at Milvian Bridge in 312. Constantine crushed the opposition handily, and during the heat of battle Maxentius was thrown into the Tiber and drowned. Soon after, Constantine was proclaimed the Roman emperor, the Augustus of the West. Apparently, the God of the Christians hears the prayers of the unwashed, since at this time Constantine was not yet a baptized Christian. He undoubtedly had some acquaintance with the Christian religion since his half sister, Anastasia, was a devoted follower of Jesus. He eventually converted to Christianity but delayed his baptism until he was on his deathbed. Augustine's father also took this belated path to salvation and thus we see another example of diversity in the early church. In a strange quirk of human reasoning some Christian writers at the time called Socrates and Plato "Christians before Christ." This saying was a forerunner of Karl Rahner's famous concept, the anonymous Christian.[222] In short, pagans played important roles in the epic struggle of Christianity for survival. They were apparently members of the church in some way, even though they had not experienced the saving waters of baptism.

A point often forgotten when discussing the conversion of Constantine, is his devotion to the cross. His mother, Helena, set out to find the true cross in the Holy Lands and some argue she was successful in her quest. But one must recall, as Carroll points out, that before the 4th century, the symbol of the cross was not a popular image for the Christian church.[223] Jesus was hung on a tree; there was a sense of shame in recalling His horrible death. Symbols found in the catacombs prior to the 4th century included the palm branch, a dove, the fish, but the cross is rarely found. Constantine changed all of this since he and his soldiers were convinced that victory at the Milvian Bridge was the result of the Christian God; the cross became the symbol of power. Both the Cross and the Creed would be a unifying theme in the age of Constantine and thereafter.

Instead of becoming drunk with his own power and success, Constantine concluded that what he had accomplished at the Milvian bridge was due to 1) the power of the Christian God 2) and the superiority of the Christian religion. He would use this new religion to promote his political ends and the beliefs of his soldiers. The emperor's new way of thinking had tremendous consequences for the early church. Religious freedom for all was declared by the Edict of Toleration in 313. Yet this magnanimous gesture did not last long. By special edict in 315 he imposed restrictions on the Jews, namely, that they could not proselytize. After his 324 A.D. victory over Licinius, leader of the Eastern region of the empire, Constantine controlled the entire Roman Empire, both East and West. No social change for a large segment of humanity—the Christian people—had ever been so quick and decisive. The notion of Christian martyrs in the Roman empire was to become a thing of the past. Christian ministers were exempt from Roman taxes. The hated punishment of crucifixion was abolished. In 321, Sunday—the first day of the week—was declared a public holiday. There would be no required labor on that day. This was a time of prayer for the empire and a day of rest. Note his special deference to the Sun god in granting a public day of rest on SUNday. Christians did not object. They selected the feast of the birth of Jesus around the winter solstice: December 25th. It is customary to build churches so that the altar is facing the East, the direction of the rising sun. Thus, Christians celebrate the Eucharist and other religious functions facing eastward. Lastly, Constantine ordered the construction of new churches and the empire helped pay for these buildings. He ordered the construction of the Lateran Basilica and donated numerous gold vessels for its sanctuary. With the help of archaeology we can affirm the authenticity of several references in Eusebius' **Life of Constantine** that this emperor was a major church builder. The church of the Holy Sepulchre, dedicated in 335 A.D., represents a major symbol of how the imperial church was linked to the power structure of the empire. Armstrong, reminds us, however, that the "emperors were not, of course, the only builders at work; buildings of private donors and those erected by bishops from local resources were not unimportant...but they seem to follow rather than to set the pattern."[224]

Constantine, the church builder, also saw to it that his own children were brought up in the Christian faith. All this growth in the Christian community took place in a mere decade. Spiritual men and women saw this as a great intervention of God in the lives of men; He had changed the hearts of pagans and given the church a new, secure place in history. Many call this the time of the imperial church. Some argue, however, that not all the consequences of becoming the favored religion were positive for Christianity; lax practices occurred especially among the clergy, as we will see when studying Jerome and Augustine. It was only later under Emperor Theodosius that Christianity became the state religion.

Those who subscribe to the "great man of history" theory (G. Hegel, Thomas Carlyle) would see the new emperor acting to bolster his hold on the empire's resources and solidifying his control over his subjects. Christianity would serve his political ends. Either way, the Church was transformed in the process, and its place in society and the world was dramatically changed.

With Christianity now the favored religion of the realm, its spirit and doctrines began to infuse public life. The large number of people joining the church, however, became a source of considerable tension. Whereas the persecuted church had previously consisted mostly of convinced believers, now the people of God were overwhelmed with large numbers of half-hearted converts who wanted to be part of the latest religious movement. They saw that it was in their best interests to join Christianity and become a part of the emperor's new program for the then civilized world: the new religion of the empire was Christianity and the new center of the empire would be Constantinople, the "New Rome." Rome would no longer be the center of life and culture, according to Constantine, but rather the East would become famous and the port of Byzantium would now become Constantinople. The shift impacted the lives of Christians throughout the empire.

A strange arrangement between the new emperor and the Christian church began to unfold. The man who had become convinced about the importance of the Christian religion on the battlefield was not yet baptized, but he was telling the Christian bishops what to do. He referred to himself as the "bishop of external affairs."[225] Church officials seemed willing to go along with these arrangements as long as the emperor did not interfere with the internal affairs of the Christian faith. He did, however, and they bit their tongues. The emperor's intrusion into church affairs became clear when Constantine called the council of Nicaea in 325 A.D. He saw himself as someone anointed by God to lead the empire and the church. This meeting is considered one of the great councils in the first millennium of Christianity. The place of the meeting was the summer home of the emperor, now modern-day Turkey. All the bishops of the empire were invited, but Sylvester, Bishop of Rome (314-335), declined to participate because of his advanced age and poor health. The absence of the bishop of Rome was duly noted by church observers. As stated in Acts (15:6-9), the Apostle Peter did attend the council of Jerusalem in 49 A.D. and contributed mightily to its outcome. However, Sylvester decided to send two presbyters to represent him at Nicaea; they were given no special precedence at the council.[226] The council and its members apparently showed no special deference to the representatives of the bishop of Rome. The pope was by no means elevated to the status of Pontifex Maximus for the empire as yet. That would come later. But with its improved social status, Christianity and its members had more time and freedom to think as well as to discuss the theological issues of the day; they began to speculate about the truths of their faith. Previously Origen had laid down some of the basic principles of theological inquiry, and now with leisure time to reflect on religious issues, Christian leaders could argue about the doctrines of their faith.

What better place to start than with the Trinity: three persons, one God. But what exactly sparked the call for a council?

Heresy seems to be one of the main reasons for calling this council. An elderly cleric named Arius, Bishop of Nicomedia, challenged the Christian church in 318 to a theological debate regarding the nature of God. He held that the Word (Logos) who became flesh in Jesus was not equal to God the Father. Christ was not a true deity but rather a half-God and a lesser being; He was not equal to the eternal Creator. Moreover, the Word was created; the Son had a beginning, but God the Father was without beginning, according to Arius. This message had considerable appeal to some pagan converts and Eastern bishops, but Arius' notion of Jesus as divine hero, unequal to God the Father, was met with swift opposition from the church in Alexandria and other regions of the empire. Bishop Alexander of Alexandria stated emphatically that Arius was in error, and so he and his fellow bishops called a synod to deal with this new conflict in the church. Constantine was upset with all this quarreling in his empire; he wanted to bind the empire together; consensus and solidarity were his top priority. The emperor abhorred conflict. The synod of Alexandria, which was called in 320, condemned the teaching of Arius who was promptly excommunicated. The problem was not easily resolved, and if we are to believe the writers of the time, rioting in the streets broke out on numerous occasions because of this contentious theological issue! After a long period of repression and persecution (inter arma silent musae, "in time of war the poets are silent"), the quest for theological truth began to influence the lives of many Christians. Some of the debates were fierce, and not even the bishop of Rome could bring order to this chaos. Thus, Constantine saw that he must intervene in the affairs of the church: he called its first Ecumenical council. In 325 he invited all the bishops in the civilized world to join him at the council of Nicaea. They were his guests and he paid for all their expenses. Rather than division, he wanted agreement on important social and religious matters. Peace was his ultimate goal. Once the council convened, the emperor withdrew and let the bishops conduct their theological investigation. The result, among other things, was the writing and proclamation of the Nicene Creed which most Christians affirm today. The key dispute regarding the nature of the Son was resolved by the early church fathers: Jesus was "true God of true God, begotten not made, of one substance with the Father." An English translation of the Nicene Creed is found below:

We believe in one God,
the Father, the Almighty,
maker of heaven and earth,
of all that is, seen and unseen.

We believe in one Lord, Jesus Christ,
the only son of God,
eternally begotten of the Father,
God from God, Light from Light,
true God from true God,
begotten, not made,
of one being with the Father.
Through him all things were made.
For us and for our salvation
he came down from heaven:
by the power of the Holy Spirit
he became incarnate from the Virgin Mary,
and was made man.
For our sake he was crucified under Pontius Pilate;
he suffered death and was buried.
On the third day he rose again
in accordance with the Scriptures;
he ascended into heaven
and is seated at the right hand of the Father.
He will come again in glory
to judge the living and the dead,
and his kingdom will have no end.

We believe in the Holy Spirit, the Lord, the giver of life,
who proceeds from the Father [and the Son].[227]
With the Father and the Son
he is worshipped and glorified.
He has spoken through the Prophets.
We believe in one holy catholic and apostolic Church.
We acknowledge one baptism for the forgiveness of sins.
We look for the resurrection of the dead, and the life of the
World to come. Amen.

The Nicene Creed is considered so important that many churches recite it every Sunday at their liturgies. The council statement clearly affirms that 1) the Son is not created; 2) He is the only begotten Son; he is eternally begotten. The Son is eternal (contra Arius). Both the Father and the Son are co-eternal. 3) The Son is from the same substance as God the Father and hence equal to the Father.

Just as the Apostles' Creed was formulated to counteract the Gnostic heresies, this creed was aimed at the teachings of Arius, the bishop who claimed that Jesus was not equal to the Father. It is clear from the notes of the council that 218 of the 220 bishops accepted the new creed; the 2 bishops who refused to agree with the creed, together with Arius, were sent into exile. Heretics were not put to death at the time but their dissent would become a problem in the empire, and thus they were not welcome. Free speech was still a long way off for this segment of the ancient world.

The Council of Nicaea, the Church's first ecumenical[228] council, was a perplexing social event in Christian church history. First, it was called by a layman, Constantine, who supported the Christian faith but was yet to be baptized in its saving waters. Second, all the bishops of the empire were invited to oppose the enemy of the church—Arius—but the bishop of Rome (Sylvester) was not in attendance. Some of the most important doctrinal issues of the day were decided at this ecumenical council, and yet the bishop of Rome had little or no personal input. He was not a teacher at the council. His absence was not a strong argument for the primacy of the bishop of Rome at this time. Primacy means, to some degree, that one is present in time of need and providing essential leadership for the problems of the day. Pope Sylvester was at best an absentee landlord. Later on, he did approve the declarations of the council.

But strongly held ideas are not easily overcome by the pen of ecclesiastical emissaries, nor through the emperor's edict to exile dissidents. We ought to recall the council of Jerusalem where the circumcision party would not give up. Arius and his followers kept the ideas of Arianism alive for some time after Nicaea. Athanasius, who later succeeded the aging bishop Alexander in the East, had to deal with Arianism for many years after the council. Christians had been trying for some time to answer the question: what constituted truly orthodox Trinitarian belief. The answer was not easily formulated and numerous challenges to the truths of Christianity became evident. Later on at the Council of Constantinople, in 381, the early church gave its definitive condemnation of Arius and all of his followers.[229] The fundamental doctrines of the Christian faith had to be stated again and again for those who refused to be taught. With over a half-century of wrangling about the Triune God and the role of the Son in redemption, it is not surprising that the status of Mary, the Mother of Jesus, would cause controversy with some early theologians. Nestorius of Antioch stated that he could not accept the concept of Mary as "God-bearer, Mother of God."[230] He and his followers could not reconcile the divine and human nature of Christ and thus they asserted that the divinity of Christ was not involved in the human activity of Christ, e.g., His birth, much less his brutal suffering and death. In short, the Nestorian heresy argued that the divine nature could not be born of a woman. Mary could not be called the God-bearer. Various scholars note that Nestorius was not only hard to get along with as a person, but it appeared abhorrent to him and his followers that a woman could have been given such an exalted role in God's plan (not shared with any male). She gave birth to the divine being with no help from a man. Little was made of his sexist views at the Council of Ephesus (431), but his theological ideas were debated and condemned. He was rejected, like Arius, as unfit for membership in the orthodox Christian church.

The 4th century was a significant growth period for the Christian church. Despite Julian the apostate's attempt to restore paganism as the state religion in 361, his short reign as emperor did not alter the fundamental thrust of Christian leaders: spread the Gospel to the ends of the earth. By the end of the 4th century the majority of the empire was still non-Christian.[231]

Change is clearly a hallmark of the early church, and there was one obvious way the people of God chose to solve problems: bring the church leaders (clergy and laity) together, discuss problems openly, and make a group decision to lead the church in an orthodox direction. But as we will soon observe, not everyone saw the growing transformation of the church as a good thing; reform was needed.

CHAPTER ELEVEN:

EARLY MONASTIC LIFE:

CHRISTIAN CALL FOR REFORM

> "In those days John the Baptist came, preaching in the desert of Judea... John's clothes were made of camel's hair, and he had a leather belt around his waist. His food was locusts and wild honey."
> (Matt 3:1ff)

To the people who lived in and around the desert of Judea, John the Baptist was known for his austere way of life. His clothes were made of camel's hair and he ate locusts and wild honey (Matt 3:4). Penance, prayer, and preaching were the hallmark of his lifestyle and ministry. For a brief time he may have joined the desert community of the Essenes (a group that had withdrawn in protest to the Judean wilderness to live a more intense religious life). He differed from them, however, by his itinerant preaching and a call for repentance in the holy waters of the Jordan.

Established ca. 150 B.C., the Essene community prayed and lived separately from the secular activities of the empire in order to prepare for the end time.[232] Roland de Vaux maintains that the Dead Sea scrolls (Qumran) were a product of the Essene community, and that they give us an insight into the austere life of the Baptist.[233] Establishing a celibate male Jewish monastic group was atypical of the Hebrew biblical tradition, but the fact that sects like this emerged throughout ancient history illustrates the great diversity of religious thought and practice despite age-old customs. There is some evidence that a small number of the Essenes were married. "Marriage was permitted but due to the doctrine of holiness which they [Essenes] espoused, many men refrained from marriage...."[234] This pre-Christian monastic movement was preceded in time by the Hindu spiritual communities that wrote the **Upanishads** (means "sit down near") around 700 B.C. The Upanishad writings originated in India and mark the first evidence of monastic communities searching for spiritual enlightenment and wisdom separate from worldly activities. After a radical conversion (awakening), Buddha founded monasteries for both men and women; he lived as a mendicant until his death in 478 B.C.E. at age 80. Many non-Christians dedicated their lives to asceticism long before the time of Jesus.

The early Christian monasteries were founded much later by men and women with apparently little or no interest in the social and political issues of the time. Their goal was to build an informal monastic community, study the scriptures and prepare for the coming of the kingdom. For them the end was near. The Essenes studied the Hebrew bible and developed an intense spiritual life; they influenced John the Baptist who said: "I am the voice of one crying in the wilderness: 'Make ready the way of the Lord, make straight his paths'" (Jn 1:23).[235] Through prayer and penance he received special knowledge about God's plan for the world. He told travelers passing along the banks of the Jordan River about the need for repentance. He baptized many with a baptism of repentance, and even Jesus decided to take part in the ritual—despite the fact that He had no need of repentance, according to most Christian teachings.

Toward the end of the 3rd century, a small group of Christians saw the need to return to the insights of the Baptist and rediscover the life of penance and sacrifice for the kingdom; thus a select few withdrew from worldly concerns in order to live a more intense spiritual life. The role model was Jesus and his 40 days in the desert. One of the first to explore these new and uncharted waters of Christian living was Anthony of Egypt. Born in 251 A.D., he became the founder of

Christian monasticism,[236] according to some authors. Others argue that Paul the Hermit was the first Christian known to embrace the life of a monk. Mircea Eliade calls the work of Anthony an "innovation" which had major consequences for the religious, cultural and social life for centuries.[237] Two elements characterized the monastic movement for Anthony: separation from the world and extreme asceticism. The concepts of poverty and chastity were a part of this movement as well. Pachomius and Basil the Great saw the need for obedience to live an effective religious community life. The monks were anti-cultural and historian David Knowles[238] gives several reasons why Christian monasticism arose: 1) changes brought to the church by Constantine; 2) the church and its leaders had become wealthy and worldly; 3) Christianity was accepted as the main Roman religion and no longer could claim to be a small dedicated group of committed believers; 4) the monks concluded they would be the nucleus of the dedicated.

Born in Egypt to wealthy landowners, Anthony took charge of his parents' estate after both had died when he was 18 years old; he worked hard to continue his family's high status in the community. Yet, his reading of the Gospels in his mid-thirties led him to sell or give away most of his wealth and take up residence in the desert as a Christian hermit. He lived a harsh life in the desert west of Alexandria for about 10 years and survived on food brought to him by Christian villagers. He was alone but not forgotten. The emperor Constantine wrote him at least one letter and praised the monk's good works and the wisdom contained in his epistles; the converted soldier who hailed the Christian religion asked the monk for prayers. After being encouraged by his fellow monks, Anthony wrote back to the emperor and assured him of his prayers and blessings. At age 45 he rededicated himself to prayer and fasting at an old abandoned fort for the next 20 years.

Around 310 A.D. he left the solitude he had found in an abandoned Roman fort where he had lived alone for two decades and traveled to various cities, including Alexandria. After visiting those in prison and assisting the city's poor he gathered a group of disciples who wanted to follow his example; the concept of communal monastic life began to unfold for him. In 320 he established his first monastery in the desert and encouraged his followers with the twofold mantra of "pray and work"; this simple dictum was used to organize this band of brothers to dedicate their lives to living the Gospel. Many people from the surrounding area came to him and his disciples for spiritual enlightenment. Chadwick makes this clear when he states that the "desert fathers in Egypt in the second half of the fourth century were constantly visited by individuals who used to ask according to the regular formula: 'Speak to me a word, father, that I may live.'"[239]

The theology behind this practice is simple. Just as the bishop and other leaders in the empire were expected to be advocates for the people when they were in trouble with the police, etc., the monk was to be the peoples' patron in the celestial sphere.

Anthony's disciple Macarius created a proto-monastery of sorts that provided members with cells or huts to live in separately, while joining together for common activities such as prayer and meals when the need arose. This began the transition from hermit (Anthony) to monk (Pachomius, Basil).

St. Pachomius learned of the work of Anthony and followed the example of the desert Father. While being held by the Roman army for training and possible military service, Pachomius was given food and support by local Christians who visited him and others at the Roman soldiers' quarters. These acts of charity impressed him so much that after escaping from his military duties, he converted to Christianity. More of an organizer than Anthony, he built his first monastery ca. 323 and at his death had established 9 monasteries for about 3,000 men who wanted to live an ascetic life of prayer, penance, and manual labor. Within one generation after his death, over 1,000 monasteries dotted Egypt from north to south. The fact that he refused to be ordained a priest, did not stop him from spending part of his monastic life defending the orthodox church from Arianism. Some bishops voiced their displeasure with some monastic tendencies, namely, indifference to secular society and civilization as well as their failure to participate in the normal prayer life of the church (sacraments). These issues would be resolved by the time of Augustine when religious orders had their own ordained priests to service their communities. Moreover, Basil the Great (d. 379) was known for his epoch-making teaching which asserted the social purpose of the ascetic movement. He wanted his monks to attend to the Gospel's demand for love and service to one's neighbor.[240]

These ascetics from Egypt came to the conclusion that the church had become corrupt and needed a new direction and reform. Later on in this series on church history we will study the life of St. Francis (d. 1226) and find that he too worked for church reform through personal prayer and service to the poor.

St. Anthony labored in Egypt to establish a new way of life for Christians which meant leaving the world and the worldly church. It is hard to imagine that after just two centuries, Jesus' followers had moved so far away from the solid traditions of the founder, that a major reform was being proposed, at least according to some religious observers. Anthony wanted to save his own soul and anyone else's who was willing to follow him in his native Egypt. He and like-minded people followed the vows of poverty, chastity and obedience; this new monastic view distinguished between lower and higher morality. By giving up sex, marriage, and worldly possessions, one chose the higher moral plane of Jesus and John the Baptist, according to the desert fathers. Their goal was personal: live a holy life and follow Christ (Messiah). They had only a modest interest in reform issues within the church and society. Anthony's letter to Constantine and 7 other epistles give us a glimpse concerning the need for church reform. Monks would reform the church through their good example and prayers.

Later on St. Jerome followed this same monastic tradition as did Augustine of Hippo (North Africa) in the late 4th century. Thus we have monasticism in the East and West by 400 A.D. There is no evidence that the bishop of Rome sought to control or supervise these religious movements. Pope Damasus (366-384) utilized the skills of Jerome (he was a member of the pope's staff) for a time and certainly was aware of these religious practices. Such innovative men and some women were allowed to live out their religious convictions and help the institutional church when called upon to do so. From time to time St. Jerome criticized the clergy of his time who failed to live up to their calling. His commentary on certain deacons and priests pulls no punches: "They think about dressing well....Their boots must be perfect and they use curlers in their hair; their fingers sparkle with rings...."[241] Such behavior in Jerome's eyes showed considerable degeneration of true ecclesiastical ideals. Chadwick agrees that there was a problem; he states that in "worldly terms of status and social influence, the episcopate of even moderately important cities had become an established career to which a man might aspire for reasons not exclusively religious."[242] The clerics were now middle/upper class and removed from the poor and lower classes. Hence we see some of the negative effects of Constantine's intervention, the creation of the Imperial Church, and the growing wealth of ecclesiastical officials.

Jerome showed no stomach for tackling the more difficult task of confronting papal corruption. Several years earlier Damasus had tacitly approved the use of violence to put down challenges to his claim to be bishop of Rome. In a street fight with rival Ursinus and his followers who demanded their candidate be declared pope, city officials recorded 137 deaths due to street brawls before order was finally restored.[243] Popes in the past have used or condoned violence to achieve their ends, and why not? Once they obtained the goal of becoming bishop of Rome, the rewards were enormous; they attended banquets even superior to the imperial table.[244]

Despite these failures work had to be done and so Pope Damasus urged Jerome to take on the Herculean task of translating the entire bible (old and new testament) into Latin. The old Latin version of the day was judged to be gravely inadequate. This enormous task was so monumental that it took over twenty years to complete (383-405). Today some religious authorities feel most comfortable in reading and studying the bible utilizing only St. Jerome's Vulgate.[245] Upon reviewing this new translation of the bible, St. Augustine said he did not like it; he had memorized many texts from the bible, and now he had to change. Using Jerome's vulgate can be dangerous since all the New Testament was certainly written in Greek and thus studying the bible (in English) using Jerome's Vulgate would be reading a translation of a translation—an English text not derived from the original Greek. Jerome translated the Old Testament from the Hebrew and his Latin version was considered a masterpiece for hundreds of years. Today for the English speaking Christian community, the New Revised Standard Version (NRSV) of the bible is considered "simply the best," according to John Crossan.

Martin of Tours (316-397) was another religious innovator with a keen interest in community life and the need to withdraw to rural settings to pray and work. He first joined the disciples of St. Hilary and later formed his own religious group near Tours, France (Gaul). He combined some ministry with his quest for a life of solitude and prayer. His spiritual reputation spread far and wide and soon he was asked to serve as Bishop of Tours, an offer he could not refuse.

Augustine and his followers lived a common life of prayer, study, and service in North Africa; his way of life was instrumental in founding the Augustinian religious order. Later on, in the 6th century, St. Benedict continued this monastic movement in the church and wrote a special rule of life for monks who followed his directives (Rule of St. Benedict). This was a time of other-worldly people and in their view the church was in need of change and reform. One answer to the church's spiritual decline was the growth of monasticism to preserve the pristine doctrine and practice of the founder, Jesus. It was through the work of holy monks, according to Peter Brown, that Christianity was transformed "into a religion of the masses."[246] Christianity received a needed boost from monastic reform.

CHAPTER TWELVE:

AUGUSTINE OF HIPPO

"For you have made us for yourself, and our heart is restless until it rests in you."
Confessions[247]

"Anyone who wants to understand the Catholic Church has to understand Augustine."
Hans Küng

The writings of Augustine are complex and extensive. This review of early Christianity can only touch on the most basic ideas of this intellectual giant, yet I try to give each topic a thorough analysis relative to its contribution to early Christian thought. Not everyone considers his body of work without its flaws, and so in this brief chapter I will attend to the controversial aspects of his work as well as his clear, positive contributions to the history of ideas.

The life of Augustine is really a story within a story; we try to tell the remarkable epic story of how Christianity succeeded against all odds. At the same time, the life of Augustine is so prominent in the history of the new church that his personal experiences show how, through his efforts, the church moved forward, warts and all.

Early Years

The son of Monica and Patricius (Patrick) was one of the great religious thinkers in the early church. Augustine's early life was probably typical of a young man from a working class family in North Africa.[248] Due to his parents' sacrifices and assistance from patrons he became a well educated man from a rural outpost of the Roman empire. Later on, he developed into a successful scholar and professor of rhetoric in Milan. His father was a nonbeliever who was finally baptized a Christian on his deathbed. Patrick married the future St. Monica but neither of them were very educated. He held a minor local office (decurion), and some authors think that Monica was illiterate.[249] Augustine was born near the city of Thagaste, North Africa (present day Algeria), in 354 A.D.; he probably had one brother and two sisters. The family lived in a fertile farming area called the "granary of Rome." His life as a young man was, by his own admission, rather wild and hedonistic. He ran with street gangs at night, and he stubbornly refused to study Greek despite the punishments meted out by his father and paid tutors. Augustine's bias toward Latin narrowed his vision of the world and limited his scholarly reading list to Latin authors. Latin was his language of choice and he loved to read Virgil's **Aeneid** as well as the works of Cicero. In his **Confessions** we find Augustine in praise of Cicero's **Hortentius**: "It gave me different values and priorities.... I longed for the immortality of wisdom with an incredible ardor of the heart."[250] Whether one agrees with the writers who claim he was obsessed with sex or not, it is clear that in his youth he was taken up with sexual pleasures and some excesses like many young men his age. He had a child out of wedlock when he was about 17-years-of-age and lived with the mother of his son (Adeodatus) for about 15 years. He was faithful to this woman for all those years, but he never mentions her name in any of his writings. He tells us that he did not know real love, but just "the love of loving." The young woman was probably a Catholic from his home town of Thagaste, but Augustine at this time was not baptized and did not practice the Catholic faith to any appreciable degree. He did show signs of being interested in religion, though, by occasionally attending Easter Services. The couple never entered into a formal marriage. Chadwick rightly points out that cohabitation by persons not legally married was no bar to communion in the early church provided they "kept wholly faithful to one another."[251] This provision would have applied to the mother of Adeodatus, who was a Catholic, but the ruling was irrelevant for Augustine who was not yet baptized and hence probably did not follow Christian norms or practices (communion). The point is important though when we consider the fact that the young couple probably lived with Monica for several years, and as a Christian, she could not have allowed them to live in sin while eating at her table. She also was worried about living with her son who followed the teachings of Mani, a heretic. Her concerns were with family and the church; she was able to resolve whatever religious conflicts she perceived and enjoyed the company of her grandson.

Augustine's only child was named "Adeodatus" (given by God, or Godsend), which was a common name for children in that region. By his own account the child was unwanted. It is clear that Augustine saw his actions at this time as a product of a pagan culture, but at a certain point, he embraced Christianity and entered the church under the direction of Bishop Ambrose. Because of his family's limited resources he had to find a patron who would support his advanced educational program. A wealthy man in his home town of Thagaste named Romanian, gave him the money needed to complete his education. Augustine in turn became a tutor to the man's sons but not his daughters—young girls were not given a formal education in ancient times. The new patron was a member of the Manichean sect and for about 9 years until age 28, Augustine followed the principles of Mani (d. 276), the group's founder. Manicheism taught, among other things, that matter is evil and detachment from the body was a prerequisite for true philosophical enlightenment. As a branch of Gnosticism, this school of religious thought maintained that life on earth was a constant war of good and evil; as a religious offshoot of Christianity, they embraced the dualism of mind and body. The spirit we have is good but the physical aspect of the world and body are evil. The solution to this bi-polar cosmology is to seek the spiritual world through abstinence: shun riches, reject sexual pleasure, avoid wine, meat, etc. Manichaeism took a spiritualistic view of Jesus who, they said, lived on a non-material level; he never really experienced the pain and suffering of the cross. He was never truly in the physical realm. Many argue that even after his conversion Augustine still held on to some of the dictates of Mani and managed to bring some of these ideas with him when converting to Christianity. Evans maintains that Augustine found it almost impossible "to shake off [Manichaeism] after he became a Christian."[252] After following this religious tradition for about nine years, Augustine abandoned Mani but never totally repudiated all the doctrines of Manichaeism.

Rome, Milan

Augustine decided to leave his homeland with Adeodatus and his concubine in 383; they set sail for Rome without his mother's knowledge or permission to continue his intellectual career in a more challenging environment. Monica was very upset with his decision but could do little to reverse her son's quest for fame, fortune and a little independence. He did some teaching in Rome and with the help of friends attracted the attention of Symmachus, prefect of the City. This influential Roman official helped Augustine gain a position as professor of rhetoric in Milan. It is important to note that Augustine's voyage to Italy was the only major trip he took by boat in his entire life. After living in Italy for a few years, he returned to North Africa and never left his homeland, except for a few minor trips in the general region of Numidia. He died in the port city of Hippo at age 76. His culturally limited attitudes and behavior led to a very narrow and provincial mentality, and unlike Paul the Apostle who traveled extensively, Augustine saw no need to meet non-Romans, learn new languages and study diverse cultures. The eastern part of the empire (Greek speaking) was foreign to him.

After the death of his father, Patrick, which Augustine mentions only in passing, Monica joined the young couple's household in Milan where she began planning her son's future life as an up-and-coming Roman official. In many ways her actions resemble today's "stage mother" who tries to plan her son's/daughter's career whenever possible. She introduced her son to Bishop Ambrose who Augustine said was everything a bishop ought to be.[253] Monica tried to assist her son's career by arranging a marriage to a young Christian heiress, and subsequently, his mistress of 15 years was sent back to North Africa around 386. Apparently the mistress was from a lower class family, and Monica wanted her son to marry into a social class worthy of his newly achieved academic position. Such an arranged marriage would garner a handsome dowry and help promote Augustine's career. Many writers feel Augustine showed himself to be spineless in the treatment of his concubine of 15 years. He could have married the mother of his son, but chose not to. His whining that the "woman I lived with for so long was torn out of my side"[254] rings hollow since he chose to formally marry someone else. Who caused him the pain wherein Augustine claims his heart "was lacerated?" Apparently it was Monica. From the perspective of late 4th century Roman culture, however, we must be cautious about judging Augustine and his mother too harshly. There were strong taboos at the time about marrying below one's social position and Monica was probably following these social norms. Augustine was really from the lower class at first, but through education and hard work he achieved a much higher social status than his parents; his mistress did not personally share in that social mobility. Since he was not a practicing, baptized Christian, religious norms regarding human relationships seemed unimportant to him. What Augustine and his mother were looking for was a marriage to a wealthy heiress which would produce a large amount of money and make them wealthy. The money could advance his career in Roman society where everything of value had a price tag. The search paid off and Monica was able to find him a suitable fiancée. Nonetheless, because the girl had not yet reached the age of 12 (minimum marriage age under Roman law), Augustine had to wait some time before the marriage was finalized. In an impetuous move, he took a temporary mistress to hold him over until his formal, arranged marriage could take place. Between 386 and 387 Augustine became disenchanted with his lifestyle, reflected on the values of Christianity, and decided to become a baptized Christian. After a period of Lenten fasting and prayer, he was baptized. During this time Adeodatus, newly baptized as well, stayed in Milan with his father and grandmother, but life would soon change as the family was destined to return to North Africa.

Some writers claim Augustine "callously" separated from his legal concubine (today we would call her his common law wife) and began seeing another woman. He decided to take what has been called a stopgap mistress to serve his needs since his arranged marriage had been delayed. This period of his life showed his non-Christian values and immaturity as a man in his early thirties who had to kowtow to the whims of his stage mother. These were his pagan years. His mother was not yet "Saint Monica."

Figure 9. Augustine: "Take and read."

Gradually Augustine saw the folly of Manichaeism and tried to find a way of life that would bring him true happiness. The well-known story in his **Confessions** describes him in a garden when he hears a voice "Take and Read" (Latin: tolle et lege).[255] He opens a nearby bible to St. Paul and reads "Be clothed in the Lord Jesus Christ" (Rom 13:13). He saw this as a call to break from his old ways (selfishness) and build a new life as a Christian. Through the help of teachers working with Bishop Ambrose (Simplician and Theodore), Augustine began his preparation for baptism. He says in his **Confessions** that he had a great deal of trouble giving up sex but gradually was able to attain self control. It is clear that conversion to Christianity for him meant giving up sex and being celibate; this was to be his way to God. He broke off his relationship with his new mistress, canceled his arranged marriage and with his son, became a catechumen. His mother's 30 years of prayer had been answered. After a long retreat he was baptized at age 33 by Bishop Ambrose in 387. Soon after his baptism Monica died of a mysterious illness, but with his new found faith Augustine realized her soul was now in heaven; this belief provided some consolation for her loss. He would see her again in heaven. Adeodatus, deeply saddened by the death of his grandmother, joined Augustine as they returned to North Africa after spending several months in Rome.

Upon his return to Thagaste Augustine organized a quasi-monastic community of male friends, and together they tried to live the ideals of the Gospel for about three years. For him *amicitia* (friendship) was to be the basis of all Christian community. From this religious experience emerged the Augustinian Order (Rule of St. Augustine, 400). Through the good deeds of his religious community, he gradually became popular with local church leaders and just four years after his baptism he was ordained a priest. The process of selecting a man to become a priest was unique in his day. In 391 he was in the city of Hippo to talk to a young man about joining his newly formed religious group when he met the local bishop, Valerius. Previously, the aging prelate had spoken to his congregation of the need for a priest to assist him in his parish work. So when Augustine appeared in the church at Hippo, the congregation swept him forward to Valerius, entreating the bishop to ordain him a priest. Augustine yielded and was ordained. By 395 he was the Bishop of Hippo, succeeding the retired Valerius. Aside from the general responsibilities of church services, preaching, and administration he soon became embroiled in the conflict between Orthodox Catholics and the schismatic Donatists of North Africa.

Donatus and some of his followers were singled out for persecution by Diocletian (303-305) because of their radical religious reform program within the Catholic church.[256] They wanted to purify what they considered a lax Catholic church. Like the monks whom we studied earlier, they longed for serious church reform. This motivation was derived from their founder, Donatus, who died in exile ca. 355. Years later a certain bishop named Caecilianus was ordained by the local bishop Felix. Donatists claimed the ordination was invalid since the head bishop was a traitor, i.e., he had handed over the scriptures to the Diocletian persecutors. Donatists claimed that episcopal powers depended on the moral worthiness of the cleric and in their view Caecilian's ordination was invalid. Anyone who was associated with Caecilian and his ordaining bishops was to be shunned. Thus, a major schism arose in North Africa which lasted many decades. Donatus' followers continued his work of purification after his death—it was a crusade to change the church. They wanted only holy men and women in the church. In their view too many sinners and uninspiring priests and bishops were involved in church activities. They were particularly appalled by weak Christians who agreed to hand over the sacred texts to Roman officials to be burned during various persecutions. They argued that these individuals could never be taken back into the church. Augustine and other leaders followed the Caecilianus[257] tradition and pushed for a more lenient approach to apostates. Imperial soldiers used force to suppress the Donatists in 347, and as a consequence they were put on the defensive; Caecilianus Catholics stood by and did not help them. By the time Augustine became bishop in 395, Donatists would no longer talk to Catholics; their bakers would not even sell bread to Catholics. This group of Christian purists stressed fanaticism and religious fundamentalism: their God had no use for sinners, and they had a low tolerance of human failings. The Donatists considered Catholics who followed in the Caecilianus tradition too lax because they tolerated, among other things, heavy drinkers and apostates—a sure sign they were not following the dictates of the Gospel. Augustine tried to approach Donatist leaders with the idea that Jesus called both saints and sinners to follow him; He forgave the failings of His apostles. The Bishop of Hippo used the scriptures to show that in Matthew 3:12 the wheat and weeds were allowed to grow together. Then on judgment day, God was going to determine who should be a part of his heavenly kingdom. Here we see the compassionate Augustine and a church willing to compromise. They were not rigorists; Augustine and others were centrists on this point while showing a distaste for radical hardliners. Such actions did not sit well with Donatists, and so they continued to shun Catholics.

To resolve this issue, Flavius Marcellinus, the Imperial Commissioner and a Catholic, called for a hearing to be held in Carthage, 410 A.D. This dispute had to be resolved because it was disturbing the peace of the empire. Note the famous saying: order in Rome and peace in the provinces. The meeting would allow him to hear arguments about whether Donatists violated the heretic laws[258] and should therefore be punished. The hearing drew large numbers of clergy from both sides and thus demonstrated the extent of the controversy. Church documents show that 286 Catholic bishops participated, while a total of 284 Donatist bishops signed into the hearings. Some of the bishops were judged to be illiterate because they had signed the roster with an 'X'; they could neither read nor write.[259] After both sides presented their arguments, Marcellinus determined that the heretic laws applied in this case. 1) As heretics the Donatists lost all their churches; 2) they could not hold meetings; 3) they could be fined for not attending Catholic church services.[260] Later on, these sanctions proved difficult to enforce and gradually the schismatics came to realize that social order was a top priority for the Roman empire and this conflict was causing too many problems for the emperor. During the Donatist controversy intolerance was the norm and conflict was at a high pitch in the Christian church. The peace loving group that Jesus had founded, once again, failed to follow the master's directives.

After the Donatist trial, Augustine's work was now aimed at reconciliation, but that was not going to be an easy task. Some radical Donatists were so upset with Marcellinus' decision that they committed suicide.[261] One lesson often overlooked by historians is the contrast between Augustine and the Donatist leaders. Here we have a learned scholar, a great orator, a man of the century, trying to reach out and convince a rural group of reactionaries to listen to reason and hopefully resolve their religious differences. Not even one of the greatest scholars of antiquity and later a doctor of the church could get these people to change their ways. The human group is at times completely intransigent. Not even great people can reach the stubborn and confused. Hans Küng likes to use the term "people who refuse to be taught" and that line applies to the Donatists.

Use of Force

In his mature writings Augustine championed the will over the intellect and nowhere is this more evident than in his clash with the Donatists. He used the scriptures to deal with Donatist leaders, and he cites Luke (14:21ff) to support his approach to heretics and schismatics: the parable of the wedding feast. Raymond Brown points out that the Gospel of Thomas (apocrypha) has a somewhat different version of this parable of the king who holds a marriage feast. Nevertheless, many key points are the same.²⁶² When numerous guests refuse the king's invitation to come to his son's wedding feast, he tells his servants to go out to the highways and byways and "**compel** [emphasis mine] them to come to the banquet" (Lk 14:23).²⁶³ Augustine used this text (old Latin translation, not from St. Jerome Vulgate) to justify the idea that Donatists should be forced to come into his church and listen to his arguments. He will teach them the truths about God's kingdom and his forgiveness, but it will be done in the spirit of love. The bishop of Hippo thought that the major problem in this schism was false information and non-communication: let them hear the truth, was his motto. He thought dialogue would change their ways. He accepted some form of suppression and force but did not endorse extreme measures such as torture or execution. When one of his priests was murdered by radical Donatists and another maimed, Augustine did not seek revenge since he rejected the Old Testament notion of an "eye for an eye." Vengeance was not the answer for Augustine. But we know that when Rome fell in 410 to the Visigoth leader, Alaric, Augustine considered it wise to use force against heretics and barbarians. Garry Wills observes: "A need for new discipline and toughness was felt, to which Augustine would respond, showing a dark side of his teaching on the importance of the human will."²⁶⁴ It may be a bit unfair to say Augustine's commentary on St. Luke was an invitation for future generations to deal harshly with heretics and schismatics. Yet, many take the view that Augustine's questionable exegesis of this text ("compel them") has led, in part, to the theological justification of persecution. Hans Küng takes a dim view of Augustine's suppression theory:

> Thus down the centuries Augustine, who could speak so convincingly of the love of God and human love, indeed who defined God as 'love itself,' fatally became the key witness for the theological justification of forcible conversions, the Inquisition, and holy war against deviants of all kinds....²⁶⁵

Supporters of Augustine simply state that his words are taken out of context: he clearly opposed torture and capital punishment/execution. In future volumes we will see how Augustine was used and/or abused by later generations of so-called Christians to deal with heretics and deviants in the middle ages.

Sex and the City (of God)

When Augustine began writing one of his greatest works, **The City of God** (circa 413) he was in his late fifties and had already formulated many of his basic ideas about the human body and sexuality. We look at this development in two parts: his ideas before and after his conversion to Christianity.

Many writers acknowledge that in the late 4th century there was a distinct aversion to sex by some prominent scholars who were not even Christian. This sexual ethic was not based on any religious conviction. Marcus Aurelius, for example, made it clear that he renounced sex to advance his intellectual and philosophical career. The mind-body split was obvious in his writings and behavior. Garry Wills clearly points out that Sophocles was happy to have escaped sexual, erotic love "as one flees from a crazed and ruthless despot."[266] Both Cicero and the Manichean school felt that a life of continence was the only discipline for the true philosopher.[267] Origen, the great scripture scholar from the East, castrated himself in the hope that he could reduce his sexual urges. Yes, even smart people do dumb things. These men of letters would seem to agree that the "'brainstorm' of orgasm" blocked the mind's ascent to intellectual stardom and union with God.[268] While in Milan, before his conversion, Augustine saw the need to purify the mind and give up all sexual activity: he came under the influence of the Neo-Platonic school, particularly Plotinus, and the ideas concerning the mind/body split. Sex could not be a part of Augustine's new way of life.

Augustine assimilated some of these 4th century ideas and attitudes into his thinking before his conversion, but as a Christian he went one step further. He saw sex as a major source of sin, and he viewed the world and all humans as pulled down by Adam's original sin; the drive of concupiscence made it difficult for humans to elevate themselves to the higher spiritual plane. He is said to have moaned "nothing brings a man down like the caress of a woman."[269]

After his conversion women would not be a part of his life. Oil and water do not mix; women and the new Augustine did not seem to get along. His theology would later be called Christian misogyny. First, he considered women inferior to men.[270] Why was woman created by God? Augustine thinks that the only reason could be procreation.[271] He enjoyed the company of men over women: "How much more pleasure is it for life and conversation when two [male] friends live together than when a man and a woman cohabitate?"²⁷² Augustine pays no attention to the fact that women were not educated at the time and his common law wife and mother were probably illiterate. They had little to talk about according to the well-educated Augustine. Lastly, the Bishop of Hippo blamed Eve for the fall from grace, so women took a hit there as well. "The expulsion of Adam and Eve from paradise, according to him, was purely the fault of Eve. He taught that Satan, in the form of the serpent, tempted Eve because she was more gullible than Adam."²⁷³ It is this heritage of misogynist thinking—not Paul's baptismal equality—which was handed down to clergy, monks and women for a thousand years that is so troubling. As a doctor of the church, his views dominated the Christian landscape until Aquinas emerged in the 13th century. St. Thomas continued the theme that women were inferior to men, using texts from St. Paul (erroneously) and Aristotle to suggest that women are subject to men but equal.

Augustine took the view that the sexual impulse was all part of the curse bequeathed to all mankind because of Adam's fall.²⁷⁴ He writes that the sex act "throws a man's mind down from the tower."²⁷⁵ In his attempt to understand the nature of human existence he gave priority to the intellect for a time; the will was secondary. Later on, he reversed the ranking and placed the will first; it is the key faculty. It is, according to Augustine, man's will to love and care for others which distinguishes him from all other creatures. He held that this will to love and care for others was the bond of society. One could argue that he was a sociologist before sociology since he dealt with the key subject of the human group: solidarity. Without mutual caring the group cannot survive. Moreover, for Augustine, love is the definition of God (Deus est Caritas).²⁷⁶ Jesus' compassion for the widow of Naim is at the heart of Augustine's theology.

In short, the human being must will to be like God and love with all his heart—but she must try to avoid sex as much as possible. He preached this doctrine even to married couples: they were to show affection without having sex.²⁷⁷ In another place in his writings the bishop of Hippo presented the laity with this challenge: sex is to be engaged in only for the begetting of heirs.²⁷⁸ Thus, one can see that the legacy of Augustine is very different from that of Paul, the Apostle to the Gentiles, who always reminded the people of God that the body is a "temple of the Holy Spirit"(1 Cor. 3:16). It was not bad or evil. That would mean God's creation was in default even after redemption brought by the suffering, death, and resurrection of Christ. The sexual legacy of Augustine has been a problem for the Church for hundreds of years. Many theologians would like to forget this part of his theology and praise him for his overall superior insights regarding love and mercy. No one's perfect, but we cannot be cheer leaders for church bishops and bashful theologians. Augustine's twisted ideas about sex came from his pagan lifestyle as a young man, the Manichaean years, the culture of the times (neo-Platonic), his personal hang-ups, as well as the failure of colleagues to correct his inadequate theology. He was seen as the only theological giant until the time of Aquinas—some 800 years later. For hundreds of years Augustine was the only true theologian the church had to offer. Many used his ideas and arguments at the Second Lateran Council in 1139, to argue that priests who marry are not properly serving the church. This date marks the time when the Roman Catholic church requirement of celibacy was in full force. That would solve the church's sex problems once and for all, or so they thought. Of course, other factors entered into the Lateran's decision to require celibacy. But the move toward forced celibacy was one of the grave errors of the Roman Catholic Church, and the people of God have suffered from its effects for a thousand years. There is a saying in social science that is relevant here: situations that are defined as real, are real in their consequences.[279] When sex is defined as life on a lower plain, a distraction from priestly duties and to be avoided, then the consequences are going to be real and negative. Stay away from sex....run from it. Be a celibate. In the teachings of Augustine the body is not considered evil and sex can be tolerated, but this is an inadequate statement regarding Christian sexuality. Even though this conceptualization was flawed based on NT considerations, it became common doctrine for church leaders and had real negative consequences for later generations. Married people were viewed as a lesser kind of Christian. Those consequences weakened the church's teachings on marriage and the family for centuries. These new Lateran policies implied that priests were better off not marrying and fathering children.

Augustine and the Bishop of Rome

Augustine had dealings with several popes during his years as Bishop of Hippo. Wills tells us that "his dealings with the papacy would always be formal but distant."[280] He became a bishop in 397 while Siricius was Bishop of Rome (384-399); they knew each other and had a fairly cordial relationship. It is important to note that Siricius was the first Bishop of Rome to claim the title of "pope."[281] Before this, his title was simply the Bishop of Rome." The word "pope" comes from the Greek "pappas" and is a loving and honorific name for "father." In the East it was used by Christians to refer to their own bishop. Due to the new law passed by Siricius, we find that from the "end of the fifth century, the bishops of Rome claimed the term [pappas] exclusively for themselves."[282] Here we see yet another example of how the church in the West rode rough shod over the sensibilities and cultural practices of the Eastern churches. As if this were not enough, Siricius became the first pope to write "decretals" (letters with the force of law) to all the churches. He promulgated laws without broad consultation. In these letters he answers questions submitted by a certain bishop and thus informed all readers that he is responsible, as successor to Peter, for all the churches. Some feel the document reads like a letter from a man who thinks he is an absolute monarch.

Pope Innocent I, the son of Pope Anastasius I, likewise asserted the primacy of the Roman See during his 16 year reign (401-417). It is clear that there is a tradition of married popes whose sons were later elected bishop of Rome. Innocent I asked church leaders that all important matters be submitted to Rome for review, as did some of his predecessors. On the issue of the liturgy, Innocent I stressed that the Roman liturgical customs were to be normative for all Christians—another slap at the Eastern churches. The Roman ecclesiastical court was to be the last court of appeals in Christian disputes. Decades earlier, his predecessor, Julius (d. 352), asserted that Rome was the court of appeals for all major disputes. Now Innocent I proclaims it is the last court of appeals. This political posturing and boasting about Roman preeminence would soon be tested. It is not surprising that we find this sardonic comment by Augustine: "The Church extends throughout the world, Rome excepted."[283]

The teaching of the controversial Celtic monk named Pelagius led to one of many confrontations between Rome and the bishops of

North Africa. During Augustine's final years as bishop, church officials were busy trying to deal with doctrinal attacks which they felt were heretical and dangerous for church orthodoxy. The Pelagian teachings were a major source of controversy because of their stand on original sin. Holding to a strict doctrine of Stoicism and self control (followers exalted the power of the human will), Pelagius did not acknowledge the true effects of original sin, according to orthodox church leaders. Augustine came forward asserting the importance of Adam's original sin in condemning humanity and how his fall affected all mankind. Because of original sin (a term coined by Augustine) we all deserve eternal damnation, but through Christ and his divine grace we have been saved. The only good that man does is by the grace of God. Pelagius was not buying it; he denied the notion of original sin transmitted from one generation to another. He held that man commits sin by following the immoral example of others and through weakness of the will. For these theological errors and others, the African bishops had him excommunicated in 417. Augustine felt that Pelagius did not acknowledge the role of grace in performing good works, that is, the loving kindness of God poured into our hearts which leads us to do good. Pope Innocent I agreed and declared Pelagius and his disciples guilty of heresy. The case was closed—or so people thought.

With the death of Innocent I and the election of the new Pope, Zosimus (418), the fast talking and persuasive Pelagius was able to hoodwink the bishop of Rome into reopening the case against him. Upon further review, the pope stated that the African bishops had acted hastily, and that as far as he was concerned, Pelagius had cleared himself of all heresy. Rome was the last court of appeals, so it looked as if Pelagius had won his case.

The action by Zosimus infuriated the bishops of North Africa, including Augustine. Apparently at that time local bishops could confront the pope, just as Paul withstood Peter to his face(Gal. 2:11). At Carthage in 418 A.D. the bishops of Africa asserted that as far as they were concerned the censure and condemnation of Pelagius by them and Innocent I must stand. They stated that the current bishop of Rome, Zosimus, was in error! The African Bishops again condemned Pelagius and this forced Pope Zosimus to retreat from his previous position. He had no choice because an apparent schism was brewing and the pope was its cause.

Moreover, the African bishops went one step further. They contacted the Emperor Honorius who issued a rescript from Ravena condemning Pelagius and his followers. In essence the Emperor told everyone that Pelagius was a heretic and that his actions were disturbing the peace of the provinces. Thus the bishops of North Africa saved the church from heresy, corrected the pope, and fortunately persuaded Zosimus to see his error and back down. The pope issued his famous **Tractoria** and like other church leaders at the time, he finally condemned Pelagius and his teachings.[284] Dissent was alive and well in the early church, as bishops confronted erroneous papal policies. It was good for the people of God to assert their opinions and this helped save the church from grave error, namely, the Pelagian heresy. In Appendix B there is a contemporary case study dealing with a two-year confrontation between Pope Benedict XVI and various Cardinals and bishops. The Pope stated in 2005 that the Catholics cannot use condoms to prevent the spread of AIDS. His fellow bishops have asked the Pope to retract his statements and join them in advocating the use of condoms to prevent the spread of AIDS. At this writing the dispute has not been resolved. Will Pope Benedict issue a retraction similar to Zosimus? Time will tell.

After the Pelagius' conflict, perhaps both parties looked forward to a cooling off period and relative calm. That was not to be. The African church dealt decisively with one of its unruly priests named, Apiarius, who was excommunicated by his superior, Bishop Urban. In 419 Apiarius traveled to Rome to appeal his ouster to none other than Pope Zosimus who listened attentively to the priest's complaint. It seems that appeals to Rome in the 5th century were becoming commonplace. Thinking that the cleric may have been mistreated, the pope sent delegates to North Africa to investigate the matter. But in a hastily called council at Carthage (22 bishops attended) the major leaders of North Africa's church declared that the pope did not have jurisdiction in the case! The pope and his advisors countered that the Council of Nicaea gave the bishop of Rome jurisdiction over such matters. Augustine with other African bishops maintained that Nicaea gave him no such power. The case was eventually resolved when Apiarius repented of his sins and later was assigned to a new post. Thus, the so-called North African challenge to the supremacy of Rome never fully materialized in the Apiarius case. But in a few years the African bishops would find themselves embroiled in yet another dispute that would lead to a further confrontation with Rome.

As if these two controversies were not enough, Pope Celestine, elected in 422, had to rule on the legitimacy of an African bishop named Antonio, bishop of Fussala. Although highly thought of by Augustine at one point, Antonio was found guilty of "tyranny and violence" toward his flock and therefore Augustine wanted him removed. The North African synod agreed with Augustine and deposed the prelate. Bishop Antonio, like some of his predecessors, traveled to Rome and presented an appeal to Pope Boniface in 421. The sickly pope apparently restored him to his post, but soon after this decision Boniface died. The new pope, Celestine, who was a friend of Augustine, agreed to review the case and ultimately sided with the African bishops that Antonio should be deposed. These confrontations help us see that local bishops held strong views even when they came in conflict with the bishop of Rome. They did not back down. True, at this time, Rome claimed to be the last court of appeals, but strong words and confrontational actions often arose between the pope and local bishops who challenged papal decisions. They said he lacked jurisdiction in some cases! Boniface was hoodwinked! Recall St. Paul's words: he opposed Peter to his face (Gal 2:11). The above conflicts seem to have led to a satisfactory outcome. It is clear that there is nothing in the writings of Augustine that speak to the issue of Petrine primacy. The question of papal primacy never really arose during the time of Augustine.[285] In short, it was not the bishop of Rome, but rather the Ecumenical Council, that had supreme authority in the church, according to Augustine. We will see later in the 14th century that this doctrine was labeled "conciliarism" and it would be beaten back by papal partisans. It is obvious that the notion of papal infallibility had no meaning at all in the early church. How could it…the bishops of Rome were constantly making mistakes while conducting the important business of the church. Fortunately, they were corrected and the church moved forward—warts and all.

Summary and Conclusions (Chapters 10, 11,12):

    31. Constantine helped the church develop as an organization; power and wealth had its good and bad points.

    32. The importance of the cross as a Christian symbol owes much to Helena and Constantine.

33. The monastic reforms of Anthony and others helped reform a worldly church; the common people had great respect for the new ascetic movements.

34. Paul, Constantine, and Augustine made the early church a dynamic force in the Roman Empire. Augustine's teachings had positive and negative effects on church development.

35. Augustine's views on sexuality and the use of force were used by later generations to harm others. Nonetheless, Augustine would never have approved the Crusades and the Inquisition.

CHAPTER THIRTEEN:
CONCLUSION

"There is no reconciliation without transformation."
Mark Gevisser, author of
Thabo Mbeki: The Dream Deferred

The epic story of how a small band of religious men and women grew the Jesus movement into a world religion is remarkable. First as a Jewish sect, and later, a mostly gentile church, this new religion took about 300 years to develop into the dominant religion of the Roman empire. Constantine used them to solidify his rule over an empire of 60 million people.

When books are written about early Christianity they tend to have two common themes: they try to focus on the unique message of Jesus' preaching and how his followers were transformed into effective disciples of the Good News. These final thoughts will pull together the prominent features of the new religion, Christianity, and how it was able to achieve some of the essential goals of the founder in a very hostile environment.

1. The public life of Jesus began with a small band of disciples drawn from a remote area in the Roman Empire around the Sea of Galilee. Jesus and his followers came from the lower social classes, and many

of his followers were uneducated. As a Jewish prophet, Jesus sought to reform the Jewish religious establishment of his time by teaching, confrontation, and compassion.

2. The preaching and marvelous works of Jesus had a profound impact on his followers. After his death and resurrection a large number of his followers—men and women—were greatly transformed and sought to convert others to Jesus' way of life. They lived their lives according to the Gospel's principles and spread the message of the Jesus movement to family and friends. They saw Christianity as a new way of living and acting. Jesus was a caring person and his compassion had an impact on their lives. With Jesus, they rejected the artificial and legalistic notion of the Pharisaic tradition that had taken hold of the contemporary Greco-Roman culture. Jesus' followers had a sense of religious empowerment: Jesus changed the law of Moses and proclaimed a new covenant; they would bring flexibility and change to the people they served as well. Women played an important role in the ministry of Jesus and Paul—a big change for this period in history.

3. The first committed followers of Jesus consisted of God-fearing Jews who came to the realization that He was the longed-for Messiah announced in the OT. Most Jews at the time rejected this notion and eventually excluded Christians from the synagogue.

4. St. Paul dramatically changed the direction of the Jesus movement soon after the death of Christ. As an educated Pharisee he fully understood the nature of Judaism and the unique contribution that Christianity made to the Roman Empire. As a convert and true apostle he took it upon himself to lead an uneducated group of Galilean peasants against all odds—and in so doing became the defining icon of the new religion. He saw to it that Christianity was open to Gentiles as well as Jews. Such a program was not without conflict and personal suffering. But it was the move to include gentiles that ultimately transformed the Jesus movement and allowed it to grow.

5. Paul's extensive travels led him to many parts of the Roman empire so that by 100 A.D. there were probably eight to ten thousand men and women following the principles of Christianity. It was in Antioch that the disciples were first called "Christians" (Acts 11:26). Church growth was enriched by religious women who were called apostles and deacons; they were leaders of various house-churches.

6. By the beginning of the 2nd century the Jesus movement had a set of sacred texts—the four Gospels and Paul's letters. They had by then expanded to about 8 to 10 thousand members and their principal rituals were baptism and the Lord's supper; many besides the apostles were designated to celebrate the Eucharist. Hymns were an important part of their prayer services as they met in house-churches(Phil 2:5).

7. Almost all of the major disciples of Jesus were killed by enemies of the new religion. The gospel message was a radical break from contemporary Jewish traditions and Christ (Messiah) was a threat to both religious and secular leaders. Numerous Christian martyrs helped to convince others to join this new religion and many pagans were baptized because of the strong faith and courage of these believers. Christians died; pagans converted and this demonstrated the truth of a modern paradox: addition by subtraction.

8. The Jesus movement understood that it was guided by the Spirit sent to them by the risen Christ (Messiah). Peter, James, John, Paul, and Mary of Magdala worked together to utilize every means possible to spread the truths of this new religion. Everyone had a task to perform. The first three decades after the death of Christ showed intense spiritual growth and commitment. The foundation was being laid. Women played a major role in the expansion of Christianity.

9. Because early Christians refused to worship the emperor, many died as martyrs. The Martyrology has recorded their names and many shrines were erected to memorialize such heroic bloodshed.

10. At first, the Jesus movement attracted mostly Jews to its new way of life. The Messiah came from an observant Jewish family and all his first disciples were converted Jews. Gradually gentiles became the dominant force in the Christian house-churches. With Melito of Sardis came the charge that Jews were guilty of "deicide"; a whole generation of Christian preachers attacked Jewish families and punished Jewish religious leaders. Antisemitism started early in the Christian church and continued for hundreds of years. Few spoke against this prejudice and hatred in the first few centuries of Christian development, certainly not the bishop of Rome.

11. Gnostic Christians were a religious force that the early church had to reckon with. There is a theory in religious research that states: first heresy, then orthodoxy. It is part of the age-old principle: thesis, antithesis, synthesis. Jesus' ideas shocked the world; people tried to

live his teachings. Various disputes arose about what Jesus said and did. What did Jesus want? Each age tried to solve these questions and move on. The Gnostics were the antithesis (deviance, heresy) that stirred early Christians' thinking about the nature of God, Jesus' role in redemption, and the continuing debate about spirit and matter. Gnostics made the Apostolic church think about its beliefs and make sure it was on the right track. The result: creeds, synods, and councils helped formulate orthodox doctrine. The proposed solution was not always the right answer; so future generations had to reformulate ideas and develop better ways of thinking and doing. One thing seems abundantly clear: the conclusion of the Council of Jerusalem was the correct way to proceed. On the other hand, the notion that Jews were guilty of "deicide" was a terrible way to formulate what had happened at the crucifixion, and it took hundreds of years for the church to see the light on this problem. The suppression of Gnostic texts in the early church helped to resolve certain tensions, but the loss of this rich Christian tradition has hurt our appreciation of early Christianity and its diverse legacy.

12. Beginning with a solid oral tradition, the Jesus movement used house-churches to reflect on the words and deeds of the founder. Later on, the unique truths of Messiah were written down for future generations, namely, in the letters of Paul, the four Gospels, Acts and Revelation. We have the community of believers first and then the scriptures. This group of God-fearing people came to the conclusion that certain sacred texts were fundamental to Christianity and thus they created a NT canon of 27 books.

13. By avoiding extreme ideologies (rigorists, Donatists, circumcision party, etc.) the early church came to realize that it had power to forgive sin, lift the burden of guilt, and learn from Greek philosophers. By reading the signs of the times church leaders made changes as they saw fit because Christians understood they were given the power to build the church for each succeeding generation. Mistakes were made and subsequent believers had to correct errors so that the church could grow and prosper. They were not afraid to admit their mistakes and errors—even the pope had to retract his errors.

14. Constantine experienced a life-altering vision on the battlefield which convinced him of the importance of the Christian religion. Once he became head of the Roman empire—60 million people—he favored

the Christian religion, built some of their churches, and finally died a member of the new faith through a deathbed baptism. Christianity was now the Imperial Church. By this time the number of Christians had grown to at least 4 to 5 million.

15. Early Christian monasticism took hold because the church was in need of reform. Building on the insights of various pre-Christian movements, St. Anthony and others felt it was necessary to separate themselves from civic and church activities to live a more pure form of Christian witness. Augustine was unique in that he was active in church affairs all his priestly life, but looked to religious community for support in his apostolic endeavors. Celibacy was central to the monastic way of life during these early reforms.

16. Augustine was one of the greatest thinkers of all time. He wrote over 5 million words on various social and religious topics; today his books line the shelves of all the major universities and libraries of the world. Like Paul, he had his faults but had never persecuted the church during his life of youthful exuberance. His flaws were in the area of suppression, sex, and misogyny. The strength of his teachings center on compassion, independent thinking, passionate teaching, and hard work. He wrote about 125,000 words per year using sermons, letters, books, etc. to get his message across. That meant his Roman lamps burned late into the night in the town of Hippo.

Conflict was at the core of early Christian life, but through reason and true charity, some major problems were resolved. Others were not confronted nor were they dealt with in a Christian way, e.g., antisemitism, bishop of Rome's quest for power. During 400 years of growth and turmoil, Christians had to choose between circumcision and freedom, Gnostics and Apostolic tradition, papal dictates and Christian insight. In short, it was a cafeteria world—then and now. One had to be careful about what teachings to accept and follow. Paul, Origen, Jerome, and Augustine helped in this process.

APPENDIX A:

WAS JESUS MARRIED?

Only recently have writers asked the forbidden question: was the single, celibate life of Christ real? Books about this subject appeared as early as 1970, but it was the 1973 Broadway musical "Jesus Christ Superstar" which clearly suggested that Mary Magdalene and Jesus were a couple. Think of the lines from the song, "I don't know how to love him...." The arrival of Daniel Brown's novel **The Da Vinci Code** not only asserted that Jesus and Mary were romantically involved but that their love child was able to continue the blood line of Jesus after his death on the cross. Brown's novel has led people to think that the child of this union was the holy grail—the human cup that held the blood of Christ. What can be said about these rumors and innuendos about Christ? The short answer is that, no, there is no solid historical evidence that Jesus was ever married or that he had children.

    1. Before 1980 few theologians or scripture scholars bothered with the question about Jesus' personal relationship with women. Questions on this subject were off limits. Only non-believers concerned themselves with such gossip. But questions continued to trouble Christians. Let us first consider the canonical writings and see what they have to say. Mary Magdalene, and others, are mentioned in the Gospel as people who

provided for Jesus out of their own resources. She had some wealth and accompanied Jesus on his final journey to Jerusalem. As a witness to the crucifixion, she, with Joseph of Arimathea and others, laid the body of Jesus in a tomb. On the following Sunday an angel appeared to her, and later she became the first witness to the Resurrection (Jn 20:1-2). When she saw the Risen Lord, she uttered, "Rabboni" which means "teacher" and did not say "my spouse" or "husband" which would have indicated they were married. She was considered an apostle, and Mark's Gospel states that Jesus appeared to her first following his resurrection. This is what we know of Mary Magdalene from the New Testament, but accounts from the non-canonical literature show there is considerable evidence that Jesus and Mary had a close personal relationship. They seemed to be a couple. The ancient texts found in 1945 near the town of Nag Hammadi (Egypt) show us some interesting writings from the Gnostic Christians which were originally penned around 125 A.D. In 1896 the Berlin Codex, a compellation of more Gnostic texts found in Egypt, records the discovery of another group of ancient writings from the same period. In all these documents we find for the first time "Gospels" written after the death of Christ but apparently destroyed or suppressed as the canon of the NT was being formulated in the 2nd and 3rd centuries. Both the church and the Roman empire had reason to get rid of these documents. These documents, especially the Gospel of Mary, which was written in Coptic, suggest that Mary of Magdala was very close to Jesus and perhaps one of his intimate friends. This is the only Gospel we know of that is attributed to a woman. Other relevant texts in these Egyptian discoveries give us another version of life before and after the death of Christ and are part of the evidence we must take into account as we build the true picture of early Christianity. But can we believe these documents? Should they be rejected as mindless drivel by heretics? Probably not. Why did some early Christians want to suppress these writings? It is clear they had done a good job of hiding them for 1900 years. What does this new literature suggest? What questions do they raise?

2. As an adult Jewish male, Jesus should have been married by age 20 unless he was following the traditions of the Essenes—a mostly celibate monastic group with only a few married couples. Yet, Jesus is presented in the Gospels as a mature Jewish man and not married. Some argue that this arrangement was unusual and very atypical of the

Jewish family traditions of the time. Yet, we should note that John the Baptist, a prophet and most likely a member of the Essene religious community for a time, was single and lived the life of a quasi-hermit.[286] "I am the voice of one crying in the wilderness, make ready the way of the Lord" (Jn 1:19). St. Paul, a Pharisee and student of Gamaliel, was thought to be unmarried, but this tradition is now being questioned. Recently, writers have developed a series of arguments suggesting that Paul had once been married.[287] First they use the writings of Clement of Alexandria who maintained that Paul was once married but had somehow become separated from his wife.[288] Second, tradition dictates that at his conversion Paul was a mature man and a Pharisee; he would have been required to marry by age 20 or be in violation of strong religious norms. The exception would be a person who had withdrawn from the world and lived a monastic life, i.e. the Essene community. Wills states that Paul's wife could "have died, left him, or been sent away under Jewish law."[289] Being celibate was no problem in the ministries of Paul or John the Baptist. In fact Paul had great credibility and visited high ranking Roman officials on the island of Cyprus. Being a single man with no children would not necessarily be a problem for Jesus. It was not an issue with John the Baptist nor Paul.

3. Why did the church suppress certain documents? It is clear that there were numerous Gospels written in the first and second century and the church decided Matt, Mark, Luke and finally John would be the four most treasured documents for Christians; they would be included in the NT canon. Other Gospels were dismissed since at that time leaders wanted Christians to focus on the central message of the NT (27 books) and not on apocryphal writings. Thus, many texts were done away with; some were considered too closely allied to heretical groups like the Gnostics and they were rejected on that score. One must not overlook the fact that officials of the Roman empire (recall the Donatist controversy) burned many Christian texts and so the loss of these documents could be the result of secular actions as well as church policy.

4. There is no historical evidence that Jesus was married and/or had children. No text in the bible identifies Mary of Magdala and Jesus as husband and wife. This is the argument of silence. People think that because nothing is said about Jesus' private life, there must be something fishy. Some think there is something missing. Did the anti-

sex group in the early church want to keep the memory of Jesus so "other worldly" that He would be remembered only as a lone Messiah and Son of God? If so, it would have been difficult to suppress all information about Jesus' marriage and family life, if it ever existed, and then continue this myth for generations after the time of Christ. The young church was not well enough organized to arrange such a massive cover up. The church did not have the capacity to control a charismatic group for this extended period. The first Gospels appeared about 40 years after Jesus' death, and this early period of Christianity is marked by simple language and unsophisticated communication.[290] Paul's first known epistle was written around 51 A.D. and nothing about Jesus and his married life ever appeared in the Pauline corpus. The four Gospels do not mention any marriage. The Acts of the Apostles and St. Paul's letters had plenty of opportunity to touch upon this aspect of Jesus' life; they record nothing. The argument against a married Jesus: nothing is said because nothing happened.

   5. Mary and Jesus had a special relationship. Mary of Magdala was a close follower of Jesus, and Luke 8:1ff tells us that she and others provided for Jesus out of their own resources. She probably came from a well-to-do family living in Magdala that made money in the fishing and cloth dyeing business.[291] The bible does record that she was the first to discover the empty tomb (Jn 20:1). Jesus first appeared to Mary Magdalene (Jn 20:16; Mk 16:9) and He instructed her to tell the apostles the good news that He had risen from the dead. This is a striking event: of all the people Jesus knew during his earthly life, He chose to first reveal himself to Mary after his resurrection. Not Peter, not James, but Mary. She was sent to tell the other Apostles the good news. Why? Was she his closest friend and did he want her to know first that he was truly alive and risen from the dead? The Gospel of Mary states that Mary was his favorite disciple and that he loved her more than the others. Moreover, these documents show that Mary played a central role in the life of Jesus and his chosen band. That does not mean Jesus had a sexual relationship with her as many would like to think. The Gospel of Mary says that Jesus and Mary kissed and that this close relationship upset some of the male followers. Peter asks "Did he choose her over us?"[292] Peter, apparently, was jealous of Mary and refused to believe that Jesus gave her special knowledge about the kingdom. What is clear is that we must throw off the romantic view of

early Christianity: the great spirit of harmony in the early band of Jesus' followers. There was no small amount of strife and struggle in the early church. Some contend that it is difficult to establish the veracity of the Gnostic gospels and many dismiss these writings as idle speculation. The message cannot be believed since it does not correspond to the authentic teachings of the apostles. Either way, the Gnostic texts do not state that Jesus was married.

6. Was there a parallel church? According to this line of reasoning one group of followers presented the life of Christ in an other worldly genre and another segment gave the so-called true, human side of his life and activities. What evidence do we have of this dualism? There is none but much speculation has been offered about the "grail mother" and how Pope Innocent III dealt harshly with believers of this myth as late as the 13th century. A group of Christians living in France held to this view of Mary as Jesus' wife into the middle ages. Some maintain this belief today.

7. Biblical scholar John Crossan does not believe Jesus was married. He claims that Jesus was too poor to be married and have children. That is a strange comment since many people live in poverty, marry, and have children. Moreover, Mary of Magdala had some wealth which Greeley[293] suggests she could have utilized to support Jesus and his ministry.

8. The most controversial evidence regarding Jesus and his possible marriage to Mary of Magdala arose recently with the discovery of an ancient tomb near the Talpiot apartment complex, in Jerusalem. Jacobovici[294] and his colleagues reported that they had found what appeared to be the 2000-year-old family burial place of Jesus. In 1980 a team of archaeologists uncovered 10 ossuaries or limestone bone boxes, six of which were inscribed with these names: Jesus, son of Joseph; Maria (or in English, Mary), Matia (Hebrew word for Matthew), James (ossuary stolen and later found), Judah, son of Jesus, Mariamene (a name for Mary Magdalene). DNA testing of the materials found in the Jesus ossuary and that of Mariamene showed the individuals were not related. Since tombs normally contain either blood relatives or spouses, the authors suggest that Jesus and Mary Magdalene were a couple and married. Judah would have been their son. James was clearly a brother of Jesus (Mk 6:3). Matthew, the disciple, was probably a relative of Mary, the mother of Jesus. Some have argued that this tomb and the

names could fit many families at the time and hence it is "coincidental" that this tomb seems to fit perfectly the broad characteristics of what we know about Jesus' family in the Gospels. Various statistical studies have concluded that there is only 1 chance in 600 that the Talpiot burial site is not Jesus' family tomb, given the distribution of such names and combination of names in the 1st century Roman empire. Princeton scholar, James Charlesworth, has stated: "I have reservations, but I cannot dismiss the possibility that the tomb was related to the Jesus clan."[295] If one accepts this conclusion, that we have found the remains of Jesus and his family, the following would seem to be true: 1) Jesus was married; 2) he and Mary Magdalene had a child; 3) there was no bodily resurrection of Jesus (could have been just spiritual); 4) there was no virgin birth of Jesus (defined as Jesus' mother Mary remained a virgin before, during, and after the birth of Christ). All these ideas are rejected by a large segment of the Christian community and thus we have no broad consensus about whether Jesus was married.

9. While Jesus was ministering with his disciples there was never any mention of the fact that he had a wife or children. Peter had a wife and his sick mother-in-law was healed by Jesus. Topics like this found their way into the scriptures. Paul was single at the time of his conversion and discovered that he could serve the Lord better through celibacy (1 Cor 7:27). Many of the Essenes were not married and chose celibacy as a way of life. For the Essenes at Qumran, being single was a way of life that was chosen for the sake of the kingdom. Many felt the end of the world was near and marriage was too "this worldly" a lifestyle.[296]

In conclusion, all the ancient and modern literature consulted in writing this book fail to mention explicitly anything about a marriage between Jesus and Mary Magdalene. Karen King of Harvard concludes her work on the subject in this way: "Looking at the history of early Christianity, there is no evidence at all that they [Jesus and Mary] were married."[297]

APPENDIX B:

POPES, CONDOMS, AND AIDS:

WHEN RELIGION BECOMES A SOCIAL PROBLEM*

R. John Kinkel, M.A., Ph.D.
Oakland University
Rochester, Michigan

Paper presented at Midwest Political Science Association Meetings, Palmer House, Chicago, Ill., April 3-6, 2008 (Present April 3, 4:45, 54-6). Rev. June 2008.

*Most of the work on this study was completed during a visiting faculty appointment at Miami University, Oxford, Ohio (2007). Contact Dr. Kinkel, Sociology, Oakland University, Rochester, Michigan. Recent books by author: Chaos in the Catholic Church (2005), Letters to Pope Benedict (ed.) 2008, Cinderella Church: The Story of Early Christianity (forthcoming 2008).

I am grateful to the following for reviewing the manuscript and offering helpful comments: Norma Josef, Danielle Kinkel, Jonathan Kinkel, Francis Strunk, and Richard Hansen.

ABSTRACT

Several major religions ban the use of condoms to prevent the spread of HIV/AIDS. This paper examines the who, what, where, and how of one denomination, the Roman Catholic church, which maintains that no Catholic in good standing can use condoms to prevent AIDS. Using Kimball's warning signs of dysfunctional religion, the paper points out the inadequacy of Catholic teaching as articulated by reform-minded Cardinals and bishops; they argue that abstinence and fidelity are not the complete answer to the problem of spreading AIDS. These high ranking officials say that condoms must be a part of Catholic church's AIDS policy. While Pope Benedict and others state that a condom is simply a method of birth control, pure and simple, some clerics assert that such analysis is flawed and that the commandment "Thou shalt not kill" trumps all previous teaching and theological speculation. A condom can prevent death and preserve life. While publicly objecting to Pope Benedict's teaching, these clerics have formed a de facto social movement in the church with all the true characteristics of a mechanism for social change. They assert that the pope is wrong and must change his position on this matter. Two years ago the Vatican stated its plan to review current teaching on this matter but with no published report as yet, many think Rome is stonewalling, unwilling to alter its previously stated position. The teachings and procedures of the Catholic church are discussed and evaluated as to whether we can conclude that papal policy is a global social problem.

Key Words: HIV, Condoms, AIDS, prevention, Popes, religious ideology, social movement, social change, conservative.

Introduction

The Roman Catholic church is reviewing its long-standing ban on the use of condoms to prevent the spread of HIV/AIDS. In May, 2006 Vatican expert John Allen[298] stated that a "forthcoming Vatican document is set to state that use of condoms by a married couple, where one partner is infected with HIV/AIDS and the other is not, can be acceptable to prevent the transmission of the disease." So far, no official document has seen the light of day. Thousands of attendees at the August 2006 International AIDS conference in Toronto petitioned the pope to lift the Vatican ban on using condoms to prevent the spread of AIDS. They contend such action could make a real difference in curbing the spread of HIV/AIDS throughout the world. How will the Pope respond to this international social problem now that he, and his colleagues, have had over two years to think about it?

Since Pope Benedict ordered a review of Catholic teaching which currently bans the use of condoms to prevent the spread of HIV/AIDS, Vatican watchers have been perplexed. Some think we are now in a position to ask with Charles Kimball, "is religion the problem?"[299] How long can the church continue to delay its decision on condoms and AIDS? Can it dawdle when human lives are at stake? This paper examines how a major Christian church could reject a safe and effective means to assist in the prevention of a deadly disease; second, we explore the rationale for past church policy; lastly, we speculate on whether this church is capable of altering its stated position on dealing with a major social problem: the spread of HIV/AIDS.

Method

Using the Harvard Case Study Method, this paper explores how the Catholic church has taken a stand against protecting human life, despite the fact that many church officials have objected to such a policy. This approach allows teachers and learners the opportunity to analyze and synthesize conflicting data and points of view, to define and prioritize goals, to persuade and inspire others who think differently, to make tough decisions with uncertain information, and to seize opportunity in the face of doubt.[300] Two principles employed by religion scholar Charles Kimball as warning signs of dysfunctional religion will inform this case study investigation: 1) absolute truth claims by religious groups and 2) blind obedience. When zealous and devout adherents of a religious tradition elevate teachings and beliefs to the level of absolute truth and blind obedience, they open the door to the possibility that their religion will become evil.[301] I wish to make it clear, however, that this paper is not saying any religion is evil per se. The thrust of this research agenda is to point out, with the help of Kimball's research, some of the "warning signs that alert us to the potential for evil behavior. When one or more of the warning signs discussed here are in place, it is all too easy for sincere people and well-intentioned religious groups to harbor destructive attitudes and justify deplorable actions based on what is deemed essential to their life of faith."[302] Henceforth this paper examines just how close the Catholic church has come to being a source of grave harm to its members' social and physical well-being.

Background: Previous Church Teaching

This paper does not try to evaluate the Roman Catholic church's controversial stand on artificial birth control which has been articulated most notably by Pius XI (1930), Pius XII (1951), Paul VI (1968) and John Paul II (1993). Their teachings have been critiqued, praised and condemned by numerous authors. One thing is clear: the Catholic church's teaching on birth control is not infallible and can be changed.[303] It suffices to say that in the United States, 80 percent of Catholic married couples ignore this papal ban on birth control and in Europe we find similar trends.[304] Our only concern in this paper is to explore how the pope's absolute ban on the use of condoms may be transformed into a new ethical policy now that the AIDS pandemic has marked its 25th year. The goal here is to examine how this major social problem has forced the Catholic church and its leaders to rethink its views on the use of condoms to prevent AIDS; we likewise wish to point out the lengthy process whereby Vatican officials finally came to the realization that a review and change in current policy may be needed. One obvious issue we will look at concerns the many people who have died of AIDS in the last decade and whether the Vatican's dilatory actions have directly resulted in many unnecessary deaths especially in South America, Africa, Asia and other developing countries.

Impact of HIV/AIDS

The recent controversy involving popes and condoms probably would not have come to light if the HIV/AIDS issue had not emerged as a worldwide pandemic of gigantic proportions. Generally, Vatican officials were quiet in the 1980s regarding AIDS and condom use, but they were not alone. President Ronald Reagan did not use the word AIDS in any of his speeches until the mid-1980s—long after AIDS was identified as a major problem by the Center for Disease Control and Prevention in 1981.[305] Funding to support HIV/AIDS research was not a high priority even by 1990 since many in the U.S. Congress erroneously believed that the problem was confined to the gay community with limited impact on the general population. However, the Western World took notice that AIDS can affect anyone when Mary Fisher addressed the Republican National Convention in 1992. The daughter of the late multimillionaire Max Fisher told how she had contracted AIDS from her intravenous drug using husband. She said that people must be able to protect themselves from contracting AIDS at all costs. Thus, by the early 1990s Western leaders (including the Vatican) knew full well that the general population was at risk for HIV infection and immediate action was required.

Epidemiologists began to point out how the virus spread (i.e. blood transfusions, intravenous drug use, sexual intercourse, etc.); thus, it also became clear in the medical community that public policy action was needed, despite the intractable nature of homophobia. The National Institutes of Health stated in the early 1990s that condom usage proved extremely helpful in reducing the risk of contracting AIDS. Numerous studies[306] demonstrate that condoms are not foolproof, but they can make a significant difference in the spread of AIDS. Hence the general recommendation: use a condom when having sex.

Yet, during the lengthy reign of Pope John Paul II (1978-2005), the teaching of the Vatican was clear: Catholics could not use condoms to fight AIDS since they were a forbidden method of birth control and thus would violate church discipline. In his encyclical **Veritatis Splendor** (1993) and in other pronouncements, the Pope declared that all forms of artificial birth control were "intrinsically evil" and could never be tolerated by the Catholic church. This came as a surprise to many observers since he was the first pope to ever use the term "intrinsically evil" to describe artificial birth control (reported by

Cardinal Avery Dulles on EWTN Catholic channel); second, he put forward this view knowing full well that the church has never declared that unprovoked warfare is intrinsically evil—arguably, a condition far more evil than having sex using a condom. In short, John Paul II preached that he opposed the use of condoms for birth control and he rejected the idea that they could ever be used to prevent the transmission of AIDS. Most of the non-Catholic community rejected this papal pronouncement; indeed, the backlash may have even cost John Paul a very prestigious award: the Nobel Peace Prize.[307] The Pope had been criticized in numerous circles for opposing the use of condoms to slow the spread of HIV/AIDS. Kimball's signs of dysfunctional religion were beginning to emerge in the 1990s: absolute truth claims and demand for blind obedience when peoples' lives are at risk.

The Growing AIDS Problem

With the start of the 21st century two things began to impact church officials and their traditional teachings. Many scientists and public policy analysts deplored the stance of the Catholic church on this matter and global data began to make world leaders aware that the AIDS crisis was a tragic problem that kept growing each year. A United Nations study using 2001 data helped to put the world on notice about this social problem. 1) Nearly 40 million adults and children are infected by the HIV virus worldwide; 2) about 25 million have died of the disease since 1981. Although recent research has adjusted these figures to somewhat lower levels than previous estimates, the AIDS problem is still defined as an enormous health care problem. This crisis has created some 12 million orphans—mostly in poor, developing countries.[308] The number of orphans will balloon to 18 million by 2010. The UN and other organizations have asked all nations and charitable organizations throughout the world to help in the treatment and prevention of this problem. The Catholic Church, in contrast, has refused to change its stance and has stated repeatedly that Catholics cannot use condoms to prevent AIDS. To its credit, the church continues its efforts in providing treatment for AIDS victims and it is well known that "Catholic organizations mercifully provide around 25 percent of the care AIDS victims receive worldwide."[309] The Catholic church deserves high marks for its work in treating AIDS patients but its AIDS prevention program needs a major overhaul.

In order to reiterate the church's stand on condoms, a prominent member of the Roman Curia, Cardinal Alfonso Trujillo, has declared that condom use by Catholics is morally wrong. As President of the Vatican's Pontifical Council for the Family, he certainly had the full support of the pope in stating without reservation in 2003 that the church's ban on condoms was unequivocal.[310] The use of condoms to prevent AIDS was therefore unacceptable. In seeking to emphasize his point, Trujillo claimed that the AIDS virus could pass through the latex condom and thus it offered little or no protection against the virus. The World Health Organization (WHO) and numerous scientists declared this statement to be totally false and asked the Vatican to withdraw it immediately. Catherine Hankins, chief scientific advisor to UNAIDS, contended that Vatican statements "are totally incorrect. Latex condoms are impermeable. They do prevent HIV transmission."[311] Nevertheless, Rome's leaders remained steadfast in their position. Church skirmishes with science and the modern world are well known: the Galileo controversy that the earth is the center of the universe, the ancient view that usury is a grave sin, the theory of evolution according to Cardinal Schonborn, etc. As Trujillo's comments indicate, the Catholic church and its officials continue both to maintain disingenuous views of the truth, and at the same time ignore the possibility that good people could very well die as a result of such misrepresentations.

As if the clash with AIDS workers was not enough, it has become apparent that priests in Africa have told poor people in the villages that condoms are laced with HIV/AIDS and should not be used.[312] In a recent interview with a former Peace Corps volunteer who worked in Tanzania (2000-2003), I further learned that African priests in Tanzania often gave Sunday sermons condemning the use of condoms to prevent AIDS. The Vatican's anti-condom policy had clearly reached the local churches in Africa where there are now 143 million Catholics.[313] Many are dying of AIDS. The Vatican's program of disinformation has now reached the local churches.

Fortunately, according to Nicholas Kristof, not all Catholic agencies follow church directives. "In El Salvador, I talked to doctors in a Catholic clinic who explain to patients how condoms can protect against AIDS. In Zimbabwe, I visited a Catholic charity that gave out condoms - until the bishop found out."[314] Throughout this controversy many scholars have criticized the church for its irrational stance and argued that its teachings probably contributed to the deaths of millions. Garry Wills' views are shared by many: People are dying of AIDS all around the world now especially in places like Africa and Indonesia... the Pope refuses to allow people to have contraception [condoms], he's killing them. He is responsible for murder...This is killing people on a grand scale, and it's a horrendous scandal, much greater than any sexual molestation scandal."[315]

While Pope John Paul II was gravely ill from Parkinson's disease and close to death in 2004, the church did nothing to encourage discussion on this question, it simply reiterated its ban on condoms.

Voices from the Local Churches

With little change on the horizon regarding this growing global problem, church leaders and pastors began to question the Vatican's stance on condom use and AIDS. One of the first bishops to question the Vatican's views on condoms/AIDS was Bishop Kevin Dowling of South Africa. In 2001 he argued that the use of a condom can be seen not as a means of preventing life, but rather as a means of stopping the transmission of death to another person.[316] For this he received a number of rebukes from the South African papal nuncio. Some years later, in 2004, officials from Spain's Conference of Catholic Bishops argued that there should be a place in church moral theology for the use of condoms to prevent the spread of AIDS. This is the responsible thing to do, they said. These opposition forces were quickly noted by Vatican officials and pressure was applied to squelch dissent. The full body of Spain's conference of Bishops rejected the ideas of this small reformist group and sided with the pope. It became clear, however, that a church social movement was taking shape. All was not well in the papal apartments and many seemed to feel a policy change might be appropriate. Thus, opposition forces took a crucial step toward church reform: they went public and drew media attention.[317] All the parts needed for a social movement were beginning to fall into place, at least according to one social theory. That is, a social movement needs strong and powerful leaders to confront the status quo; they must mobilize the population; there is a coalescence of groups working for change; the media becomes useful in communicating the issues.

A few months after Spain's conference of bishops spoke, Felipe Arizmendi of Mexico presented his views to the press. In late 2004 the bishop said that condom use to prevent AIDS was a lesser evil when compared to the spread of AIDS, and that people have an obligation not to infect others. Then, in a surprise move, the reformists gained coalescence when Cardinal Georges Cottier, the theologian to the pontifical household, joined the progressives and stated that change was needed. The movement for change gained momentum when he joined the dissidents to say that church policy must be revised. Cottier told the Italian press in February 2005 that condoms could be used by a married couple but only for the purpose of preventing the spread of HIV/AIDS.[318] Thus, those at the highest level of the Roman Catholic church were voicing their opposition to papal teaching. However, it was no surprise to read that Pope John Paul II urged abstinence and fidelity to reduce the spread of AIDS just before he died; he had again rejected the use of condoms by Catholics.[319] Nevertheless, the evidence for the church's claim to absolute truth and blind obedience was eroding. Opposition forces were growing.

With the death of John Paul II and the election of Benedict XVI some leaders in the Catholic church and most of the scientific community were hoping for a change in policy. AIDS workers were hopeful that "there may be room for maneuver when it comes to the new Pope's position on condom use."[320] Yet, in a June 2005 speech to African bishops, the new pope stated that the "spread of HIV and AIDS in Africa should be tackled through fidelity and abstinence and not by condoms."[321] There was nothing new here; he was following the line of the previous administration in making his first public statement on the matter. It was clear: obedience was required. Nonetheless, the voices of opposition grew louder. Their tactics were clear: speak out and use the media to let church officials know they are wrong.

In the Fall of 2005 Bishop Kevin Dowling of South Africa once again asked the Vatican to change its stand on the use of condoms to prevent AIDS. He stated that the Vatican ban on the use of condoms was morally unacceptable.[322] Not to be outdone in theological insight, the highly respected Cardinal Godfried Danneels of Belgium weighed in, and it became clear that the social movement for change was now in high gear. During a press conference in late 2005, Danneels stated in no uncertain terms that one must use a condom if he/she has AIDS in order to obey the commandment "Thou shalt not kill" (Deut 5:17). The laity quickly joined forces with the bishops. Marcella

Alsan, a woman physician who has worked extensively in African Catholic hospitals, wrote that the church's opposition to the use of condoms "may mean not only untold human suffering, but the loss of millions of human lives."[323] While the Catholic church maintained its traditional moral stand, many pointed out that this rigid stance was killing people. Surprisingly, the Vatican blinked.

The tipping point in the debate came in April 2006, when 79-year-old Cardinal Carlo Martini, retired Archbishop of Milan, entered the fray, stating that the Vatican should allow the use of condoms for married couples if one partner is infected with the HIV/AIDS virus.[324] It is a "lesser evil," he said. The key point that apparently caught the Vatican's attention was the well-publicized report that many monogamous married women were being infected with AIDS by their promiscuous husbands. Thus they should be allowed to protect themselves from HIV by not being forced to have unprotected sex with their husbands—an act that ultimately would leave their children orphans. High ranking church officials were now using the argument of self-defense to push for a new church policy. Within a week of Martini's remarks the Vatican stated that it was preparing a document on the "question of condoms and AIDS, and that it would be released soon."[325] More than two years have passed, and there is no decision and no published document. Indeed, the Vatican reported in November 2006, that Cardinal Javier Barragan finished his 200-page report on condoms and AIDS, but Pope Benedict still has yet to make a final decision on this controversial topic. Another crucial point is that since the Vatican's announcement that it was reviewing the issue of condoms and AIDS, there have been no more voices of dissent. It appears that no bishop will critique the pope's teaching while his special committee purports to review the issue. Many feel that the Vatican is trying to kill the issue by putting it in the research box. This tactic has worked so far.

Social Problems, Church, Change

What have we learned in this case study about the Roman Catholic church during this particular crisis? The lessons are many.

(1) As a self-described teacher of moral theology the church has shown itself to be very slow in understanding the nature and scope of

numerous modern social problems, e.g., AIDS, the priest sexual abuse crisis, women in the church, priest shortage, etc. Its social teachings and views on the family are not easily adjusted to changing times because of its centralized governance structure and the dominance of the ultra-conservative branch of Catholic theology at the highest levels of Roman Catholic bureaucracy. Such was not the case in the early Christian church. The Council of Jerusalem (50 C.E.), Council of Nicaea (325 C.E.), just war theory, and Pope Cornelius' policies toward (ca. 251 C.E.) "lapsed" Christians all show a moderating, centrist ideology in church decision making.[326] Rigorists in the church were essentially ignored. The first response of most contemporary Vatican officials, however, is to assert traditional teaching and reject new ideas that could require change. The church is prejudiced in the strictest sense of the word, that is, it pre-judges most new ideas and then rejects them because they do not fit its traditional conservative view of reality. Nothing has really changed in some quarters of the Vatican in the last 40 years. We should recall the coat of arms of anti-reform conservative Cardinal Alfredo Ottaviani (d. 1979): "semper idem"—always the same.

(2) However, members of the Roman Curia, e.g. Cardinal Trujillo, make things up as they go along. This, some say, is to protect Holy Mother church. They either hire bad people who give them wrong information or simply tell white lies to keep old truths from unraveling. According to them, previous popes cannot be wrong; they have the Holy Spirit on their side. Leaders of this type are an embarrassment to many Roman Catholic church members around the world and cause many to leave the church—especially young people. Such intransigence on the AIDS-condoms issue has cost many lives, as well. Many people in the Roman Curia should be dismissed for the way they have responded to the AIDS crisis. None, of course, will lose their jobs; they are the loyal soldiers fighting the good fight against cultural relativism. The church claims to be against the "culture of death" but its current stand on condoms/AIDS facilitates the deaths of millions throughout the world. Many of these deaths are preventable. The church is now part of the culture of death, which it condemns.

(3) Despite the presence of massive church incompetence which has probably led to the deaths of millions, strong leaders have emerged

who refuse to submit to authoritarian church policy; they present their views in their own countries to priests, bishops and laity so as to correct official church teaching. They ask the pope and curia to listen and change.

(4) These officials in the Church have become a true social movement for change, trying to bring the church's ultra-conservative clique to its senses for not teaching proper Catholic theology. These Papal elitists are teaching false doctrine. That is the critique of numerous Cardinals and bishops who are on the church's payroll and object to the pope's HIV policy.

(5) Continued objections by strong leaders have the following effect: they show the absurdity of the church's stand. These actions demonstrate that the church needs Catholics around the world (laity and clergy) to pressure the pope and the Roman curia for change; these forces ultimately help to bring reform in a corrupt and dysfunctional organization.

This crisis demonstrates that there is a good model for church reform and it comes from the bottom up and not the top down. By holding public debates instead of calling secret meetings to bare one's soul to the pope, religious leaders initiate change and help the world's suffering. The process of permanent church reform may be just beginning.

New Church Stymied

The early 1960s brought an influx of innovative ideas to the Roman Catholic church through the process of the Second Vatican Council (1962-1965). Pope John XXIII wanted to bring the church up-to-date with a program he called "aggiornamento." First, the notion of religious freedom was proclaimed; second, liturgical renewal became a top priority; the Council stated that the Church should be viewed first and foremost as the "People of God" and not primarily a hierarchical structure; better relations with Jewish leaders were made possible with the discontinuation of the Tridentine mass which was insulting to Jews and an obstacle to ecumenical progress. But, as council expert Hans Küng rightly points out in his **Memoirs**, he and other scholars underestimated the power of conservative forces to once again take over the Vatican power structure after the council ended.[327] Led by ultra-conservative Cardinal Alfredo Ottaviani (d. 1979), these ecclesiastical hardliners would stop at nothing to block meaningful change in the church. Their first post-Conciliar victory came in 1968 when they convinced Pope Paul VI to ignore the papal birth control commission recommendations for a change of policy and to join conservatives to keep the church's absolute ban on artificial birth control with few exceptions.[328] During the next 10 years Pope Paul faced criticism even from moderates and many felt he never recovered from the rejection of progressive bishops who objected to his birth control encyclical. In 1972 the beleaguered pope remarked that the "smoke of Satan" had now entered the church. What Pope Paul was alluding to has never been fully understood.[329]

Conservatives took this to mean that liberal ideas were destroying orthodox church doctrine and belief. Progressives countered that evil forces within the church were trying to turn back the teachings of the Ecumenical Council—one of the most authoritative teaching bodies in the Catholic church. With Paul VI's death in 1978 two leaders emerged: Cardinals Luciani and Wojtyla. Albino Cardinal Luciani was elected pope in 1978 but died under suspicious circumstances after only 33 days in office. No autopsy was performed. His plans were for curial reform, a clean up of Vatican finances, and a review of church birth control policy. Obviously he never had the opportunity to carry out any of these reform programs. The next pope, John Paul II (Wojtyla), came from the conservative Polish branch of the Catholic church; it is well known that he supported the Church's ban on artificial birth control even before Pope Paul's 1968 encyclical, **Humanae Vitae**, and may have helped write it.

Thus, Cardinal Karol Wojtyla of Poland—long a bastion of devotional Catholicism—was elected the new pope with an apparent mandate to go slow on Vatican II reforms. By 1978 thousands of priests and nuns had resigned from ministry, dissent from church teachings was commonplace, and liberation theology became a popular topic in seminaries, colleges, and local churches. Catholic progressives in the USA proclaimed: stop the war (Vietnam), stop Third World oppression, stop Vatican II obstructionists. The new pope wagged his papal finger and ushered in a new phase of Catholic conservatism with simple authoritative answers to complex problems. Why should women want to be priests? Mary was not a priest and they should want to be like her. Down with liberation theology; it smacks of Marxism. No married priests...Jesus was not married! His simple answers to complex problems carried enormous weight. After he was shot by Ali Agca and almost killed in St. Peter's square, 1981, the pope became a cult figure; no one dared challenge his teaching authority. He was the closest thing to God-on-earth, according to some Catholic newspapers. Leaders in the Catholic church joined forces with fundamentalist religious groups and for the next 25 years it became difficult to object to any issue that the pope supported. Cardinal Joseph Ratzinger, a former Nazi conscript, was recruited to confront any Catholic theologian who stepped out of line. The Vatican's new enforcer was quickly labeled "God's Rottweiler," and the Panzer Cardinal. This German Prelate aimed his theological guns at liberal priests, laymen, and nuns alike. The pendulum had swung to the far right. Claims to absolute truth and blind obedience were at a high pitch in the curia's choir.

Radical conservative forces of all religious persuasions became so prominent during this period in history that the American Academy of Arts and Sciences funded a major study to try and understand the rise of fundamentalist religion and its implications for the future of America.[330] The 8,000 page report, published in five volumes (it covers research undertaken from 1988-1993) states, among other things, that the doctrine of fundamentalism affirms that "religious authority is absolute, admitting neither criticism nor reduction."[331] With a focus on religious texts (Bible) and the pronouncements of religious leaders (e.g. Popes, etc.), fundamentalism has become an anti-modern movement which adheres strictly to traditional religious teachings without compromise. Recent fundamentalist religious leaders maintain that it was their duty to defend truth against the new and radical theologies of the '60s.

The Catholic church bought into this conservative movement and made **Opus Dei** its favored son. Founded by controversial Spanish priest Jose Escriva, who during his lifetime was a strong supporter of Fascist Francisco Franco, this secretive organization has now grown to its current membership of 80,000. It was no surprise to find out that Pope John Paul II made **Opus Dei** his own personal prelature in 1982; members were accountable only to him, not the local bishop.

Defending proclaimed truth became one of the Catholic church's chief goals. Some have argued that nothing has really changed in some quarters of the Vatican in the last 40 years. We should recall again the coat of arms of anti-reform conservative Cardinal Alfredo Ottaviani (d. 1979): "semper idem"—always the same. As a doctrinal purist he took the militaristic view of Catholicism that proclaims that one must defend church dogma to the grave. He was obsessed with power and control. But ironically, when Paul VI declared in 1970 that Cardinals who had reached 80 years of age could no longer vote in conclave for a new pope, Ottaviani went on Italian television to object to this papal directive; indeed, the Cardinal had just turned 80. So much for the conservative moniker: always obey the Vicar of Christ on earth.

Today too many Catholic bishops share this fundamentalist ideology to some degree. Members of the Roman Curia such as Cardinal Trujillo distort church doctrine. Ideology, not true religious insight, all too often dominates Catholic discourse. Even the Catholic laity have joined in the chorus. Phyllis Schlafly, a well known right-wing Catholic ideologue, opposed C. Everett Koop's recommendation to then President Ronald Reagan that condoms and sex education should be employed to contain the AIDS epidemic. She quickly went on "television and essentially said that she would rather see her children become infected with sexually transmitted disease than to know there was such a thing as condoms."[332] The runaway conservative freight train just keeps rolling along.

Fortunately, we have some innovative ways of analyzing these institutional shortcomings and identifying how they negate any possibility for solving problems. Gene Burns[333] suggests that three concepts are helpful in understanding the nature of Catholic culture, and by extension, the religious fundamentalism problem we have identified. The concepts are: ideology, core, and periphery.

The discussion regarding condoms and AIDS moves to the area of ideology when idea systems (viz., theology) use a set of norms and values to try and keep social structures as they are (no change regarding condoms and AIDS). The use of condoms is sinful. It is against the natural law. That's it. They interfere with God's plan for procreation. The Catholic social structure clearly involves ideological teachings and normative standards: good Catholics should obey the pope—do not use condoms. The values presented are clear: do not interfere with the natural process of transmitting life. The ideology completely ignores the other side of the coin: do not transmit death. The Cardinals and bishops who have challenged the pope's position on condoms and AIDS want to alter the core of Catholic teaching on condoms, that is, they want to alter those factors that are essential if one wants to be a Catholic in good standing. Furthermore, papal critics want to move the current teaching on condoms and HIV/AIDS prevention to the periphery of Catholic norms and assert that "Thou shalt not kill" (Deut 5:17) trumps all discussion regarding condoms and AIDS. Additionally, they want the pope to side with them, namely, that "Thou shalt not kill" is the core. So far the Pope has given no indication that he will change.

Benedict's Challenge

The current pope has made the Vatican position clear in 2005, but many church leaders have informed him that they oppose this ban, and thus, the ideological battle continues. The pope has the power in the Catholic culture realm, according to Burns, to define what the core is and "sanction flagrant (or even subtle) dissent from that core."[334] This is why certain bishops have asked the pope to reevaluate his teaching and proclaim a new direction in church policy. They do not want to break from the church (schism); they want the church to break from an old, death-producing tradition. The old tradition banning all condom use should end, according to church dissidents and a new period of moral theology should begin. We have new norms, they say. Catholics and non-Catholics are waiting to see how the Vatican responds. Reformers are challenging the pope's claim to absolute truth and his requirement of blind obedience. This is a sign of religious growth, according to Kimball, and I think he would argue the Catholic church is showing signs that it is trying to move away from being a dysfunctional religion.

For many Roman Catholics around the world the pope's stand is an embarrassment and causes many to leave the church. Catholic theologian and writer Richard Rohr suggests that Catholics believe the Roman Curia has misunderstood the core principle of all religion: it is not sin-management but rather concern for human suffering.[335] He thinks most Western clerics have failed to understand the essence of religion's first principles and that Catholics have fallen into this error again in the 21st century. What is clear to most modern observers is that the Catholic conservative onslaught has had negative consequences.

Fundamentalist religion is essentially anti-modern and this makes the church's quest to solve its own organizational problems fatally flawed. The church apparently will not change its stance on artificial birth control, it rejects the notion of married priests, and asserts that women must know their place. When confronted with the terrible realities of sexual abuse by priests, U.S. Catholics witnessed their church leaders orchestrate a denial and cover up. Hide the facts and blame the media. That fiasco cost $2.2 billion in legal settlements. Now we have administered, through the above analysis, the **coup de grâce** to Catholic fundamentalists. Church leaders are reeling because their ideological stance has led to a dead end—the perpetuation, rather than the alleviation, of human suffering and death. Those who continue to claim moral and theological superiority must be put out of their theological misery. Church leaders back a policy that puts Catholic families around the world at risk for getting AIDS—especially the poor and uneducated. This must stop, according to reformists.

In response, centrist Cardinals and bishops within the church bureaucracy want to change Vatican policy. They do not want the reputation of the church to continue its decline or say nothing while innocent people die unnecessarily. They do not want people to leave the church due to badly outdated policies. The conservatives who took control of the church in the late '70s, supposedly to save it from liberals, have been unable to move from their theological catatonic state, except to advocate that the church maintain its absolute ban on condoms for AIDS prevention. They refuse to seriously consider the moral and ethical ramifications of Catholic hardliners. Their answer to the AIDS crisis, fidelity and abstinence, is inadequate to growing numbers of Bishops and Cardinals, not to mention world leaders at large. Papal intransigence on the AIDS-condom issue has cost many lives, but can we really begin to fathom the number of casualties?

Johns Hopkins University physician Thomas Quinn has collected AIDS data (year 2000) from around the world and estimates that about 16,000 new HIV infections occur each day.[336] More recent studies suggest a lower number of about 7,000 new HIV infections per day worldwide due to improved estimates in India and effective healthcare interventions.[337] Thus using the most recent lower calculations, it is evident that in the last 700 days while papal theologians speculated on the propriety of condom usage, at least 4,900,000 more people have been infected with HIV/AIDS worldwide. Some of these victims are the 1.2 billion Catholics around the world who have been instructed to follow papal directives banning the use of condoms to prevent AIDS. The church has failed to move quickly to join humanitarian forces in order to reduce new AIDS infections. Papal intransigence is killing people. Timely action by the church 5 years ago could have saved millions of lives. Many clerics in the Roman Curia should resign for the way they have responded to the AIDS crisis. None, of course, will be fired because, as noted above, they are fighting (alongside Pope Benedict) against the "dictatorship of relativism."[338] The church claims to be against the "culture of death" but now we see its conservative doctrines help contribute to millions of AIDS casualties, leaving many to ponder: will the church let more moderate forces within the church enter the pope's circle of influence and thus bring needed change? We may soon find out.

In the face of the Church's shocking indifference to human suffering related to the AIDS crisis, strong leaders have emerged who refuse to submit to authoritarian church policies. They present their views in their own countries to priests, bishops and laity to correct official church teaching. They ask the pope and curia to listen and make the church holy once again. These Church officials call for reform and have become a true social movement for change, hoping to expose the flaws of ultra-conservative forces within the Vatican. Church traditionalists are not teaching true Catholic values, they say. These traditionalists are teaching false doctrine. Continued objections by strong leaders have the effect of exposing the absurdity of the church's stand. These actions demonstrate that the church needs Catholics around the world (laity and clergy) to put pressure on the pope and the Roman curia; these forces ultimately help to bring change in a rigid and dysfunctional organization. For one thing, they have forced the pope to review his stated policy.

This crisis demonstrates that there is a good model for social change and reform: it comes from the bottom up and not the top down.[339] By holding public debates instead of calling secret meetings to have a heart-to-heart talk with the pope, religious leaders hope to bring change and help to those suffering in the world today. The political process of permanent church reform is just beginning. The church cannot afford another "condomgate."

Theological Breakthrough?

Many who are unfamiliar with the machinations of Vatican bureaucrats ask how the church could consider changing its ban on condoms which seems inevitable. What was the particular insight that led church officials to consider change and possibly lift the absolute ban on the use of condoms? The embarrassing truth is that Church theologians and officials have resurrected a 900 year-old principle (refined in the 1700s) that is well known to anyone who has studied Catholic theology: the principle of double effect attributed to Thomas Aquinas.[340] In essence his doctrine, when applied to the condom/AIDS issue, states that a married person can intend at least two things when deciding to use a condom during sexual intercourse: prevent conception or prevent the transmission of a serious disease. As long as the Catholic wills to prevent the disease (a good) and does not will contraception (the evil)[341], they can engage in sexual intercourse as a married couple without violating church law.[342] The Catholic church may invoke this principle in changing its stance on condoms and state that it is permissible to use them under these very specific conditions. The argument of self-defense is also persuasive since women should be allowed to protect themselves from an HIV infected husband who demands sexual relations. The central issue in the above discussion is why it took the church over 10 years to address the gravity of this social problem when the theological principles needed to solve such an issue were readily available to church leaders. During the long reign of John Paul II, it is clear that the constant teaching of the church was that condoms = contraception and therefore were forbidden. "End of discussion" was the familiar mantra. The church was locked into a theological time warp. The fundamentalist flaw was arrogance—we are in charge; we said it is true; it must be true… we have God on our side. For many this line of reasoning proved to be indefensible and thus many church leaders forcefully opposed this ban. That was to no avail. With a change 5 years ago instead of the year 2008, the church could have saved many lives, perhaps millions of lives, through its powerful teaching and ministry. But with conservatives dictating church policy over the past three decades, we find blunders like this piling up with no end in sight. Nicholas Kristof rightly observes that "when historians look back at the Catholic Church in this era, they'll give it credit for having fought Communism and helped millions of the poor around the world. But they'll also count its anti-condom campaign as among its most tragic mistakes in the first two millennia of its history."[343]

Conclusion

This paper has investigated the Catholic church's ban on the use of condoms to prevent AIDS. Kimball's warning signs of dysfunctional religion—claims to absolute truth and blind obedience—are sprinkled throughout this case study of how a major church has failed to deal with a modern social problem: the use of condoms to prevent AIDS. While popes have reiterated old doctrines, social movements within this organization have tried to change policy by confronting the Vatican's claim to absolute truth and the requirement of blind obedience. The big question that remains for many Catholics and observers of this struggle is: has the Vatican learned its lesson? Will conservatives consult more effectively with local bishops and the laity? Will they hire qualified professionals to research issues and advise the Curia on the proper policy to advocate regarding Catholic morals? Will they decentralize the church's structure so that many diverse voices can be heard?

The pope traveled to the U.S. in April, 2008 and delivered a major speech before the UN in New York. This would have been an excellent opportunity for him to announced a change in Vatican policy regarding the use of condoms to fight the spread of AIDS. Instead he spoke of general moral principles, human rights, and social justice. He did not apply any of these high level theological ideas to a single social problem. His failure to retract any of his previous statements regarding the use of condoms and AIDS is reminiscent of Pope Zosimus and his clash with bishops in the 5th century. Augustine and the bishops of North Africa demanded that the bishop of Rome retract his statements and condemn Pelagius for heresy as they had done. Eventually Zosimus saw the light. Will Benedict respond to the call for reform by his fellow bishops and Cardinals? After over two years of deliberations he ought to give them and the rest of the world an answer.

Notes

[1] http://pewresearch.org/pubs/778/a-portrait-of-american-catholics-on-the-eve-of-pope-benedicts-visit
[2] See Tracey Rich, "Who is a Jew," http://www.jewfaq.org/whoisjew.htm
[3] Richard Schaefer, *Racial and Ethnic Groups* (Prentice Hall, 2006), p. 376.
[4] The term "proto-orthodox" comes from the work of Bart Ehrman, *After the New Testament: A Reader in Early Christianity* (Oxford University Press, 1999), p. 405.
[5] Chris Armstrong, "The Future Lies in the Past," *Christianity Today* (February, 2008), p. 23.
[6] Alejandro Bermudez, "A Minimalist on Catholic Education," *N.Y. Times,* April 17, 2008.
[7] Raymond E. Brown, *An Introduction to the New Testament* (Doubleday, 1996), p. 503.
[8] Ibid.
[9] See "From Jesus to Christ – The first Christians," PBS, *Frontline* (1998) and the work of Allen Callahan.
[10] James Carroll, *Constantine's Sword* (Houghton Mifflin, 2001), lists three periods in the study of Jesus in the last two centuries: Schweitzer, Bultmann, and the focus on Jesus as a Jewish prophet (Meier).
[11] L. Michael White, *From Jesus to Christianity* (HarperCollins, 2004), p. 95.
[12] This is essentially the view of Bart Ehrman but not that of John Dominic Crossan who argues Jesus rejected the eschatological message of John the Baptist in favor of an egalitarian and wisdom teaching more congruent with his peasant background.
[13] See Christopher Price: **http://www.christianorigins.com/miracles.html**; Josephus, *Antiquities* 18.63-64.
[14] Taken from *The Works of Flavius Josephus,* translated by William Whiston (Hendrickson Publishers, 1987).
[15] See Andrew Greeley, *Jesus* (Forge Books, 2007), p. 99.
[16] Joseph Ratzinger (Benedict XVI), *Jesus of Nazareth* (Doubleday, 2007), p. 19.
[17] An ancient Coptic tradition asserts that Jesus spent a good deal of time in Egypt and knew of various religious traditions practiced there (feed the hungry, cloth the naked); see Mircea Eliade, *A History of Religious Ideas,* Vol. 1-3.
[18] See Bart D. Ehrman, *From Jesus to Constantine* (The Teaching Company, 2004) for details.
[19] This is an example of a blood curse which was well known in antiquity. Some Jews did call a curse upon themselves but the multi-generational curse is upon those who ignore God's truth.
[20] L. Michael White, op. cit., p. 84.
[21] Term formally used by Catholics on Good Friday, meaning faithless and deceitful.
[22] *Commonweal,* January 18, 2008.

[23] Bart Ehrman, *From Jesus to Constantine Part I*, transcript, The Teaching Company, 2004), p. 3.
[24] Quoted in Hans Küng, *Christianity: Essence, History, and Future* (Continuum, 1996), p. 314; see footnote on Joseph Ratzinger, "Volk und Haus."
[25] Hans Küng, *The Catholic Church: A Short History* (Modern Library Books, 2001), p. 10; Raymond Brown states that some writers doubt Mt. 16:18 contain words spoken by Christ: this passage is not found in Mark, Luke, or John and the use of the word "church" is a later development. The text is often used for ideological purposes to argue that the Bishop of Rome is the successor of Peter.
[26] Henry Chadwick, *The Early Church*, (Penguin, 1993 rev.), pp. 237-238.
[27] http://www.angelfire.com/ms/seanie/PeterRome.html
[28] Garrett G. Fagan, *The History of Ancient Rome* (Penn State University, 1997), lecture 45.
[29] Küng, *The Catholic Church*, pp. 11-12.
[30] Claudio Rendina, *The Popes*, translated by Paul D. McCusker (Pharos Publications, 2002), p. 26-27. The practice of using the word "pope" to refer exclusively to the bishop of Rome began in the 4th century.
[31] Seven devils is a metaphor for illness; see Meera Lester, *The Everything Mary Magdalene Book* (Adams Media, 2006), p. 7.
[32] Brown, op. cit., p 359.
[33] Edward Gibbon, *The History of the Decline and Fall of the Roman Empire* (The Modern Library, 2003/1753) p. 237ff.
[34] Küng, *The Catholic Church*, p. 5.
[35] Thomas F. O'Dea, *The Sociology of Religion* (Englewood Cliffs, N.J.: Prentice-Hall, 1966), p. 68.
[36] Brown, op. cit., p. 526
[37] J.N.D. Kelly, *Dictionary of the Popes* (New York: Oxford University Press, 1986), p. 7.
[38] White, op. cit., p. 123.
[39] Ibid., p. 111; during the transition period no doubt the hypothesized Q (Quelle or source) document emerged which aided the authors of the canonical Gospels.
[40] Brown, op. cit., , p. 286.
[41] J. Murphy-O'Connor, *Worship* 51 (1977), p. 56ff; see Brown, op. cit., p. 538.
[42] White, *From Jesus*, p. 119
[43] Brown, op. cit., p. 512
[44] The Diaspora is defined here as the exile of Jews from Judea to Babylon in 586 B.C.
[45] Not to be confused with James the brother of the Lord (James the Less) who was stoned to death by order of the Jewish council in 62 A.D. according to Josephus; he was the acknowledged head of the Jerusalem church (see Brown, *An Introduction*, p. 302).
[46] http://philologos.org/bpr/files/a015.htm
[47] White, *From Jesus*, p. 346; Judith M. Lieu, *Christian Identity in the Jewish and Graeco-Roman World*. Oxford University Press, 2004. See chapter 5. Also see Walter Bauer, *Greek-English Lexicon of the New Testament* (University of

Chicago Press, 1999).
[48] Edwin Yamauchi, "On the Road with Paul," *Christian History*, Issue 47 (1995), p.18.
[49] Ibid.
[50] He was a true Roman citizen according to Raymond Brown but Michael White questions Paul's citizenship.
[51] Cited by E. Yamauchi, "On the Road," p. 17.
[52] Technology: knowledge that people use to form a way of life in their social surroundings, e.g., tool making, cement, the wheel, etc.
[53] Peter Berger and Thomas Luckmann. *The Social Construction of Reality* (Doubleday, 1966).
[54] White, *From Jesus*, p. 153
[55] Thomas Bokenkotter, *A Concise History of the Catholic Church* (Doubleday, 2004 rev.), p. 19.
[56] Raymond Brown, op.cit., p 306; some prefer calling this a conference and not a council.
[57] Gibbon, *The History of the Decline*, p. 241.
[58] Brown, *An Introduction*, p. 309.
[59] http://www.usccb.org/nab/bible/galatians/galatians1.htm
[60] See White, *From Jesus*, p. 148, with some adjustments by me.
[61] http://www.catholic.com/thisrock/1993/9312qq.asp
[62] See Garry Wills, *Why I am a Catholic* (Houghton Mifflin, 2002).
[63] Brown, *An Introduction*, p. 609.
[64] White, op. cit., p 260.
[65] See Bart Ehrman, *The New Testament: An Historical Introduction to the Early Christian Writings* (Oxford University Press, 2004), p. 395ff.
[66] **http://mariannedorman.homestead.com/Women.html**; see Marianne Doman article; also note K. Bailey, *Theology Matters*, Jan 2000.
[67] Brown, *An Introduction*, p. 574.
[68] Quoted by James Carroll, *Constantine's Sword*, p. 80.
[69] Brown, *An Introduction*, p. 663.
[70] Ibid., p. 654.
[71] Ibid., p. 662, see footnote, 26.
[72] Ibid., p. 663.
[73] A redactor is simply a copyist who tries to embellish and alter the text according to his point of view. This process is called redaction. The book of Genesis is a classic example of redaction and this was to reflect the various religious traditions present over time. Pauline redactors say "this is Paul" and they are not totally correct.
[74] Brown, op. cit., p. 610.
[75] Ibid., p. 609.
[76] Ibid., p 524, footnote 39. An interpolation is a relatively small insertion in the original text that is done for ideological purposes.
[77] See Bart Ehrman, *From Jesus to Constantine* Part I.
[78] Benedict XVI, *Jesus of Nazareth* (Doubleday, 2007), p. xiv.

[79] Jerome Murphy-O'Connor, "Interpolations in 1Corinthians" CBQ 48 (1986), 90-93.
[80] Wayne Meeks, et al. (Editors), *HarperCollins Study Bible* (1993).
[81] J. Fitzmyer, et al., (eds), *New Jerome Biblical Commentary* (Prentice Hall, 1990).
[82] Brown, *An Introduction*, p. 609.
[83] Hans Conzelmann, *1 Corinthians: A Commentary on the First Epistle to the Corinthians* (Fortress Press, 1975), p. 246.
[84] Conflict theory argues that society and its components are not about solidarity and consensus, but rather competition; in this case the proto-orthodox won and women lost.
[85] See Küng, *The Catholic Church*, p. xxi, et passim.
[86] Bart Ehrman, *The New Testament: An Historical Introduction* (Oxford University Press, 2004), p. 399.
[87] See **http://www.pbs.org/wgbh/pages/frontline/shows/religion/maps/primary/thecla.html**; see Catholic Encyclopedia, "Thecla."
[88] Ehrman, *After the New Testament* (Oxford University Press, 1999), p. 278.
[89] See *In Search of Paul* (HarperCollins, 2004) by John Crossan and J. Reed. This section draws on their insights.
[90] Ehrman, *The New Testament*, p. 400.
[91] Henrich Greve, "An Ecological theory of spatial evolution," *Social Forces* 80:3 (2002), p. 847ff.
[92] Garry Wills, *Why I am a Catholic* (Houghton Mifflin, 2002), p. 70ff.
[93] II Cor 12:2.
[94] Garry Wills, *What Paul Meant* (Viking, 2006), p. 10.
[95] **Quod ubique, quod semper, quod ab omnibus creditum est.**
[96] See White, *From Jesus*, p. 307; Brown, *An Introduction*, p. 334.
[97] Brown, op. cit., p. 111; see footnote 18.
[98] White, op. cit., p. 113.
[99] A mile in the Roman Empire was 1000 paces (a pace was equivalent to two steps which measured five feet) and so a mile=5,000 feet, somewhat less than our 5,280 feet.
[100] http://www.bibles.com/brcpages/MaryMagdaleneApostle
[101] See Küng, *Christianity*, p. 233; this discussion depends on insights from Küng and Brown.
[102] Küng, *Christianity*, p. 120.
[103] Brown, *An Introduction*, p. 303, footnote 64; this early church document written circa 100 A.D. was thought to be lost for all time but in 1873 it emerged through the research efforts of P. Bryennios.
[104] Justin, ***First Apology***, chapters 61-67.
[105] This is the contention of Raymond Brown and Karen King.
[106] White, *From Jesus*, p.211
[107] Ibid.
[108] Brown, *An Introduction*, p. 645.
[109] http://www.apostolic.net/biblicalstudies/pastoraltheology.htm
[110] See Küng, *The Catholic Church*, p. 65.

[111] Cited in Küng, *Christianity,* p 129, f.n. 58.
[112] Josephus, *Wars of the Jews*, VI, 9.3.
[113] Ibid.
[114] See Elaine Pagels, *The Gnostic Gospels* (Vintage Books, 1989), pp.33-56).
[115] Armstrong, *Christianity Today*, Feb. 2008, p. 23ff.
[116] Gibbon, op.cit., p. 238
[117] J.M. Roberts, *Rome and the Classical West* (Oxford University Press, 1998), p. 115.
[118] Bart Ehman, *From Jesus to Constantine* (The Teaching Company, 2004).
[119] Rodney Stark, *The Rise of Christianity* (HarperSanFrancisco, 1996), p. 7.
[120] Origen, Against Celsus, 8.69.
[121] Stark, *The Rise*, p. 7.
[122] Adolph von Harnack, *The Mission and Expansion of Christianity in the First Three Centuries* (Putnam, 1908), p. 247.
[123] Stark, op. cit., p. 9ff; See Richard Carrier blogs on Stark.
[124] Garry Wills, *What Jesus Meant* (Penguin, 2006), p. xi; he says the NT Greek is not elegant. Words are strung together to communicate the basic meaning.
[125] See Catholic Encyclopedia, "Cornelius, Bishop of Rome"
[126] http://tatumweb.com/churchrodent/terms/celsus.htm
[127] Mircea Eliade, *A History of Religious Ideas* Vol. 1 (University of Chicago Press), p. 136.
[128] L. Michael White, *From Jesus to Christianity* (HarperCollins, 2004), p. 379.
[129] Gibbon, op. cit., chapter 15.
[130] Tertullian, ***Apologeticum***, ch. 39:7.
[131] Carroll, op. cit., p. 167
[132] Bart Ehrman, *After the New Testament* (Oxford University Press), p. 45.
[133] Eliade, op. cit., Vol 2, p. 366
[134] Clement of Alexandria, "Misellanies."
[135] See Joyce Salisbury, *Perpetua's Passion* (Routledge, 1997).
[136] See J. Liebeschuetz, "The Diocletianic Revival, " *Continuity and Change* (Oxford University Press, 1979), p. 251.
[137] Comments by Wayne Meeks, in ***From Jesus to Christ***. PBS Documentary, 2004, Part IV.
[138] C. John Cadoux, *The Early Christian Attitude to War* (1919). Cited in: http://www.lewrockwell.com/vance/vance60.html
[139] Ibid.
[140] Eusebius, *The History of the Church* (Penguin, 1989), p. 102.
[141] See L. Michael White, *From Jesus,* p. 46.
[142] Ibid.
[143] Edward Flannery, *The Anguish of the Jews* (Paulist Press, 1985), p. 60.
[144] Brown, *An Introduction*, p. 222.
[145] See Matt 15:8
[146] Louis Feldman, "Is the New Testament Antisemitic," *Moment*, December 1990, pp. 32-34.
[147] See Paul Jones, "From Intra-Jewish Polemics to Persecution," *Encounter* (Spring,

2006), p. 16ff for more details.

[148] Coffman Commentaries on the Old and New Testament; http://www.searchgodsword.org/com/bcc/view.cgi?book=joh&chapter=016

[149] Justin Martyr, Trypho, chapter 16.

[150] Ibid., ch. 26.

[151] Carroll, op. cit., p. 191-192.

[152] Melito of Sardis, "On the Passover," in *Current issues in Biblical and Patristic Interpretation (Eerdmans, 1975)*, Gerald Hawthrone (ed.).

[153] Bart Ehrman, *From Jesus to Constantine*, The Teaching Company (2004 transcript), Part 1, p. 139.

[154] Carroll, op. cit., p. 219

[155] Michaele Kress, "Jewish Christian Relations"; http://www.myjewishlearning.com/history_community/Jewish_World_Today/ContemporaryInterfaith/Jew_Christian_Relations.htm

[156] Documents, Vatican II, *Nostra Aetate*, par. 4.

[157] Küng, *The Catholic Church*, p. 181.

[158] Ernst Troeltsch, *The Social Teaching of the Christian Churches* (MacMillan, 1931), p. 37.

[159] Hans Küng, *The Catholic Church*, p. 22

[160] Richard McBrien, *Lives of the Popes* (HarperCollins, 1997), p. 35.

[161] Ibid.

[162] J.N.D.Kelly, *The Oxford Dictionary of Popes* (Oxford University Press, 19986), p. 8

[163] White, op. cit., p. 340

[164] McBrien, op. cit., p. 36.

[165] Küng, op. cit., p. 22.

[166] McBrien, p. 41

[167] The dispute has been labeled the "Quartodeciman" controversy and shows early on the tension between the Eastern and Western churches.

[168] Henry Chadwick, *The Early Church* (Penquin, 1993), p. 118.

[169] Ibid.

[170] Kelly, op. cit., p. 21.

[171] Küng, *The Catholic Church*, p.10.

[172] Brown, *An Introduction*, p. 221

[173] Kelly, op. cit., p. 27.

[174] Chadwick, op. cit., p. 130.

[175] See Raymond Brown, *An Introduction*,"Letter to the Colossians," p. 599ff.

[176] http://www.crivoice.org/biblestudy/bbjohn21.html

[177] http://www.iep.utm.edu/g/gnostic.htm

[178] Raymond Brown, *An Introduction*, p. 92.

[179] Chadwick, op. cit., p. 35.

[180] Marvin Meyer, Editor and Translator, *The Gnostic Gospels of Jesus* (HarperSanFrancisco, 2005), p. vii.

[181] Ibid., p. 34.

[182] Brown, op. cit., p. 88.

[183] White, *From Jesus*, p. 398.
[184] Ibid.
[185] Ibid, p. 398
[186] Chadwick, op. cit., p.39.
[187] See the "Gospel of Mary," in Meyer, op. cit., p. 56. The discovery of 52 Gnostic texts at Nag Hammadi in 1945 helped scholars understand what have been called "lost Christianities."
[188] The allegorical interpretation of the bible argues that bible passages can mean something different from what the literal meaning of the words imply.
[189] See Tim LaHaye and J. Jenkins, *Left Behind* (Tyndale, 1995).
[190] Karen King, The Gospel of Mary of Magdala (Polebridge Press, 2003), p. 107.
[191] Irenaeus, "Against the Heretics," Book 1, chapter 25.
[192] Bruce Metzger, *The Canon of the New Testament* (Clarendon, 1997), p. 187.
[193] Brown, op. cit., p. 13.
[194] Metzger, op. cit., p. 109-110.
[195] Eliade, op. cit., Vol. 3, p. 27
[196] This insight depends on the work of Richard Carrier: http://www.infidels.org/library/modern/richard_carrier/NTcanon.html
[197] See Richard Carrier, quoted below; also read Metzger, op. cit., p. 154ff.
[198] McBrien, op. cit., p. 65.
[199] Those sacred writings outside the official canon and "hidden away."
[200] Eusebius, *History of the Church*, p. 127; Everett Kalin, *The New Testament Canon of Eusebius*, pp. 403-404.
[201] Brown, *An Introduction*, p. 189.
[202] Küng, *Christianity*, p. 119.
[203] Brown, op. cit., p. 645
[204] Ibid., footnote 17.
[205] Ibid.; see Merkle for similar view: http://filemanager.silaspartners.com/dox/9marks/9news/feb079news.pdf
[206] Ignatius letter to Smyrnaeans, 8.1-9.1
[207] Küng, *Christianity*, p 123.
[208] Cyprian, Letters, LXXII,: extra ecclesiam nulla salus,
[209] E. Schillebeeckx, Ministry: Leadership in the Community of Jesus Christ, 1981; see Robert McClory, "Dutch Proposal," *National Catholic Reporter*, Feb 22, 2008.
[210] Peter Brown, *Augustine of Hippo* (University of California Press, 2000), p. 132.
[211] See document "Church and Ministry"; http://www.liturgy.co.nz/worship/matters_assets/Church_and_Ministry.pdf
[212] See the Catholic Encyclopedia, "Second Lateran Council, 1139."
[213] Richard McBrien, *Lives of the Popes* (HarperCollins, 1997), p. 85.
[214] Kelly, op. cit., p. 17.
[215] The Catholic Encyclopedia, *apokatastasis*.
[216] Gibbon, op. cit., p. 451.
[217] Wilko van Holten, *Anglican Theological Review*, Summer, 2003; also see "Hell and the Goodness of God," *Religious Studies* 35 (1999): 37-55.

[218] The Greek words he probably heard were "Εν Τούτω Νίκα" ("in this, be victorious!", often rendered in Latin, 'In hoc signo vinces.' Eusebius states that Constantine saw the cross in the sky and heard the saying in Greek.
[219] http://theologytoday.ptsem.edu/jul1977/v34-2-editorial1.htm
[220] This is a clear example of a Christian talisman, i.e., the utilization of a symbolic object to confer on its bearer supernatural powers and protection.
[221] Chadwick, *The Early church*, p. 125; Carroll and Barnes dispute this assertion that he was the underdog.
[222] http://www.ttc.edu.sg/csca/CS/2001-Apr/Norman%20Wong.pdf
[223] Carroll, op. cit., p. 175.
[224] Gregory Armstrong, "Imperial church Building," *The Biblical Archaeologist*, Vol. 30, No. 3 (Sep., 1967), p. 90.
[225] From the work of Hugo Rahner, S.J.; http://www.ignatiusinsight.com/features2005/hrahner_csec_sept05.asp
[226] J. Kelly, *The Oxford Dictionary of the Popes*, p. 28.
[227] The "filioque" meaning "and the Son" was added to the Creed at the Council of Toledo in 589 A.D. but was never fully accepted by the Eastern churches.

[228] Meaning "worldwide" i.e., including all the bishops in the civilized world.
[229] Carroll, op. cit., p. 191.
[230] The Catholic Encyclopedia, "Nestorius."
[231] http://www.britannica.com/eb/article-26708/ancient-Rome
[232] See James D. Tabor: http://www.religiousstudies.uncc.edu/JDTABOR/DSSEssay.htm
[233] Ibid.
[234] http://jewishmag.com/14MAG/ESSENES/essenes.htm
[235] James Charlesworth (ed.), *The Bible and the Dead Sea Scrolls* (Baylor University Press, 2006), p. 17.
[236] See Catholic Encyclopedia, "St. Anthony of Egypt."
[237] Eliade, op. cit., Vol. 2, p. 413.
[238] David Knowles, *Christian Monasticism* (World University Library, 1977).
[239] Chadwick, *The Early church*, p. 178.
[240] Ibid., p. 178
[241] Cited in Rendina, *Lives of the Popes*, p. 52.
[242] Chadwick, op. cit., p. 174.
[243] Küng, *The Catholic Church*, p. 90
[244] Rendina, op. cit., p. 58.
[245] R. Clifford, 'The Authority of the Nova Vulgata,' *The Catholic Biblical Quarterly*, 63 (2001), p. 197ff.
[246] Peter Brown, "The Rise and function of the Holy Man in Late Antiquity," *J. of Roman Studies*, Vol. 61 (1971), p. 99; Eliade, op. cit., p. 414.
[247] "…quia fecisti nos ad te et inquietum est cor nostrum donec requiescat in te" Book 1, Chapter 1.
[248] Peter Brown, *Augustine*, p. 44.
[249] James O'Donnell, *Augustine: Confessions* (Cambridge U., 1995) Vol. 3, p. 115.

[250] Augustine, *Confessions*, chap. 4
[251] *St. Augustine Confessions* (Oxford University Press, 1992), trans. Henry Chadwick, p. xvi-xvii; this cohabitation norm comes from canon 17 passed by the Council at Toledo in 400 A.D.
[252] Augustine, *City of God*. Translated by Henry Bettenson with introduction by G. Evans, p. xxiii.
[253] Augustine, *Confessions*, V. xiii, 23.
[254] *Confessions*, VI, 25.
[255] See *Confessions*, VIII, 12.
[256] Keep in mind the term "Catholic" was first used by Ignatius of Antioch (d. 107)
[257] Caecilianus was ordained by Bishop Felix of Aptunga who apparently had wavered under intense Roman persecution and so Donatists considered this ordination invalid; they viewed these churchmen as traitors.
[258] Heretic laws were renewed in 405 by Emperor Honorius and penalties could be severe; http://penelope.uchicago.edu/Thayer/E/Roman/Texts/secondary/BURLAT/11*.html
[259] Garry Wills, *Saint Augustine* (Penguin, 1999), p. 108
[260] Ibid., p. 109
[261] The "hut people" were fanatical Donatists who used clubs to protect their holy shrines; violence was their way of dealing with sinners.
[262] Brown, *An Introduction*, p. 248
[263] The New American Bible reads: "Go out to the highways and hedgerows and make people come in that my home may be filled" Lk 14:23).
[264] Wills, *Augustine*, p. 99
[265] Küng, *The Catholic Church*, p. 47; Ratzinger (now Pope Benedict XVI) wrote his doctoral dissertation on Augustine's ecclesiology and used his Vatican position and power before becoming pope to sanction unsuitable theological inquiry. Some of his witch hunts proved groundless e.g. Jesuit Fr. Jacques Dupuis. Augustine in the wrong hands can be lethal. Ratzinger has called Augustine his master.
[266] Wills, *Augustine*, p. 49
[267] Ibid., p. 41.
[268] Ibid., p 132
[269] Augustine, *Soliloquies;* see Vern Bullough, f.n. 38; http://www.humanismtoday.org/vol6/bullough.pdf
[270] Cited in Uta Ranke-Heinemann, *Eunuchs for the Kingdom of Heaven* (Penguin, 1991), p. 55.
[271] Ibid., p. 203.
[272] Ibid., p. 88.
[273] Ibid., p. 185.
[274] Ibid., Willis, *Augustine*, p. 130.
[275] Ibid.. p 132; it is from Dialogues with myself, 1.17.
[276] Joseph Ratzinger (now Pope Benedict XVI) wrote his first encyclical on the theme "God is Love" (Deus cartitas est) and has been influenced greatly by Augustine's theology; his doctoral dissertation was on the ecclesiology of Augustine.

[277] Wills, *Augustine*, p. 66
[278] Ibid., p. 41
[279] W. I. Thomas, "The Relation of Research to the Social process" in Morris Janowitz, ed., *W. I. Thomas on social organization and social personality* (University of Chicago Press, 1966 [1931]), p. 301.
[280] Wills, *Augustine*, p. 63.
[281] Küng, *Christianity*, p 313.
[282] Ibid.
[283] Augustine, *Letters*, 36.4.
[284] See Catholic Encyclopedia, "Zosimus."
[285] See Küng, *Christianity*, p 314.
[286] http://www.americancatholic.org/Newsletters/SFS/an1299.asp
[287] Garry Wills, *What Paul Meant* (Penguin, 2006), p.100
[288] Eusebius, 3,30,1.
[289] Wills, op. cit., p. 100
[290] See G. Wills, *What Jesus Meant*, p. 34.
[291] See Greeley, *Jesus*, p. 57.
[292] See *Gospel of Mary of Magdala* by Karen King.
[293] Greeley, op. cit., pp. 57-58.
[294] Simcha Jacobovici and Charles Pellegrino, *The Jesus Family Tomb* (HarperCollins, 2007).
[295] *Time*, Jan. 16, 2008.
[296] see Josephus, *Antiquities*, 18.
[297] Karen King, *The Gospel of Mary of Magdala* (HarperCollins, 2003); "Da Vinci Code" **http://news.nationalgeographic.com/news/2004/4/8.**
[298] Allen J. *National Catholic Reporter*, May 5, 2006, p. 9.
[299] Charles Kimball, *When Religion Becomes Evil* (HarperSanFrancisco, 2002), p. 17.
[300] William Ellet, *Case Study Handbook* (Harvard Business School Press, 2007).
[301] Kimball, op. cit.; he lists five warning signs but I utilize only two.
[302] Ibid., p. 7.
[303] http://members.aol.com/revising/change.html
[304] R. John Kinkel, *Chaos in the Catholic Church*. Philadelphia: Random House/Xlibris, 2005, p. 19; http://www.pbs.org/wgbh/amex/pill/timeline/timeline2.html
[305] "First Report of AIDS," *Morbidity and Mortality Weekly Report*, CDC, June 1, 2001, p. 430.
[306] WHO, and National Institutes of Health, 1994; www.cdc.gov/HIV/pubs/facts/transmission.htm
[307] BBC News www.**news.bbc**.co.uk/1/hi/health/3176982.stm
[308] "Report on the Global HIS/AIDS Epidemic," UNAIDS, Geneva, 2002. *Newsweek*, May 15, 2006, p. 53. Also see http://www.msnbc.msn.com/id/15829203/
[309] Marcella Alsan, M.D., "The Church & AIDS in Africa," *Commonweal*, April 21, 2006.
[310] Alfonso Trujillo, "Family Values versus Safe Sex," Pontifical Council for the

Family, December 1, 2003.

311 Quoted in BBC NEWS October 9, 2003; **http://news.bbc.co.uk/2/hi/health/3176982.stm**; of course, nothing human is perfect; condoms prove 2% defective in U.S. studies.

312 Steve Bradshaw, *The Guardian*, October 9, 2003.

313 Data from *The Catholic Almanac*, 2006.

314 Nicholas Kristof, 'The Pope and AIDS,' *New York Times*, May 8, 2006.

315 Interview with Amy Welborn: http://amywelborn.typepad.com/openbook/2006/03/pope_garry.html

316 Newsweek, July 20, 2001. Also, Nolen, Stephanie. "**South African bishop defies Vatican on condoms**", *Globe and Mail,* 7 April 2007.

317 John McCarthy and Mayer Zald, "Resource Mobilization and social movements," *American Journal of Sociology*, 82:6 (1977), p. 1223. Coalescence is key: group comes together.

318 Catholic World News, February 1, 2005.

319 Daniel Williams, "Pope Rejects condoms as a counter to Aids," *Washington Post*, January 23, 2005, p. A23.

320 Declan Butler, *Nature*, April 21, 2005, p. 944.

321 Quoted in BBC News, June 10, 2005; see http://news.bbc.co.uk/2/hi/europe/4081276.stm

322 See full story in *National Catholic Reporter,* November 30, 2005.

323 Marcella Alsan, M.D., "The Church & AIDS in Africa," *Commonweal*, April 21, 2006.

324 See BBC News, April 21, 2006.

325 Nicole Winfield, 'Vatican studying condoms and AIDS,' *Washington Post*, April 25, 2006.

326 Henry Chadwick, *The Early Church* (Penguin, 1993), p. 119.

327 Hans Küng, *My Struggle for Freedom: Memoirs* (Eerdmans, 2003), p. 24. Same thing happened at Nicaea and Council of Jerusalem.

328 Robert McClory, *Turning Point* (Crossroads, 1997).

329 http://www.biographybase.com/biography/Paul_VI.html

330 New York Times, March 8, 1993.

331 Martin Marty and Scott Appleby (eds), *Fundamentalisms Observed* Vol 1 (University of Chicago Press, 1991), p. 137.

332 William Martin, *With God on Our Side* (Broadway Book, 1997), p. 251. Cited in *Head and Heart,* Garry Wills, p. 492.

333 Gene Burns, "Studying the Political Culture of American Catholicism," Sociology of Religion, Vol. 57, 1 (Spring, 1996), 37-53.

334 Ibid.

335 **http://cacradicalgrace.org/resources/rg/sept-oct_05/RGv18i5_RR_QuestionsVsAnswers.pdf**; or see http://jmm.aaa.net.au/articles/15625.htm.

336 http://www.hopkins-aids.edu/publications/report/may98_8.html

337 http://data.unaids.org/pub/EPISlides/2007/071119_epi_pressrelease_en.pdf

338 This is a favorite saying of Benedict XVI.

339 Frances Fox Piven, ASA Presidential Address, 2007.

[340] *Summa Theologiae* (II-II, Qu. 64, Art.7).
[341] Of course, Catholics who reject the church's ban on contraception avoid such scholastic rationalizations.
[342] "When Condoms aren't Contraceptives," J. Fuller and J. Keenan; http://www.beliefnet.com/story/183/story_18346_1.html
[343] Kristof, op.cit.

Index

A

AIDS 4, 164, 178, 179, 180, 181, 182, 183, 184, 185, 186, 187, 188, 192, 193, 194, 195, 196, 197, 212
Anicetus 98, 99, 104, 212
Anthony of Egypt 143, 211, 212
Antioch church 37, 212
Antitheses 118, 212
apocrypha 91, 118, 157, 212
apostle 19, 22, 33, 34, 37, 43, 45, 48, 49, 51, 58, 59, 60, 77, 130, 168, 173, 212
Apostles Creed 110, 111, 112
Arius 138, 140, 141, 212
Augustine 31, 44, 48, 66, 68, 82, 93, 94, 104, 110, 117, 121, 123, 124, 125, 131, 134, 136, 145, 146, 147, 148, 149, 150, 151, 152, 153, 154, 155, 156, 157, 158, 159, 160, 161, 162, 163, 164, 165, 166, 171, 197, 210, 211, 212

B

Barnabas, epistle 34, 36, 37, 38, 39, 64, 91, 92, 116, 212
Benedict XVI 11, 20, 164, 186, 204, 206, 212
Bishop of Rome 20, 21, 73, 97, 100, 102, 104, 137, 161, 162, 205, 208, 212
Brown, Raymond 26, 46, 60, 101, 122, 157, 205, 206, 207, 209
Bultmann, Rudolf 14
Burns, Gene 192

C

Callistus I 84, 104
canon 34, 37, 51, 68, 77, 113, 114, 115, 116, 117, 118, 119, 120, 131, 170, 173, 174, 210, 212
Carroll, James 80, 92, 133, 204, 206
Carthage 20, 74, 81, 100, 117, 120, 121, 129, 156, 163, 164
catacombs 76, 135
Catholic, meaning 64
Celsus 74, 208
Christianity Today 10, 204, 208
Clement I 62, 67, 93, 97, 98, 110
Codex Sinaiticus 116
Colossians 41, 45, 46, 106, 118, 209
condoms 164, 179, 180, 181, 182, 183, 184, 185, 186, 187, 188, 192, 193, 194, 195, 196, 197, 212
Constantine 35, 71, 72, 74, 83, 84, 96, 102, 116, 117, 119, 126, 132, 133, 134, 135, 136, 137, 138, 140, 144, 146, 147, 165, 166, 167, 170, 204, 205, 206, 208, 209, 211
Corinthians 26, 27, 40, 41, 46, 47, 110, 118, 127, 207

Cornelius 34, 37, 73, 82, 121, 129, 188, 208
cross 106, 134, 135, 151, 165, 172, 211
Crossan, John 147, 176, 207
Cyprian of Carthage 20, 100, 129

D

Danneels, Godfried 186
Decius 82, 86, 100, 128
Diaspora 18, 29, 205
Didache 60
Diocletian 82, 134, 155
Dowling, Kevin 185, 186

E

Ebionites 106
Ehrman, Bart 18, 49, 69, 92, 113, 204, 205, 206, 207, 208, 209
Essenes 14, 142, 143, 173, 177
Eucharistic prayer 27

F

forgiveness of sin

G

Galatians 38, 40, 41, 118
Genesis 10, 91, 106, 206
Gentiles 26, 27, 30, 33, 34, 37, 38, 53, 72, 89, 96, 97, 105, 160, 168
Gibbon, Edward 37, 131, 205, 206, 208, 210
Gnostics 51, 106, 107, 108, 109, 110, 170, 171, 174
Gospel of Mary 109, 110, 173, 175, 210, 212
Gospel of Peter 117

H

Helena 135, 165
Hellenists 30, 89, 105
Herod Antipas 19
Holy Sepulchre 136

I

Ignatius, Antioch 33, 52, 57, 67, 79, 104, 123, 212
interpolation 46, 47, 206

J

Jamnia 90, 114
Jerome, Saint 47, 87, 97, 110, 136, 146, 147, 158, 171, 207
Jerusalem 14, 15, 17, 19, 20, 22, 24, 29, 32, 33, 34, 36, 37, 38, 39, 50, 54, 63, 64, 66, 67, 73, 91, 96, 137, 140, 170, 173, 176, 188, 205
Jerusalem, Council of 29, 36, 96, 170, 188
Jerusalem, destruction of 50, 66
Jesus 11, 12, 13, 14, 15, 16, 17, 18, 19, 20, 21, 22, 23, 24, 25, 26, 27, 30, 31, 32, 33, 35, 37, 41, 43, 44, 45, 47, 49, 51, 53, 54, 56, 57, 58, 59, 61, 62, 65, 66, 67, 68, 69, 70, 72, 73, 74, 75, 76, 77, 78, 79, 83, 85, 86, 87, 88, 89, 90, 91, 92, 93, 95, 96, 98, 101, 103, 105, 106, 107, 108, 109, 110, 111, 112, 113, 114, 115, 118, 119, 121, 123, 125, 126, 134, 135, 138, 139, 140, 141, 143, 146, 148, 151, 154, 156, 157, 160, 167, 168, 169, 170, 172, 173, 174, 175, 176, 177, 191, 204, 205, 206, 207, 208, 209, 210, 212
Jews 9, 10, 14, 16, 18, 23, 24, 25, 27, 29, 30, 33, 34, 38, 39, 50, 54, 66, 72, 73, 78, 80, 87, 88, 89, 90, 91, 92, 93, 94, 108, 109, 135, 168, 169, 170, 189, 204, 205, 208
John the Baptist 11, 15, 19, 21, 106, 142, 143, 146, 174, 204
John XXIII 93, 189
Josephus 16, 204, 205, 208, 212
Junia 43, 61
Justin Martyr 61, 75, 78, 81, 84, 91, 127, 209

K

Kimball, Charles 179, 180, 181, 183, 193, 197, 212
King, Karen 177, 207, 210, 212
Kochba, Bar 91
koinonia 64
Küng, Hans 11, 48, 101, 123, 149, 157, 158, 189, 205, 207, 208, 209, 210, 211, 212

L

LaHaye, Tim 109, 210
Lateran, council, second 126, 127, 136, 161, 210

M

Manichaeism 151, 152, 154
Marana tha 25
Marcion 98, 107, 108, 109, 118, 119
Mark 15, 20, 32, 53, 54, 55, 56, 68, 101, 115, 116, 117, 119, 120, 167, 173, 174, 205
martyrs 76, 77, 80, 81, 82, 83, 86, 94, 95, 114, 128, 129, 135, 169
Mary Magdalene 19, 22, 31, 44, 58, 61, 108, 109, 172, 173, 175, 176, 177, 205
Matthew 20, 53, 54, 55, 56, 88, 89, 101, 115, 116, 117, 119, 120, 156, 176

203

Meier 204
Meier, John 14, 204
Melito of Sardis 92, 169, 209
Milan 72, 83, 150, 152, 153, 159, 187
Milvian bridge 135
monks 144, 145, 148, 155, 160
Muratorian fragment 115

N

Nag Hammadi 110, 119, 173, 210
Nain, widow 16, 17
Nero 21, 45, 79, 80, 85, 97
New Rome 137
Nicaea 69, 75, 96, 102, 104, 117, 126, 137, 138, 140, 164, 188
Nicene Creed 138, 139, 140
nonviolence 84

O

Origen 43, 48, 70, 92, 96, 116, 119, 121, 123, 129, 130, 131, 137, 159, 171, 208
Ottaviani, Alfredo 188, 190, 192

P

Pachomius 144, 145
patriarchy 30, 47, 49, 50, 66, 110, 123
Paul 10, 11, 19, 20, 23, 25, 26, 27, 33, 34, 35, 36, 37, 38, 39, 40, 41, 42, 43, 44,
    45, 46, 47, 48, 49, 50, 51, 53, 54, 59, 60, 61, 62, 64, 66, 67, 68, 69, 70,
    73, 76, 77, 78, 79, 89, 91, 96, 97, 104, 106, 108, 110, 112, 114, 115, 116,
    117, 118, 120, 122, 123, 124, 125, 127, 129, 144, 152, 154, 160, 163,
    165, 166, 168, 169, 170, 171, 174, 175, 177, 181, 182, 183, 185, 186,
    190, 191, 192, 196, 205, 206, 207, 208, 212
Pauline privilege 39, 40
Pelagius 68, 162, 163, 164, 197
Perpetua 81, 82, 208
Peter, St. 83, 100, 104, 191
Petrine text 20
Phoebe 27, 43, 61
Pliny the Younger 16, 73, 80, 85
proto-orthodox 10, 40, 50, 51, 98, 120, 204, 207
pseudepigraphy 41, 42, 45

R